ISBN 978-0991139606
Published by Shavertron Press
San Francisco, California

Printed in the United States of America
Visit us on the Internet at www.shavertron.com

Design and Layout: Lora Santiago
Cover Illustration: Max Fyfield

"The Mimeograph Years"
Issues 1-11

SHAVERTRON

"The Only Source of Post-Deluge Shaverania"

Richard Toronto
Editor

SHAVERTRON PRESS

Introduction

In case of Nuclear War, your Shavertron subscription will automatically expire…" —The Editor

Shavertron—The Only Source of Post-Deluge Shaverania—was a scrappy (some said scruffy) cut-and-paste fanzine that debuted in the autumn of 1979, during the last decade of the Cold War. Its roots, however, went all the way back to the dawn of the Cold War and Richard Shaver's *Shaver Mystery Magazine,* which produced nine issues between 1947 and 1949, and its successor, *The Shaver Mystery Club Letterzine,* which published 16 issues, beginning in 1950.

The thread connecting *Shavertron* to this storied past was the relationship between its eventual editor, and Dick and Dottie Shaver, who lived in Summit, Arkansas at the time of the editor's first contact. Shaver became the de facto mentor of this up-and-coming editor. Okay, I'll get to the point—I was that would-be editor. Had I founded *Shavertron* while Shaver was still alive, it would have been a completely different fanzine, but the thought never occurred to me. For one thing, I never imagined Shaver would *die*—or that our rambling correspondence would end after three and a half years.

Shaver was pretty cantankerous in his letters, and looked old and beaten in the photos he sent—but not old and beaten enough to *die.* He was only 68 years old, for Pete's sake, which is downright middle-aged these days. During the four-year interregnum following his death, Ray Palmer died too, and with that the last tenuous thread to the Shaver Mystery snapped. It was a dark time indeed; or a glorious one, depending on which side of the fence you were sitting. Science fiction fandom breathed a collective sigh of relief as Palmer, Shaver, and the Mystery were swept into the dustbin of history, where it was hoped they would remain.

And so it was that I felt moved to do *something*…to keep things going. Other than thinking about it, not much happened…thus time marched on. In 1977 I wrote an article titled, "Do Brain Damaged Robots Rule the Earth?" Yes, it was about Richard Shaver. It appeared in *Beyond Reality* magazine that same year under a pseudonym. Still, this wasn't enough to slow the Mystery's steady descent to the boggy bottom of Oblivion.

Why it took four years *after* Shaver's death for me to come up with a Shaver Mystery fanzine is beyond me. I guess I was a late bloomer. The fanzine idea had an ulterior motive. My original plan was to locate historical material to write Shaver's life story. What better way to find this type of material, I reasoned, than to publish a Shaver Mystery fanzine to rally old time Shaver buffs? In 1979 they still existed. Now they're as rare as white rhinos. It was a good plan but with an unexpected result. *Shavertron* took on a life of its own, and the book wouldn't materialize for another 35 years. When people tell you that time flies, they aren't kidding.

Dottie Shaver continued to live in the Summit rock house after Dick's death, and we were in regular contact by phone and mail. When I told her about my plan to start a fanzine dedicated to Dick, Dottie became the catalyst that kick-started the first issue. Checking my mailbox one day, I found an envelope from Dot stuffed with scraps of paper, return addresses that Shaver had cut from his mail and put into a box. They were names of fans— fans of the Shaver Mystery. This became my mailing list.

The next hurdle was choosing a name. In 1979 the word TRON was a common signifier of a futuristic machine (in no way related to its Scottish ancestor, the tron or trone, a weighing machine to measure bulk items). The TRON was part of our emerging computer age, which was getting underway. Add TRON to any word and *violà*—you've seized the future a la 1979. It was the perfect addition to "Shaver," the subject of the zine. Thus *Shavertron* became the vehicle for Dick Shaver's future legacy. The computer-generated lettering on the masthead (taken from a sheet of stick-on letters purchased at the local stationery store) confirmed the zine's rightful place in the computer age. It was heady stuff, then. After pasting up the first issue—two sheets of copy paper printed back to back and stapled—I primed the pump by sending a copy to every name in Shaver's return address "file." This is how *Shavertron* launched with no fanfare under the radar of mainstream SF fandom.

In *Shavertron*'s first editorial, I likened "the Shavertron" to the Telaug, a telepathic machine (mech) of the cavern world from Richard Shaver's science fiction yarns. I even called the editorial column in the first few issues "Telaug Talk" or "Telaug Central," continuing the "mech" theme.

Thinking back those 35 years, I suspect Dottie was feeling nostalgic for the times she spent with Dick publishing *The Shaver Mystery Magazine*. She often reminisced about them in her letters. Though *Shavertron* was a far cry from *The Shaver Mystery Magazine*, it was enough of an echo that Dottie became a steady partner, supplying materials for each issue. She salvaged them from Shaver's shack in her backyard, where his dwindling collection of paintings, manuscript carbons, sketches, and photos sat collecting dust.

By the time issue number 8 rolled around, science fiction fandom had discovered *Shavertron* and was none too pleased with what it found. Brickbats that were familiar to Dick Shaver, Ray Palmer, and the Shaver Mystery were now redirected at *Shavertron*. In truth, my circulation was so small (a run of 100 copies per issue) that I was flattered that another editor noticed me at all. My reviewers seemed to write their remarks while in a state of high agitation, which meant their reviews were full of colorful language—none of which praised *Shavertron*.

Richard Geis, editor of the November 1982 *Science Fiction Review* wrote a lengthy report for the SF fen:

"Mimeographed with the help of an electronic stencil machine, *Shavertron* is a disorganized paste-up of bits and pieces—newspaper stories, clips, editorials letters, ads….

"Toronto and his readers believe Richard Shaver was onto something with what is known as The Shaver Mystery—remnants of a master race living in caverns far below, able to affect human minds on the Earth's surface by means of ancient evil machines…Etc. One could say if you're an anal retentive paranoiac, this is right down your hole.

"I had trouble even finding Toronto's name, and his single copy price and/or subscription rate are apparently a secret he doesn't share."

Okay. I take umbrage here. Am I just deluding myself or did Geis just describe a typical fanzine? You know, the kind that includes editorials, newspaper stories, letters, ads—all that crazy, anal-retentive stuff?

Ed Bates of *The Informant* wasn't much kinder: "Though it is indeed printed and illustrated, the layouts are nearly impossible to follow…everything is scattered seemingly at random. This is the only active fanzine dedicated to the late author, Richard S. Shaver, and it is worth struggling through if you are a fan of his…but what can you do when this is the only game in town?"

Yes, *Shavertron* was the only game in town. Is that why Shaver Mystery fans subscribed to a fanzine that was "impossible to follow?" NO! It was not! *Shavertron* became something of a legend in its own small way, publishing 29 issues throughout its decade-long career. That's something of a record for most fanzines. During that time it pulled together an eclectic mix of artists, writers, and fans willing to support it. A few were a little strange, is true, but we tried to be all-inclusive. Mostly they were fans of Dick Shaver, Ray Palmer, and Charles Fort, fans that enjoyed the fun of a good old-fashioned mystery…*any* kind of mystery. In its own corner of the fanzine world (admittedly small) *Shavertron* reigned supreme as *The Only Source of Post-Deluge Shaverania* from 1979 to 1992 (if you include the Interregnum Years 1987-1990).

When *Shavertron* ceased publication 25 years ago, I closed the door on the old fanzine and never looked back. But while scanning the issues to assemble this first volume, I studied each page as I made them more presentable (some were browned with age, Xeroxed copies, or just poorly printed to begin with). I was surprised just how much I'd forgotten about its history.

I'd forgotten that I modeled *Shavertron* after John Keel's *Anomaly,* a fanzine I enthusiastically followed throughout the early to mid-1970s. *Anomaly* was a mix of Fortean and flying saucer reports, pepped up with short articles and oddball newspaper clippings—whatever sparked Keel's interest. And so it was with *Shavertron*. Whatever interested me and *S* readers went into each issue. There really was no master plan.

Dottie Shaver continued to send photos, artwork, notes, and addresses of fans. Thirty-five

years later, some of this material found its way into the books she knew I would eventually write: *War Over Lemuria* and *Shaverology*. As *Shavertron* progressed, a crew of lively contributors signed on for the ride. Some, like Jim Wentworth (Alex Saunders), Vaughn M. Greene, Frank Brownley, Mike Cohen, Alan Wiseman, and Eldon K. Everett were part of the Shaver Mystery's old guard and used to contribute to *Amazing Stories'* lettercol, or to Rap's *Forum, FATE, Search,* and *Mystic* magazines.

Shavertron spent the first 11 issues finding itself. Other than the familiar masthead, consistency was not its strong suit. Even the masthead changed with issues 7 and 13. Realizing my mistake, I brought back the original design and stuck with it. Departments appeared and disappeared, but steadied over time. "Rap's Corner," "Pure Bliss," "Rays from the UK," "Giants in the Earth—Revised," all these signature features appeared in the first 11 issues.

RALPH FINLEY

Shavertron's visual evolution was the work of its contributing artists. The ebb and flow of its artists changed its appearance at each stage of development. In the earliest issues, the first artist to step up to offer help was a long-time friend, Ralph Finley. He contributed interior art from the very beginning, and cover art for issues 5 and 6. Mary Martin later adopted Ralph's "Hollow Hassle" cover from *Shavertron* 5 for her *Hollow Hassle* fanzine. Ralph's pen and ink sketches with their Big Daddy Roth and underground comics influence, gave *Shavertron* its earliest personality. His work continued to appear throughout *Shavertron*'s lifetime. Ralph made a comeback with his Dick Shaver pen and ink drawings for my 2013 book, *Shaverology*.

With issue 8 a new look began to emerge. This came from the Danish illustrator Max Fyfield. Though I'm not sure how we originally met, Fyfield's influence grew considerably within a very short time. He gave *Shavertron's* covers a semi-pro look. Max's "Jersey Devil" appeared on issue 8, his "Hole at the Pole" on issue 9, his iconic Dick Shaver caricature for *Shavertron's* 10th anniversary issue, and his "Shambala" cover on issue 11. As time went on, Fyfield began to write for *Shavertron*,

contributing several articles and movie screenplays about his unrequited love for Gina Lolabrigida. The illustration for his article "Fear and Laughter on the UFO Trail" in issue 9 remains a classic, and in the same issue he bared his soul in "Profile of an Artist."

MAX FYFIELD

Other artists would eventually join the *Shavertron* staff, but since they appeared in issues 12-29, they'll be covered in parts 2 and 3 of this three volume collection.

This particular volume is called "The Mimeograph Years" because many of the issues were printed on a Gestetner mimeograph machine owned by my employer at the time. I got more use out of that Gestetner than my boss, but it reproduced poorly, forcing me to replace all the photos in this book with scans of the originals. The decision to break up the 29 issues into three volumes is due to the large number of pages, and the need to organize them into different stages of *Shavertron*'s development as the years went on.

Only one person in the world has a complete set of all 29 original *Shavertron* issues: my friend and fellow Shaver scholar Jim Pobst. Jim filled in the gaps in my collection, which were considerable. Thanks to Jim, this volume became possible.

And now, behold the Shavertron…

Richard Toronto
San Francisco, California, October 2013

SHAVERTRON

"The Only Source of Post-Deluge Shaverania"

Autumn Equinox
1979

Issue 1

TUNNEL MONSTER OF CABBAGETOWN?

TORONTO
CANADA

The Sunday Sun, March 25, 1979

By LORRIE GOLDSTEIN
Staff Writer

There's an eerie city lying beneath the streets of Metro, a city none of us knows much about.

Ernest has been a visitor to that silent world of sewers, drainage pipes and the ruins under old houses, and the memory of what he saw there will haunt him for the rest of his life.

"I wish you'd never come here," he says as he sits in his small, neat Cabbagetown apartment with Barbara, his wife of 19 years. "If I tell you what I saw, people will think I was drunk or crazy, they'll never believe me."

On a summer day last August, Ernest, 51, firmly believes he saw some kind of "creature" while crawling into a small cave near his Parliament Street apartment looking for a kitten from a litter he'd been caring for. But about 10 feet inside he says he saw a living nightmare he'll never forget.

"It was pitch black in there...I saw it with my flashlight. The eyes were orange and red, slanted...it was long and thin, almost like a monkey...three feet long, large teeth, weighing maybe 30 pounds with slate-grey fur."

Ernest speaks reluctantly of what happened next...

He is convinced the thing spoke to him.

"I'll never forget it," he said. "It said 'Go away, go away,' in a hissing voice. Then it took off down a long tunnel off to the side...I got out of there as fast as I could. I was shaking with fear."

Ernest didn't come to the Sun with this story. The Sun found him after hearing about his experience from a reliable contact who works with a relative of Ernest's, one of the handful of people to whom he has confided the experience.

He would agree to talk about it only if his last name was not revealed.

"I'm in the phone book," he said. "I couldn't stand being called by a bunch of cranks."

"I believe Ernie saw exactly what he says he did," said Barbara. "He was terrified when he came back to the apartment and he doesn't scare easily. Look, he's been known to have a drink in the past — like most people, and to occasionally tie one on, but he's not a drunk and he wasn't drinking at all that day."

Checks with friends, relatives and acquaintances in the neighborhood supported Barbara's evaluation of her husband.

I accompanied Ernest to the spot where he said he had seen the creature.

It is at the bottom of a narrow passage between the building where he lives and the one next door. The only way to reach the tunnel entrance is to clamber 15 feet down the wrong side of a fire escape, which had once served as an exit to the street but today simply leads to a narrow chamber with walls on four sides.

The tunnel entrance runs under a slab of concrete at the foot of the chamber. Inside, there is a narrow passageway, branching off to the left about 10 feet back.

The corpse of a cat lies half-buried in the tunnel, reminding Ernest of the "strange noises, like animals in pain," he heard coming from the chamber last summer.

The concrete slab has collapsed on one side during the winter, making it impossible for even a small adult to get inside.

"I saw it where the tunnel turns," Ernest said. "The last I saw, it was heading off into the dark. The passageway seemed to drop down very quickly and go a long way back."

Ernest believes the tunnel leads to the sewer system that runs beneath Metro and that the entrance beneath his apartment may have been only an access point used by the creature to the surface.

Metro's sewer department agreed to inspect the tunnel since it could be a safety hazard. Children might try to enter it.

A long-time sewer worker told the Sun it was possible, although not probable, that the tunnel led into the sewers.

He said the tunnel was probably the result of poor drainage over the years which has caused erosion under ground, hollowing out the passage.

"Who knows where it leads, or how far it goes?" he said. "You'd have to get in there and the way it is now, it would take a lot of work."

Despite the strangeness of Ernest's story, the worker did not scoff at the tale.

"People who work on the surface just don't know what it's like down there," one said. "It's a whole different world. Who would have thought a few years ago that people would live in sewers, and yet that's what they found in New York a few years back. Even in Toronto, we've occasionally had to pull mattresses from the chambers beneath the manhole covers where the winos have been sleeping."

Another worker said he'd heard of animals like beavers and raccoons occasionally getting into the system but never anything like that described by Ernest.

"I don't know what he saw down there," he said. "But I'll tell you one thing. If we could get in there, I sure as hell wouldn't want to go down alone."

--from Mary LeVesque

SHAVERTRON has been informed that Mr. Jim Wentworth, author of GIANTS IN THE EARTH, will have an article appearing in SEARCH this winter called "Why I Continue to Believe in the Shaver Mystery". Mr. Wentworth is one of the original SM Club members.

...EDITORIAL...

Editor--Richard Toronto

The SHAVERTRON, like the fabled Telaug so often described in the works of Richard Shaver, is an instrument created to make you see more. It is a literary mech (machine) made to loosen up those rusty parts of the brain that once housed thoughts of Dero, Tero, "occult" happenings, UFO, mind control, the Underworld, the Elder Race, holes-at-the-poles, welding guns, mystery voices, pre-Deluge history, rock books, ray mech, Ray Palmer, the sci-fi stories of Richard Shaver and his peers, ancient language, tamper, devolution, aging through radiation, the end of the world as we know it, lost cities, and anything else that relates to the cosmology of our universe as envisioned by Richard Sharpe Shaver.

We here at SHAVERTRON, with your help, intend to fill the vacuum in which the Shaver Mystery now finds itself since the untimely deaths of Richard Shaver (1975) and his erstwhile editor Raymond Palmer (1977). The great Shaver Mystery had alot to do with the making and breaking of many people in its day; we have no doubt, however, that both Palmer and Shaver had alot of fun with it despite the weird problems.

Palmer, an unrecognised genius of the sci-fi genre and pulp mag business, always promoted lively debate, published accounts of Dero persecution and foul play, and looked at the Mystery from every angle. We intend to do the same! We invite all who are interested to send in newsclips, new findings of cave entrances, verification of Shaverian predictions, letters or quotes from Shaver (who, in the last years of his life, became a prolific correspondent to hundreds of people throughout the country).

From that Fateful time that an irate reader of AMAZING STORIES invoked Einstein's Law of Relativity to stop publication of further stories of the Mystery at Ziff-Davis, Richard Shaver steadily vanished from the public eye until he died in relative obscurity in 1975. The oblivion in which he languished in those years just might be diminishing now. All

of his work has been out of print for years, yet many of his theories and ideas are just now beginning to materialize, and SHAVERTRON hopes to publish material that will prove (or disprove if need be) these theories and conceptions.

In future issues of SHAVERTRON, things to look for will be a heretofore neverbefore seen in print manuscript fragment by Shaver called "Salivanhoe" (or "The Electric Corpse"), helpful hints on how to photograph pre-Deluge artifacts, Shaverian Quips and Quotes, and unpublished interviews taken during the last years of his life.

Naturally, SHAVERTRON is meant to be an open forum for any and all Shaver Mystery fans AND foe ...especailly all those original members of the Shaver Mystery Club from the late 1940's and early '50's. So let's hear from you... we welcome ALL suggestions and contributions. And please don't forget to send along a legal sized SSAE for your next issue. If response is good, SHAVERTRON will increase in size. Advertising is also welcomed...send for prices.

Richard Toronto

---

ray-mech dept! 5/15/76
Band Didn't Take LSD

Vallejo Times-Herald

FOWLER (AP) — LSD was not the cause of hallucinations suffered by nineteen junior high school band members, medical officials said Monday.

The youths suddenly became ill and suffered hallucinations May 1, and the doctor who treated them thought they may have been slipped some LSD.

But tests for 25 drugs, including LSD, proved negative, T.J. Conley, administrator of Fowler Municipal Hospital reported.

The 19 Mitchell Junior High students from Atwater were hospitalized only a few hours. Some became hysterical and feared they would be killed by people who went to their aid.

SHAVERTRON is published at irregular intervals by Devopress. There are no subscriptions, no fee, no future? Send SSAE for next issue.

"SHAVERTHOUGHT"... letters from the Rock House

Science -

So far as I know NO scientist knows that I exist or that rock books exist. Did you ever try to reach one of these mythical scientists with a mere letter from an ordinary mortal? Its impossible.

I suspect the whole breed of ossified stuffed-shirtedness. That is, I am too far out for them to notice. Its like expecting the Church of 1400 to recognise Galileo as anything but a liar...To interest science you have first to get well known for ways to make money... then they will notice you. "Science" as I have known it is strictly a sort of lackey or servant to the big-wheel money men. Individually they don't seem to exist.

I suspect all real science is FIRST discovered by amateurs then appropriated by corporation groups ...like Kohoutek...which they mistreated with false publicity and got themselves another red face which is a perfect record on comets for "science"...always wrong. 1/19/74

the Hollow earth -

There is a lot to support this idea of an interior world... and there is evidence that the earth itself had man-made suns orbiting it BEFORE it had a sun...that is.. before it became a satellite of the sun. Earth also had "sun ranches" orbiting it up until recent times.. they were destroyed in one or another of the moon-falls.

The whole picture is very big and fantastic..truth itself is far more fantastic than ANY sci-fic or fantasy.

Whether the earth has a hollow core is hard to decide for one's self ...I ride the fence squarely in the middle on it...its quite possible. 4/1/72

Editor's Note-Shaver spent hours every day writing what must have amounted to thousands of letters from the mid-60's til his death. Readers are invited to share any forms of Shaver communication.

rock books & money -

This whole thing needs all the friends it can get but what it needs most is someone with moolah to give it some needed publicity and circulation of info.

I don't have any...I'm on Soc. Sec. and supplemental checks from "Old Age Ass"...which is modernese for Welfare I guess.

Ass. is short for assistance.. meaning they dont want to but somebody makes them in the Great White Fathers Palace...I eat peanut butter alot, you know...and my bed is a foldaway sofa. I try...but the world isn't really my oyster.

Whatever became of oysters... I remember when they were as big as my hand...oh well.

Dick S   3/4/74

⟨ All quotes are taken from letters ⟩
  graciously supplied by Mike Cohen.

Einstein's Brain Traced to Wichita

New York

Portions of Albert Einstein's brain, which was removed during an autopsy after the scientist's death in 1955, have been traced to a laboratory in Wichita, Kansas.

The brain of the man who propounded the theory of relativity is being studied by scientists seeking clues to his genius.

Steven Levy, a reporter for the magazine New Jersey Monthly traced the brain to the laboratory of Dr. Thomas Harvey, who presided over Einstein's autopsy in Princeton. The magazine said Einstein requested his brain be preserved for study and after it was removed his family ordered doctors to reveal no information on the study.

The magazine said the results of a 23-year study of Einstein's brain are due in 1979.

Whereabouts of the brain have not been publicly known since the autopsy.

Contacted by United Press yesterday, Harvey said a group of scientists is studying the brain. "Yes, it's true we're studying it," he said. "We're comparing it to normal, looking for any differences we can find."

"The only thing I can say is that it's a study that the Einstein estate wants done, and that it also wants kept in scientific literature rather than in the lay press," Harvey said.

United Press

7/27/78

'Accidentals' again ?!

Writing on Mars Was Imaginary

Pasadena 7/26/76
S.F.Chronicle

Viking scientists said yesterday it was only viewers' imagination that made pictures of rock shapes and shadows transmitted from Mars look like crudely painted letters and numbers.

Figures resembling the letters B and G and the numeral 2 were seen in Viking pictures Saturday night.

Dr. Alan Binder, a geologist member of the Viking photographic team, said the B was simply the result of shadowing effects under certain sun angles. He said scientists paid no particular attention to the phenomenon because they knew immediately what it was.

"Things like this are very common on earth," he said. "We didn't take this thing seriously when we saw it. We obviously knew what it was."

Binder noted that Mars "has a long history of people connecting unrelated things." The "canals" on Mars as described by Percival Lowell in the 1890s are a famous example. Closeup examination of Mars showed no such thing.

"There is a very, very strong tendency for the human eye to connect splotchy patterns into something that the human being recognizes," Binder said.

"That is, we interpret what we see, and if we see something that looks vaguely familiar, there is a strong tendency in your mind to make it much more into the thing that you are used to seeing, and that is all that we are seeing in this rock."

UP & AP

⇨ ⇨ the MYSTERY hits Bulgaria HARD ⇦ ⇦ ⇦ !

Mystery Disaster In Balkan Village

Vienna

Scientists are puzzled by an unexplained natural disaster that toppled about 140 houses and left crevices up to 40 yards deep in the streets of a Bulgarian village last month, Sofia radio said yesterday.

Despite continued study, scientists cannot determine what caused the ground to split in mid-December beneath the village of Orsoya.

United Press

1-3-79

A Mushroom Six Feet Wide

Sofia, Bulgaria

A 73-year-old peasant picked up a mushroom last week that he couldn't get into the trunk of his car, the national news agency BTA reported yesterday.

The agency said Neiko Neikov of the northeastern Bulgarian town of Shoumen found the puffball mushroom with a diameter of 6.56 feet. It weighed 19 pounds.

He also found six other puffballs weighing 6.6 to 8.8 pounds, BTA said. *10/25/78 United Press*

--from Mary LeVesque

Lost Caves

There are no "lost" caves more *absolutely* forgotten than the catacombs beneath Lexington, Ky. According to G.W. Ranck's *History Of Lexington, Kentucky*, these crypts were discovered in 1776 by hunters from the pioneer settlement at Boonesborough. They moved rocks of "peculiar workmanship" and discovered a tunnel. This was little more than crawl space, but forcing themselves through, the hunters came into a second tunnel four feet wide and seven feet high which led steeply downward.

He visited the chamber several times over the next 30 years, apparently moving bits of gold when he needed cash. It was not until June 1934, however, that Brown made his discovery public. He visited Stockton, Calif., bought a boat, and organized an expedition to explore his tunnels.

The expedition was to leave Stockton on the morning of June 18, 1934. Brown's associates—several dozen men and women—assembled at the Stockton landing on the San Joaquin River. I've not yet discovered Brown's exact plans, but assume he intended to proceed down the San Joaquin, then up the Sacramento River to the point nearest his discoveries. The party would proceed the rest of the way overland.

Beyond this second tunnel they found a chamber 300 feet long, 100 feet wide, and 18 feet high. This chamber contained altars, idols, altars—and 2,000 human mummies.

The chamber was explored again in 1786. In 1806 it was visited by the Irish travelwriter, Thomas Ashe. Then, as the modern city of Lexington grew, the entrance to the catacombs was lost. The great stone room—more than half-a-million cubic feet of it!—still lays hidden deep beneath the city.

Caves nearly identical to those explored by White and Thomason were discovered in the summer of 1904, in the Bigfoot country of the California-Oregon border. J.C. Brown, a prospector, discovered a shaft-like hole in one of the foothills of the Cascade Mountains. Brown climbed down the hole and found it led to a larger, horizontal tunnel. The walls were constructed of stone blocks fitted neatly together.

Brown followed the stone corridor until he came into a large room with copper-sheated walls. The tempered copper sheets were covered with strange hieroglyphs, as were thin gold plaques stacked on the floor. The room contained oversized tables and chairs and the tables were set with golden plates.

Equally as impressive as these artifacts were the human bones the prospector found in an adjoining room. Brown estimated the bones belonged to men as much as 12 feet tall.

There was only one thing wrong— Brown didn't show up. He disappeared during the night without leaving a trace, and was never seen again.

The immediate suspicion was that Brown's tale had been a ruse to fleece the expedition members he recruited. A subsequent police investigation, however, revealed no one had given any money to Brown. Moreover, the Stockton merchants who had outfitted the expedition reported the prospector's bills had been paid in full.

'Cyclops' Skeleton Found

Sofia

Bulgarian archaeologists have unearthed the skeleton of a "Cyclops" while excavating near the town of Razlog in the southwest of the country, the Bulgarian news agency BTA said.

A brief report said the skeleton, which was found in a burial place, is 5 feet 8 inches tall and has only one eye socket in the coronal bone above the nasal cavity.

According to Greek mythology, the Cyclopes were a race of giants with single eyes in the middle of their foreheads.

BTA said the "unique discovery" was made in the ruins of a building of unknown age and specialists are making a study of the remains.

Circa 1975

4

SHAVERTRON

"The Only Source of Post-Deluge Shaverania"

Winter 1979   Issue 2

MYSTERY VOICE in SHIP CRASH

NY Post 6-13-73

The Coast Guard inquiry into the June 2 collision between the Sea Witch and the Esso Brussels continues today as investigators search for the owner of a "mystery voice" which radioed a warning before the impending crash.

The message was received by a harbor pilot, Capt. George Loud, who yesterday told the three-member board he had been navigating a freighter near Staten Island when he had heard over his radio: "Stay clear of the Sea Witch, she's lost her steering. She's going to hit a tanker."

A few seconds later, Loud said, he heard the radio say: "There she goes." The captain testified that after hearing the broadcast, he had scanned the horizon and had witnessed the collision between the American Export container vessel and the Belgian tanker.

The toll now stands at 10 dead, and 6 Brussels crewmen missing and presumed dead.

Faulty Steering

Previous testimony during eight days of hearings has indicated, and the Coast Guard has confirmed, that a faulty steering mechanism in the rear of the Sea Witch was responsible for the collision.

The chairman of the examining panel, Rear Ad. James W. Moreau, said he thought the "mystery" radio message "sounds like someone on a vessel nearby." He asked the press "to assist us in finding the source of the communication" and said that any information should be forwarded to the Coast Guard commandant in New York.

Capt. Donald Waldeck of the tugboat Jane McAllister testified he had heard over his radio shortly before the crash: "May Day, May Day, this is the container vessel Sea Witch. We've lost our steering gear and we're going to have a collision."

Tentative Finding

After hearing testimony Waldeck's Moreau refused to speculate on whether the unknown voice heard by Loud had come from the Sea Witch. He said: "This may be it."

Moreau said he had wired Coast Guard headquarters in Washington that the "tentative finding" of the board of inquiry attributed the loss of steering in the Sea Witch to a failure of a coupling in the steering mechanism.

In addition, the message recommends that "all inspected vessels with similar steering gear installation be immediately advised of possible defect."

During the hearing at the U.S. Customs House on Bowling Green, a Sea Witch sailor, Johan Johanson, testified that the container vessel had been top-heavy when fully loaded. From M. Cohen

BURLESQUE by R. Shaver

and the Shaver Mystery

DRAWING BY RICHARD S. SHAVER

Pilot Goes Berserk 4-1-77

ZAMBOANGA CITY, The Philippines (AP) — Without a word, a veteran airline pilot left the controls of his plane Thursday, picked up an automatic rifle and sprayed ammunition into the passenger compartment, killing eight persons, officials said.

The crew and servicemen on the military charter flight subdued the pilot, and the copilot, Rolando Suarez, landed the plane in this southern Philippine city.

The dead were a flight attendant and seven of the 34 passengers, all members of the Philippine armed forces. Fourteen service yen were hospitalized, as was the pilot, Capt. Ernesto Abuloc, described as in his 40s. Doctors said Abuloc suffered bruises during the scuffle.

Nine hours after the shooting, Abuloc was reported incoherent and in shock, handcuffed hand and foot and under heavy guard.

Following our contention that all art is an unnatural display of utter idiocy or group madness...we give you the "Apotheosis of the Ballet", whatever that big word apotheosis means, I never could find out.

If you don't believe that all art is nuts, go to the opera ...in German or Italian. Hah. You don't know what-n-H it's all about either, and you don't go.

You know what I think art really is? ...Burlesque. Now there was real art. All the rest is just an imitation of the real thing. Hah! Whatever became of burlesque? There was only one honest artist. He painted truth... Toulouse Lautrec. All the rest are just imitators, wishing they had his guts! Hah! I wonder what Toulouse drank?

6-2-77

Similar Suicides

Tokyo

Five women, aged between 31 and 57, committed suicide by leaping in front of trains in separate incidents in Tokyo yesterday, police said.

Reuters

RICHARD TORONTO

As your editor sits here pasting up this issue of SHAVERTRON, it is becoming more apparent to him what a many-sided creature Richard S. Shaver was, and continues to be. There are so many aspects to the so-called Shaver Mystery that it is difficult to decide where to begin. Would you readers care to hear more about his research into the rock books (those ante-diluvian artifacts that occupied more than 20 years of his life); or would a discussion of his science-fiction stories interest you more; or scientific debates on the aging process and its causes, the make-up of the universe (full of exd), the inhabitants of the caverns beneath our feet, his artwork and his contribution as an artist, or the many and varied aspects of his life as a man???

Well, I'm only guessing, but it seems to me that what most people think of when Shaver pops into their minds is the famous "Mystery" of dero/tero fame. Of caverns and ray-mech and secrets so terrible that no one dare speak their names...except for Richard Shaver, who believed he was doing the world a service by informing them of something they did not want to believe. This made him a very alienated and bitter man.

Shaver was a revolutionary with no true followers in the revolution-ary sense...no one would pick up arms to overthrow the evil he continu-ally exposed...(although Ray Palmer often declared that there were those who died for the Mystery). Shaver expounded a new world view...or rather, amalgamated bits and pieces of historical events and related them to our own 20th century. It was a world order of slaves, unknowing slaves at that, who are chained by an alien race of beings that are detrimental to our way of life.

A revolution was in order, he said, to overthrow the despicable leeches of our history on this planet...and he was the man who would rally us to the banner, the banner of freedom. The only way he found to do this, however, was through his science-fiction stories. Thus, his revolutionary followers were his fans, and those all but abandoned him by the late 1950's. But that did not stop him from continuing his strug-gle and research into the True goings-on here on earth. By the 1960's, he was a beaten man...beaten by the forces that he wanted to overthrow... beaten by Devolution, one of his pet concepts. Devolution, according to Shaver, was the fact that the race, our race, was now beginning a slow turn around in its Darwinian upsurge to greater superiority; that we were going backwards ,becoming more primitive creatures. He could have been right.

He despised the educational system, the government, the Churches, and the media. They were the puratrators of the "false syllogism", based upon false information injected into our civilization's veins by the dope-weilding dero. He blamed this faction's sabotage for his "elimi-nation" from the science-fiction arena, where he could continue his fight against these overwhelming odds. But his worldwide revolution failed... or did it? Are we any closer to uncovering what Shaver tried to bring to light? Or are we that many years closer to devolutionary oblivion in the four short years since his death?

Keeping in mind all these complex pieces of Richard Shaver's life, we have instituted a couple of new features: one is a listing of his vast portfolio of published sci-fi stories (as compiled by Jim Pobst of British Columbia, Canada.) We'll start with his epics from AMAZING STORIES, since that is where it all began; readers will find that the old pulps can still be found lying around old book and magazine stores, often for a very fair price.

The second new feature is an article by Eldon K. Everett from Seattle, Washington, who did some Shaverian research himself into the rumors of lost caves in the Tacoma area. We wholeheartedly encourage any reader who

con't. p. 4

THE DUPUIS PAPERS

by ELDON K. EVERETT

What about the Tacoma Caves? Well, starting around 1870, the Northern Pacific Railroad and others started importing thousands of Chinese laborers into the Tacoma area. This was illegal, of course, but it was done anyway.

With the Chinese there came opium smuggling galore on this Northwestern counterpart to the Barbary Coast. Crime and vice (most of it laid to the pitiful Chinese) got so far out of hand, that in 1885 the 30,000 righteous citizens of Tacoma grabbed their guns and drove the several thousand Chinese out of town, most of the Orientals trekking 40 miles up the Bay to Seattle.

It was common knowledge that the Chinese had carried on their evil trafficking through some old caves they had discovered. The legend of these caves, honeycombing the entire Peninsula, persists to this day.

In December, 1938, Carl Dupuis deposited a 1400-word document called THE MYSTERIOUS CHINESE CAVES with the Washington State Historical Society. Two typescripts of this document (Doc. # 979.7781//D929X) are currently in the society's files. One of them is a recent copy, the other apparently is Dupuis' original. The copy is of the first as it stands. But the original is incomplete! The last few pages, ostensibly an interview with an aged citizen of the area, have been lost or stolen.

The material which follows is from the remaining pages of the document:

During the spring of 1936, Tacoma City Light workers were placing an electrical conuit underground in an alley between Pacific Ave. and "A" Street, just back of the State Hotel.

At a point approximately 75 feet south of 7th St. the crew crosscut a tunnel some ten feet below the ground. William Zimmerman, of 4305 S. L Street, entered the tunnel. It was three feet wide by five feet high and tended in a southwesterly direction, under the hotel. In the opposite direction, it angled toward Commencement Bay.

Zimmerman found that he could walk about 50 feet in either direction. Under the Hotel, the tunnel was blocked, apparently by a cave-in. Away from the Hotel, the tunnel turned sharply toward the west, and after several feet, a gradual curve to the right again. About 30 feet from the entrance, the tunnel dipped sharply, and Zimmerman reported that it would have been necessary to use a rope to descend safely on the wet floor.

Zimmerman also investigated the cave beneath the old Tacoma Hotel, now Stadium High School. A hill drops sharply behind this old building for some 400 feet. The hill is crossed by a little-used railroad spur but, for the most part, it is covered with fir trees and dense undergrowth. The cave entrance is supposed to be partially blocked, but still accessible. Climbing around on this hillside, which is 3 miles from downtown Tacoma, is pretty dangerous, but I have twice tried to locate the entrance, without success. According to legend, there is also an entrance down on the Bay, some 50 feet from the foot of the hill. This is a very deserted stretch of waterfront, covered for the most part by a crumbling seawall, and the blackened timbers of the old Tacoma docks which burned many years ago. This entrance is supposed to be underwater at high tide.

Zimmerman, so far as I know, is the only one to leave a record in print of his investigations of this cave. According to the mutilated Dupuis document, Zimmerman went back over 150 feet into the hillside, but was met by a cave-in apparently caused by the water from the firehoses when the top floors of the Tacoma Hotel burned 50 years

Con't. page 4

3

would so desire, to send us material related to the Shaver Mystery for publication. Mr. Everett also enclosed a fragment of a letter from Richard Shaver dated 1950, in which Shaver reveals some interesting insights into his writing:

"Speaking of (Edgar Rice) Burroughs, did you read my "Gods of Venus", which was modelled after the ERB "Gods of Mars"?

"I had written to Burroughs in a moment of soft-headed ambition (or was it egregious impudence?) wondering if we couldn't work out a deal whereby I could go on with the Burroughs novels as Matson went on with the Thorne Smith series.

"His secretary replied that Burroughs wasn't dead yet, so no soap. I tried to get a letter to Burroughs himself, explaining that I was using "Gods of Mars" as a model just to see what I could do with a Burroughs plot, but he never answered and his secretary probably deemed me beneath notice.

"Anyway, if you're a Burroughs fan, read my "Gods of Venus" and see what you think."

EDITOR'S NOTE: "Gods of Venus" can be found in the March, 1948 issue of AMAZING STORIES.

SPECIAL NOTICE: Don't forget to send in your SSAE for the next issue of SHAVERTRON. This is the only way your editor will know who to send what to next!

═══ — AMAZING STORIES — ═══
[1945-1957]

I REMEMBER LEMURIA...March 1945; THOUGHT RECORDS OF LEMURIA...June 1945; CAVE CITY OF HEL...September 1945; QUEST OF BRAIL...December 1945; INVASION OF THE MICRO-MEN...Feb 1946; THE MASKED WORLD...May 1946; LUDER VALLEY...June 1946; CULT OF THE WITCH QUEEN...July 1946 (w/B.McKenna); THE SEA PEOPLE...Aug 1946; EARTH SLAVES TO SPACE...Sept 1946; THE RETURN OF SATHANAS...Nov 1946 (w/ Bob McKenna); THE LAND OF KUI...Dec 1946; THE MIND ROVERS...Jan 1947; JOE DANNON, PIONEER...Mar 1947; THE CRYSTALINE SARCOPHAGUS...May 1947; SHAVER MYSTERY ISSUE...June 1947, containing i)Formula From the Underworld ii) Zigor Mephisto's Collection of Mentalia iii) Witch's Daughter iv) The Red Legion v) A Proof; MER WITCH OF ETHER 18...Aug 1947; FIRST ROCKET...Aug 1947 (by D. Richard Sharpe); OF GODS AND GOATS...Dec 1947; MEDIEVAL ILLICIT... Jan 1948; FLESH AGAINST SPIRIT...Mar 1948 by A. Blade; GODS OF VENUS... Mar 1948; ICE CITY OF THE GORGON...June 1948 (w/Chester Gier); IF WE GET A CHANCE (article)...July 1948; TITAN'S DAUGHTER...Sept 1948; DAUGHTER OF NIGHT...Dec 1948; THE CYCLOPS (article)...1949,January; STRANGE DISAPPEARANCE OF GUY SYLVESTER...Mar 1949 (by Taylor Victor Shaver and Chester S. Geier); I MURDERED YOU...June 1949 by Ruppert Carlin; WHEN THE MOON BOUNCED...May 1949 by Frank Patton; EXILES OF THE ELFMOUNDS...July 1949; ERDIS CLIFF...SEPT 1949; BATTLE IN ETERNITY... Nov 1949 (w/ Chester Geier); PILLARS OF DELIGHT...Dec 1949 by Stan Raycraft; WE DANCE FOR THE DOM...Jan 1950; HISTORICAL ASPECT OF THE SAUCERS...Oct 1957 (article).

cont from p 3

ago. He described a branch in the tunnel, turning to the right, and advanced the theory that it was likely that this branch connected with the tunnel on 7th Street. Another branch led off toward Pacific Ave. but apparantly Zimmerman followed neither of these branches for any distance.

Graham Says Devil 'Possessed' Jones

1-18-79

Washington

Evangelist Billy Graham said yesterday he believes the Rev. Jim Jones was "possessed by the devil" when he ordered his Peoples Temple followers to carry out their mass suicide in Jonestown, Guyana.

"There are forces of evil in the world that must be taken seriously," Graham told a National Press Club gathering. He pointed to the deaths of Jones and more than 900 of his followers as an event that "cannot be explained apart from the demonic."

"I believe he [Jones] was possessed by the devil," said Graham, declaring the devil "counterfeits true faith."

"There is no way one can link Jim Jones with the church," Graham said. "He used the church for his own demonic ends."

Asked what the government could do to protect people from such cults, Graham said churches don't want governmental interference but he supports "a requirement that every religious organization make public its financial statement."

Graham also said:

- He has not and will not take a stand on the Equal Rights Amendment, saying women should have "all the rights that belong to them, recognizing they are different."

- He has spoken by phone four or five times with former President Nixon since his resignation and the former president sounds more jovial each time.

United Press

Scientists Push A $1 Billion 'Death Ray'

Washington   1-22-79

Scientists are recommending that the Pentagon step up research on particle beams — streams of energy likened to lightning bolts or a Buck Rogers death ray — in a program that could cost $1 billion over ten years.

Dr. Ruth Davis, the Pentagon official in charge of research and advanced technology, said in an interview yesterday that a panel of 53 scientists studying the matter soon will send its final report to Defense Secretary Harold Brown.

Pentagon officials said Brown already has indicated willingness to spend more money on technology if it is as well justified as the particle beam research appears to be.

There are reports that the Russians already have tested a particle beam, or will shortly, and some people worry that the United States is falling behind on exotic technology.

Both the panel of scientists and U.S. intelligence forces say that neither Russia nor the United States is likely to test the weapons before the 1990s.

Particle beams fired from the ground or space at close to the speed of light — 186,000 miles a second — have been suggested as a means of stopping enemy nuclear missiles before they reach the United States.

The thinking is that beams could neutralize missiles by heat or by frazzling their electronics.

'Voice From Grave' Suspect Confesses

2-23-79

Chicago

A hospital worker, named by "a voice from the grave" as the killer of a 48-year-old woman, entered a surprise guilty plea yesterday.

Judge Frank W. Barbaro then sentenced Allan Showery, 32, to 14 years in prison for the murder. Showery pleaded guilty to stabbing and strangling Teresita Basa on Feb. 21, 1977, and to armed robbery and arson. He was sentenced to concurrent terms of four to 12 years for armed robbery and arson.

Showery's guilty pleas came during a retrial. After a long trial that ended January 26, the jury was unable to reach a verdict and a mistrial was declared.

Showery and Basa worked at Edgewater Hospital. He came under investigation in the woman's murder when a co-worker, Remebios Chua, and her husband, Jose, told police that the victim's "spirit" named Showery as the killer.

The "voice from the grave," supposedly speaking through Mrs. Chua, also told her husband that Showery stole jewelry from Basa when he ransacked her apartment.

Basa's burned body was found beneath a mattress in the apartment.

Showery was arrested after police recovered the missing jewelry from his common-law wife.

Associated Press

'DEATH RAY'

But there are big problems. So far, beams have been created only inside laboratory devices called accelerators. Davis said that controlling them would be like leashing lightning, which "zigs and zags and doesn't strike twice" because of atmospheric disruptions its passage causes.

"We still have too much basic physics and hard engineering to be done" to judge whether they can be used as weapons, she said.

But she said the 53 private and government scientists assembled by Edward Chapin of the government's Los Alamos nuclear laboratory last fall mapped out proposals for five years of research to "put the jigsaw puzzle together."

The scientists recommended increases in five areas, including ways to control and point beams, and development of super-sophisticated radar to track and switch them from one target to another with great speed.

Davis said if engineering problems could be overcome "you could hit hundreds of targets in a single second."

The panel suggested spending increases ranging from tens to hundreds of millions of dollars, depending on how far the Pentagon wants to shoot a beam. That could range from half a mile to 600 miles.

Davis herself estimated the research could cost $1 billion over ten years, based on the cost of the Pentagon's high energy laser program, which still has not been demonstrated as a possible weapon.

United Press

Baker Slays Five, Dies in Mixer

Manila   6-26-76

A baker went berserk, killing five people with two knives and wounding seven before jumping into a rotating flour mixer which crushed him to death, police in the central Philippines city of Cebu said yesterday.

Reuters

'Evil voices' led to attack

By Gary Oakes 9-5-79
Toronto Star

A housekeeper who says she was "possessed" by evil people, who put a curse on her and compelled her to attack her employer, will be sentenced Sept. 20 for wounding.

Emily Mae Hernadi, 40, pleaded guilty when she appeared yesterday before Mr. Justice William Maloney of the Supreme Court of Ontario.

Prosecutor Ken Murray said Mrs. Hernadi had been speaking amiably with her employer, Arlene Zweig of Alexis Blvd., North York, last Nov. 13 before the attack.

Later that night, when Mrs. Zweig was taking a shower, the lights went off. After she stepped from the shower and called Mrs. Hernadi, she was attacked without warning by the 250-pound housekeeper.

Murray said Mrs. Hernadi used a heavy clothes iron to beat the 123-pound Mrs. Zweig.

She also pushed her employer back into the bathtub and turned on hot water which caused first- and second-degree burns, court was told.

The glass shower doors were smashed during the attack and Mrs. Zweig suffered several cuts, including a severed artery in her left wrist.

Stopped attack

Murray said Mrs. Zweig managed to bite Mrs. Hernadi and the attack ceased. The housekeeper left the bathroom and the lights came back on. Moments later, she returned, apologized and tried to help Mrs. Zweig.

Police were called and when they arrived, Mrs. Hernadi said: "I tried to kill her. Oh God, I tried to kill her."

Mrs. Zweig spent 10 days in hospital and is permanently scarred as a result of the attack, court was told.

"It doesn't make any sense," Mrs. Hernadi told police. "I didn't have any reason to hit her."

But she said: "There's a curse in my house. There's a doll in the house. It's a curse doll."

Police later found a small, black, human-like figure in the kitchen of Mrs. Sweig's home.

It was wrapped in a pair of Mrs. Zweig's panties and a lock of her hair was with it. Photographs of Mrs. Zweig were also attached to the doll, which had seven pins stuck in it.

Heard voices

"All I hear is voices," Mrs. Hernadi told police. "They said that Arlene (Mrs. Zweig) had to die.

"I told them I didn't want to . . . they told me I had to do what they told me if I wanted to be one of them.

"It's like somebody is pressing something heavy on my head."

Asked who she meant by "they," Mrs. Hernadi replied: "They're a group. They're evil people. They make people do their bidding for them."

Murray said police found a number of books and articles "relating to witchcraft and voodoo" in Mrs. Hernadi's room in the Zweig house.

She told police she didn't know what had happened the night of the attack. "All I can remember is the blood."

Defence counsel Barry Fox said Mrs. Hernadi has made progress during the 10 months she has spent in a mental facility since the attack.

Fox said he will call a psychiatrist and a psychologist to testify at the sentencing.

Weird Mistakes at 3 Mile Plant

SF Chronicle
5-18-79

Washington

Operators trying to control the Three Mile Island nuclear power plant accident repeatedly drew the wrong conclusions from a flood of conflicting information and were hampered at every turn by equipment glitches and seemingly malicious fate, the Nuclear Regulatory Commission was told yesterday.

The NRC's special task force on the March 28 incident in Pennsylvania, releasing its first interim chronology of the near-disaster, reported that:

• An operator inadvertently blocked with his body the view of indicators that would have told him two crucial feedwater pump valves were closed. NRC sources explained after the meeting that the operator was "a big man with a large belly that hung over the instrument panel."

• Listening through an amplifier system to gurgles and thumps within a steam generator, operators decided the noises meant there was water inside, when in fact the generator was boiling dry.

• The computer printout of events during the crisis, similar to an airline flight recorder, jammed for nearly 90 minutes at the height of events. It was running two hours behind and eventually much of its data was lost altogether.

• After operators were ordered to don respirators and face masks to guard against radiation they were unable to talk to each other.

• Ordered to evacuate the control room of Unit 2 for the adjacent control room of Unit 1, only a few operators did so, and those who went left the door open.

• In the middle of the crisis, when fuel damage was occurring for lack of cooling water, operators kept the pumps off from fear that vibrations would damage the pumps. "There was a general feeling that there must be something wrong with the (temperature gauges), that the temperature couldn't possibly be that high," reported chief investigator Robert Martin.

• The NRC's regional headquarters did not learn of the accident until 36 minutes after Three Mile Island officials called, because the headquarters director was stuck in a traffic jam and could not respond to the answering service beeper.

The General Accounting Office, meanwhile, said in a report issued yesterday that human error in nuclear plant control rooms is a problem not limited to Three Mile Island.

Noting that mistakes by operators are common causes of technical problems at nuclear plants around the nation, the GAO criticized the Nuclear Regulatory Commission's rules governing the training and licensing of operating personnel.

The report said that about 90 percent of the applicants for licenses to be control room operators pass the qualifying examination on the first try, prompting the GAO to question whether NRC's test is too easy. The GAO also noted that the commission does not require utilities to report names of operators who commit technical errors. Thus the government cannot monitor the competence of the operators it has licensed.

The GAO report, requested by Senator Richard S. Schweiker, R-Pa., after the Three Mile Island accident, concluded that the NRC and various organizations investigating the Pennsylvania accident should emphasize strengthening the procedures for licensing the people who operate nuclear generating plants.

The GAO said that errors by numerous categories of people — technicians, managers, maintenance crews, and others working at the plants — also can have serious implications. But workers in these other categories are not licensed.

The GAO report said that the average control room operator in a nuclear plant is a 34-year-old high school graduate with seven years of power plant experience.

Washington Post

Shaver

PRINTS

We are thinking about reproducing photographically apprx. 13 sketches by Richard Shaver. These would be in the area of 4by5 or 6 inches in B&W. If enough people are interested, will go ahead with it. So please write if you'd care to comment.

SHAVERTRON

"The Only Source of Post-Deluge Shaverania"

Spring 1980   Issue 3

Tues., Jan. 8, 1980   ★ San Francisco Chronicle

A scientist said yesterday he can tune in brain cells with weak microwaves, changing nerve chemistry and possibly altering behavior.

The results, the researcher said, may help lead to important new techniques for studying intimate details of body chemistry. They may also help show how much and what kinds of microwave radiation — a high-frequency form of radio waves — are safe.

In tests on both living cats and brain cells of chickens, using microwaves far below the intensity usually considered effective or potentially harmful to living organisms, the ability of vital calcium ions to bind to nerve cell membranes was dramatically altered, said Dr. W. Ross Adey.

He described his research at a session on microwaves during the meeting of the American Association for the Advancement of Science.

The phenomenon could lead to a way to delicately alter brain chemistry, without drugs or surgery, using a technique whose effects appear to disappear soon after the microwaves are turned off, he said.

Adey, chief of research at the Veterans Administration Medical Center in Loma Linda, San Bernardino County, said the relatively faint microwaves also seemed to change the mental state of cats, leaving them more wakeful and alert.

Whether the new findings reveal a public health hazard at microwave levels below those now considered safe, he said, will require more research to discover.

He found the effects only at certain combinations, or "windows," of microwave characteristics. He said the impact on brain cells — and some other body tissues — occurs only when specific ranges of microwave frequencies are combined with certain rates of variation in intensity, a process called amplitude modulation.

Weak Microwaves May Alter Cells

NEW "MYSTERY" FEATURE !

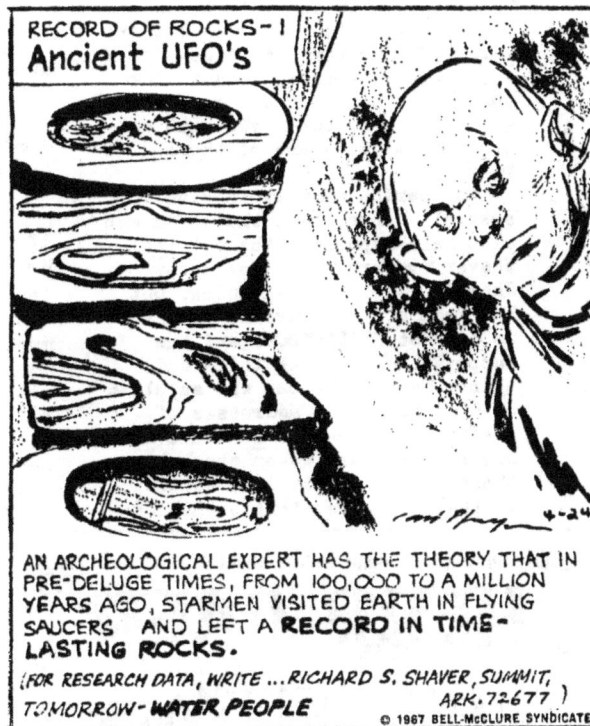

RECORD OF ROCKS—1
Ancient UFO's

AN ARCHEOLOGICAL EXPERT HAS THE THEORY THAT IN PRE-DELUGE TIMES, FROM 100,000 TO A MILLION YEARS AGO, STARMEN VISITED EARTH IN FLYING SAUCERS AND LEFT A **RECORD IN TIME-LASTING ROCKS.**

(FOR RESEARCH DATA, WRITE...RICHARD S. SHAVER, SUMMIT, ARK. 72677)
TOMORROW- **WATER PEOPLE**
© 1967 BELL-McCLURE SYNDICATE

Do you recognise this syndicated Shaver Feature?? If you do, why not drop us a line and let us all know about it? Right now, the thing is shrouded in a fog, for not all of the material we receive here at Shavertron comes with a handy instruction sheet. We have a total of six "Record of Rocks" features to run for you. Apparently, they were meant to rival the likes of Ripley's "Believe it or not"....a la Shaver. So---we will start with the first installment, "Ancient Ufos" and work our way up to number six: "Ufo Traffic", until someone recognises it and lets us in on the story.

However, he said, powerful new military radars designed to detect missiles and aircraft over the horizon sometimes produce, within one half mile of the radar, radiation of the sort he used in his laboratory. Such radars include two mammoth Air Force "Pave Paws" devices, one now nearing completion at Beale Air Force Base near Marysville and another constructed at Otis Air Force Base in Massachusetts.

The giant radars, he said, are probably safe, "but we don't really know the effect of exposing nearby populations to very faint microwaves for extended periods, many years or more."

His research on chicken brain cells, he said, is well-known to the Air Force, which he said dismissed the results "in a very self-serving way," by arguing it doesn't apply to living mammals. Subsequent research on cats, he said, confirms the effect.

Adey's work seems to mean that profound biological effects may occur under some special circumstances, even when the electric fields created by microwaves are far smaller than natural electrical activity in the body.

Adey described the surfaces of nerve cells as covered with flexible, hair-like molecules, each carrying a negatively charged atom at its tip.

The effect, he said, is like a "field of corn, waving in an electric breeze."

"If we impose a field from the outside," he said, "we are really competing with the signals the brain makes in its own cells."

The organizer of the session, Dr. Don R. Justeson of the Kansas City Veterans Administration Medical Center, said Adey's work may mean "we are on the threshold of communicating directly with the cell."

By Charles Petit
Science Correspondent

It appears that 1980 will be a prelude to a momentous decade, one that Richard Shaver would have watched with a knowing eye. RSS was an avid prophet, (some say of doom), and many of his predictions found fertile ground in fact. As the year rolls on into its first few months, we have seen great cataclysms week after week, in the way of earthquakes, floods, aircraft and political disasters. The poison Radiation spills out into our oceans and ground water, along with deadly chemicals that are causing birth defects and cancer, and our spectre of our old pal, WWIII once again looms up over us.

As I remember, RSS was one of the first anti-nuclear activists, (another good reason to blackball him from the literary arena). Ufos, after all these years, have been wrentched out of CIA files to show that these agencies are truly concerned about them, something that RSS would have enjoyed seeing after his years of harping on government cover-ups. ing on governmental cover-ups. Ufos still put on their shows of power and invulnerability, while earthly attempts to come closer to their meaning is still not coming...not one NEW development in this saga since their 1947 debut, except in their interpretation by researchers.

RSS had a very simple explanation for the ufos: "UFO really represent an intergalactic movie outfit that makes tri-dis like documentaries on various worlds. They like a captive people who can be used as FREE extras willy-nilly in wars and crucifixions and such like. So they swoop in on the planet from time to time and start a big,

wholesale extravaganza called 'World War'. Then they film it for the space sale outlets all over the galaxy. They keep a few ships flitting about to keep us all nice and ignorant of the real use they have for us as willing extras in wholesale murder mysteries..."

editorial

By Richard Toronto

We are happy to report, however, that "the only source of post-deluge Shaver Mystery info is doing well in these cataclysmic times, which only seems right for an SM zine to do.

Many Shaver fans, some who have followed the Mystery for 20-30 years, have discovered us and now read SHAVERTRON. Some helpful people have sent clippings and/or short pieces for publication. It cannot be overemphasized how much we appreciate this. S is meant to be an open forum for all fans. They are really the life blood of a zine like this. Our new letters page reflects this attitude. There were many many more notes in the SHAVERTRON box, but our size naturally cramps our style. But we appreciate every one of those letters!

One person we want to give special thanks to is the woman who also helped publish the original Shaver Mystery Magazine: Dotty Shaver. From the beginning, Dot has been of immeasurable help to us here at SHAVERTRON, and has supported us through thick and thin. Dot is the one who supplied us with names and addresses of possible readers for S. Some of our readers were taken aback by their first, unsolicited issue in the mail...we might even go so

far as to say they were suspicious of us at first, but everyone seems to know what we're doing now, and any feelings of apprehension have all but vanished. We feel that having Dot with us has given a measure of spunk and authenticity that without, we might have folded after the second issue. Many thanks to you Dotty! We love you!

Dot Shaver – 1956 –

Mr Jim Pobst has added a story by RSS to his long list of RSS's contributions to AMAZING STORIES which appeared in S no. 2... WHY THE MOON IS BLUE by 'Ruppert Carlin', July 1949. You'll find Jim's list for RSS tales that appeared in FANTASTIC ADVENTURES in this issue.

REMEMBER::: Send in your SASE's if you want to receive issue 4. We keep no file on subscribers to this zine, so a legal size envelope with your name and address is a must. We encourage unsolicited mss. from everyone...CONTRIBUTIONS, not necessarily $$, but if that's all you've got we won't argue if $ shows up. Some helpful readers have already coughed up a few frogskins here and there..it ALL helps. May KID be with you.

(From time to time, we will be reprinting excerpts from the old Shaver Mystery Club Letterzine, which appeared circa 1950-1954. Based in Chicago, this zine was meant to help RSS get out from under the load of mail from fans).

1. Where is an entrance?
"There are hundreds of entrances traceable by the names of places and towns in the far past-such as the town in Italy called 'Intramend', which meant in the elder tongue-'train going in the termina.' This town has been renamed several times in the past centuries, but the ancient name was Intramend. It was a railroad town, thousands of years ago, where people took a train into the depths from the surface. Today, the entrance would require a lot of money and excavation to uncover, but it could be done at less expense than to drill an oil well. ...If the mysterious o bstacles that rise before all such efforts did not defeat you. There is the well-known Mt. Shasta, the several quite well-known polished shafts going into the depths in South America (on government records, but now boarded up and forbidden)--there is the entrance described in the book 'Etidorpha' in Virginia. There are a great number of Indian place names which label spots where entrance to the lower world was once possible. All you need is to know the Elder Tongue Words such as IN, TRAM, and the fact that 'entrance' also means 'to go into a state of rapture', to 'carry away with ecstecy', is not an accident of coincidence but comes from the the fact that an entrance into the caverns was to be carried into the rapture of the use of the elder machines for producing pleasure. The Indian names can be decoded by a study of the elder phonetic meanings and will reveal a number of possible entrances to any sincere and intelligent person who really goes about the problem industriously and inductively. Yes, they are closed over with earth and rock, many of them impossible to all but titanic excavating efforts, or they have been walled up, by those who conceal the caverns from us, and would be uncovered by the judicious use of a few sticks of dynamite.

2. How can I get in?
"You can't without a lot of effort, and if you did the chances are a thousand to one you would not come out alive. This is understood by anyone who reads Shaver."
3. What equipment do I need for such an attempt?
"Foolhardy courage, suicidal tendencies, alot of money, several hard-headed frinds who have worked in mines and black damp, and no delusions about bringing back anything, even if you're lucky. L. Taylor Hansen found a polished shaft in Arizona but black damp kept him out. He got equipment, helmet and oxygen flasks, etc...and that was two years ago. If he came back he hasn't mentioned the fact yet. But this is the second time he has disappeared for long periods. It is two years now.

[ALL ANSWERS BY R SHAVER]

4. How do you hear voices?
"Subject yourself to variant high frequency currents- the magnetic fields surrounding high voltage-I think that what happens is the concentrated flows of electrons (or are they magnetrons in the fields around a wire) strips off the natural insulation around the nerves connecting the brains thought centers. The brain is able to receive from its parts the natural thought waves and actual electric flows which make up all thought. It is a natural receiver of all thought energies, able to read and interpret the most abstract thought...and it has been protected from outside disruptive energies by a natural sheathing of highly effective insulation. This is perforated by high velocity particles, so that the energies around, such as those that are borne upon the natural conducting medium like that surrounding all current-bearing electric wires brings you to recognisable thought messages from outside your mind. Normally these would be screened out, kept out by the normal insulative sheathing of the mind, but after subjection to certain kinds of powerful magnetic fields, such as those encountered in welding work, other electric work, one becomes sensitized by the destruction of this protection, and one hears voices. This first sensitivity is the greatest, the confused mind, receiving from everywhere all kinds of alien energies and unfamiliar thought, soon erects other greater barriers (just as scar tissue forms around a wound) and one becomes impervious to telepathic communication. But once having experienced the astounding phenomena of telepathy in all its complexity, one never again doubts the existence of powerful groups who have mastered the use of mechanical and/or electrical telepathy and use it for their own purposes. (Such devices do not operate with ordinary electricity but with a flow akin to the neural electric generated by the human body.)"
5. How do you know you're not crazy if you hear voices??
"The idea that 'hearing voices is an insane thing' entirely

ask Doc Shaver

Rich Shaver was wise in the ways of the world, and through his vast amount of experience and research into various topics, had gathered a large body of information. He used this info to help out many of the people who came to him for advice. This column aims to pass on some of that info, in the hope that it will prove to be of use to others.

[GETTING RID OF BRAIN FEVER]

"Remember what I said about brain fever...the right remedy is a long, long cold shower ... I have seen this often.. and so have you in the bughouse they cold pack you for it..doused with ice water and wrapped in blankets to keep cold.
"When you get so wound up on something..take your temp. and a good cold shower and see if it seems so reasonable.
"Just soaking your head in a bowl of cold water helps. This is a common ailment in the Pentagon, u no.
"They should all go soak their heads before they get us into some more impossible wars.
"this sounds funny but it really aint... it is a common ailment like the common cold but people dont happen to know it.
"Hotheads... are just exactly that if you took their temp."

Go to Page 4

Very few rocks have large, plain pictures in or on them. Maybe they are just plain worn out from extreme old age. And yet, because of the sheer number of rocks all over the world, there are still thousands upon thousands of rockfogo images one can find. Most are weak or difficult to perceive.

One way to restore some contrast is to look at rocks reflected in a common magnifying glass—negative magnification. A fairly bright light is needed and a dim or dark background. If some rocks are held so that the surface has shadows cast across them, many images become plain.

EASY WAYS TO SEE ROCK IMAGES / BY BILL BLISS

Making rubbings with carbon paper and thin paper will coax images out of the most unco-operative rock. Remember, the majority of rock images are small, so a hand-held magnifier with a power of 10X to 40X (or a low power microscope) will make a large number of images visible.

If you have luck with prospecting, you might find some excellent examples--like the common fine grain conglomerates. The best of those have dark blue or black or dark brown inclusions and crystals in a light-colored matrix.

If you find small, colored dots, (usually blue, green or yellow) those are index marks for the picture frames. Since almost all (the exceptions are rare) rock book images are actually SYSTEMS of images, once you have zeroed in on one, give it 1/4 turns and more images will appear. Viewing the image at different angles from the line of sight often brings out an uncanny 3 dimensional effect. And sometimes the scene changes to an aerial view.

Rock images also have what is known as the "consolidating image effect". In other words, at different viewing distances, different images are seen. This usually works well with rocks over two inches wide. The distance where the images change is commonly based on a factor of 2.

Framing can be vital in perceiving an image, so try masking off various areas, as Shaver discovered early on. Also, slow vision is very useful in perceiving dim, obscure images. It works best when there are few or no distractions. Medium or dim light helps. Slow vision also requires long minutes of concentration, repeatedly looking back on your work.

Rock images also come in extra large sizes, so photos of various mountain terrains are a good place to look for them. There is an exceptionally good one of these on page 514 of the October, 1979 issue of the National Geographic Magazine. The images are small, so looking at them through a 1/16" hole in a piece of cardboard, scanning small areas, brings them out alot plainer.

Large rock images also turn up in photos of Mars or the moon. Shaver regarded the moon as the handiest large rock pic. Both Shaver and the author have taken many rock photos, but they are not generally available except through the book, The Secret World. In a future issue of SHAVERTRON there will be an article on taking rock pix yourself. It will include common close-up techniques used on a few dozen common rocks (conglomerates are preferable).

Ed. note--Although Bill didn't mention it, he was the one who helped Rich with some of the color plates in Secret World. Bill still has a supply of rock pix slides which he sells at a nominal fee to researchers. Contact him at 422 Wilmot, Chillicothe, Ill. 61523

Cont. from page 3 ~

sourcing in self deception due to disordered mind arose when electricity itself was not discovered, and is today exploded except for those who still believe the modern age is the only time when people knew anything worth knowing. Such acts as Dunninger's are public demonstrations of the 'natural ability' to read others thought. Telepathy is another word for 'hearing voices'.

6. What connection do flying saucers have with the Caverns???

"Every connection. They transport earth goods, bring other goods from other planets, trade with the caverns, are the flying force of the cavern people, and also the ships from other planets. We will hear alot more of the flying saucers before we hear less. They are the conveyances of our actual rulers, who prefer to keep their ex-

istence a kind of open secret. Most of our real big shots have some contact with the power behind the flying saucers."

7. How have the alleged machines of the Caverns work??

"Most of the cavern machines have been wrecked in the past by ignorant mishandling, which still occurs too widely today. They are used to mani-pulating earth surfacemen's affairs to the ad-vantage of groups of people in whom we 'do not believe'."

Thanx, Jim Wentworth - for the loan

FANTASTIC ADVENTURES !

Ed. Note--As new stories are found, we will pub them in future issues so that our lists will come as close to complete as possible. One tale from Amazing we overlooked last issue is "The Insane Planet"--Feb. 49 by Alex Blade.

Following are the RSS stories that appeared in Fantastic Adventures:

An Adam from the Sixth--May 46
The Tale of the Last Man--July 46
The Princess and Her Pig--March 47
The Tale of the Red Dwarf--May 47
Witch of the Andes--Oct. 47
Slaves of the Worm--Feburary 48
The Thin Woman--March 48
Lair of the Grimalkin--April 48,
(by G.H. Irwin)
Mirrors of the Queen--July 48
Fountain of Change--December 48,
(with Chester Geier)
The Mermaid of Maracot Deep--Feb. 49
The Cyclopeans-- June 49
The World of the Lost-- March 50,
(by Paul Lohrman).

Dear Rich,
Personally, virtually any type of material you'd care to publish in future issues will be fine with me, whether it is information about the "Mystery", personal details about Shaver or whatever. I do like your idea of reproducing the Shaver sketches, so hope you go ahead with that.
Just happened to think of something Shaver said about Teros, which I've never seen mentioned in any of his writings. In one of our conversations, he said Teros were like "a mother-in-law who's always right!" I think that pretty well speaks for itself!

Yours truly,
Lou Farish,
ARK.

R--We've received a few positive replies on the RSS sketch repro's, but not enough yet to warrant a full Green Light on the project. We'd like to hear from more of you readers on this...do you want to see 12-15 of RSS's unusual sketches photographically reproduced for your collection? Then let's hear from you.

Dear Mr Richard R. Toronto,
Glad and surprised to know Dot is helping alot. Knowing your newsletter is coming out gave me a glad feeling! Many things I could write about. The deros talk to me as much as others knowing about them. Is this safe to state in a newsletter or magazine? In one or two volumes, Richard wrote the leaders (and masses) are easily mentally/emotionally rayed as their minds are too dumb to take all his data; they can't comprehend the degree of ray control on themselves.
Do you recall Richard writing in some volume that Teros had a time-travelling device? And that it was one subject he couldn't get much specific data on due to real strong dero ray interference? Well, Mr. Dick Williams told me the gov't. is in some mech-caverns and can work some of the mech. Such caverns were ones just having the devices. One of the devices, said Williams (ex-CIA) said was a time travelling device! They are using it--have been for years.
He explained it was not at all like we think of H:G: Well's time machine...works different.

I can just hear Boris Karloff say in his serious way, "Its his knowledge that must not be believed." Shaver knew the deal with me. Two-three others I've told things to thru the years said I've investigated too far ....

Sincerely,
HMS, TX.

To the Editor of LIFE MAGAZINE,
In your recent article on science fiction you described the "Shaver Hoax".
...Deros are a fact, and one does not have to be a cavern dweller to be one. Dero is an ancient word from Mantong, meaning detrimental robot, or, in English, "habitual thinker of evil thoughts" (which naturally result only in evil deeds) Hitler was a person whose thoughts and actions resulted only in harm... The hoax began as an attempt by me as an attempt to get Mantong (that language which is the mother tongue of most earth languages) into the hands of men able to force its recognition and study for the important key to the past which it is. Before Egypt the origin and the history of the human race is still pretty exclusively darkness. I give you the key to that darkness. I cannot help it if you will not make the effort to understand. It takes perhaps an hour's honest study and thought to begin to realize that Mantong is not a silly invention but something very, very big.

Richard S.Shaver
June 11, 1951

False Report Of Tito Death

Belgrade *San Francisco Chronicle* **7**
★ Sat., Mar. 4, 1978

A Yugoslav government spokesman yesterday described as absurd and completely unfounded a report that President Tito had died.

The Associated Press said in a story issued in New York that the first paragraph of an obituary on President Tito had been transmitted in error on the agency's national broadcast wire. The story was killed ten minutes later. But, in the meantime, a number of U.S. radio stations broke into their programs to report the 85-year-old Tito had died.

Reuters

Hello Richard,
I am looking for some of Dick's work which got away from me over the years and will gladly purchase if it can be located. I am looking for Volume numbers 2,3,6 and 9 of the Shaver Mystery Magazine, containing the full story of MANDARK.
Now, on another matter I must take you to task--Dick and Dotty Shaver and Ray and Marge Palmer were personal friends, and I miss them both, (Dick and Ray, that is).
You mentioned in an editorial that by the 1960's, Dick was a beaten man. I take exception to that. Dick was never a beaten man...a little discouraged now and then but never beaten, and a time or two he almost won.
One day, he and I were having a discussion and Dick said, "What I'd like to see them do is drill a hole in the bottom of the ocean and flood them bastards out!" (He meant the dero.) Well, several years later, that almost happened during the Geo-Physical Year. The USA contributor was to drill into the so-called "mantle"...they got a young engineer from Brown and Root in Texas and set at it up over the Hawaiian Deep. They started drilling like crazy but the Powers That Be were alerted and they stopped it cold. It was called "The Mohole"... look it up.

Cheers,
Bert Holland,FLA.

R--I'll make it up to you, Bert, by pointing out that Mr Eldon Evertt, of Seattle may have just what you're looking for...see his letter below.

Dear Richard,
Big News! I now have issues 1 to 9 of The Shaver Mystery Magazine. I think this was all of them... at any rate, it's got MANDARK with illustrations by RSS and Virgil Finlay (among others). Lots of articles and letters from readers, with RSS's detailed replies.
I will xerox the entire set of issues for $36.50. I know this is high, but it will take me about an hour or so of standing there feeding dimes into the copy machine...If it pays back my cost, perhaps I can make available other Shaver material from my collection.

Eldon Everett
1726 Summit Apt.1
Seattle, WA.98122

He wants to send Earth into new orbit

William E. Peterson has a bizarre plan for preventing the super cold winters we've been getting.

A 48-year-old engineer from Seattle, Wash., he wants to turn Earth into a spaceship and blast it into orbit nearer the sun.

To get a rocket engine powerful enough, Peterson has designed a "nuclear cannon" to be built in the Mojave Desert of the southwest.

As fantastic as all this sounds, Peterson says there will be incredible benefits. For example:

● Temperatures will average 5 degrees warmer all over Earth.

● The ozone layer which protects Earth from harmful sun rays will be increased as a result of the "cloud canopy" effect of the cannon.

● Deserts will be transformed into gardens due to increased rainfall from the "cloud canopy."

The nuclear cannon is patterned after the Great Pyramid of Egypt. (Peterson believes the pyramids were originally nuclear cannons built in ancient times by an advanced race.)

It will be 450 feet tall and have an eight-foot-diameter shaft aimed at the North Star. A nuclear fission explosion of one megaton will be shot through the cannon each day for a year.

One megaton is equal to the explosion of one million tons of dynamite.

Those daily blasts should be enough, Peterson believes, to change the Earth's orbit and rotation and offset the ice age some scientists predict.

The heat from the explosion will be absorbed by the stone cannon. Peterson then plans to shower tremendous amounts of water onto the cannon. The water will evaporate filling the skies with a canopy of clouds.

The clouds will pour rain onto deserts and will add to the protective ozone layer because ozone is formed when sun rays hit clouds. *12-4-79*

By DAN SCHWARTZ

A man jogging down a country road stumbles — then vanishes into thin air as his friends watch in astonishment.

A husband and wife are clearing snow from their car's windows. The husband looks up and discovers his wife has mysteriously disappeared.

A British diplomat walks behind his carriage and is never seen again.

"Incredible as it sounds, there are a number of cases of people simply vanishing into thin air," British author Paul Begg told The ENQUIRER.

Begg, who has documented dozens of these mysterious disappearances in his book "Into Thin Air," says dozens of people "simply puff out of existence" every year — and have done so for centuries.

"One of the best-known cases happened in England in the last century," he said. "One day in 1873 a health fanatic named James Worson accepted a wager from three of his friends that he could not run to the town of Coventry and back, a distance of 16 miles.

"Worson set out to win his bet and his friends climbed into a cart and followed him to make sure he kept the terms of the wager.

"For several miles, Worson jogged ahead of the cart when all of a sudden he appeared to stumble over some unseen object.

"He tripped, cried out and vanished."

Worson's friends could not believe their eyes, but an exhaustive search of the area confirmed what seemed impossible.

Worson had vanished into thin air.

In another baffling case, an early 19th-century British diplomat, Benjamin Bath-

Mystery of People Who Disappear Into Thin Air

urst, disappeared while on a mission abroad.

"He stopped at an inn, rested for a while and shortly before 9 p.m. made preparations to continue his journey," said Begg.

"In front of witnesses he looked over his horses and walked behind his carriage. Then he vanished."

A more recent case involved Jackson Wright, who stopped his car in New York's Lincoln Tunnel one winter day in 1975 to clear snow from the windshield. His wife Martha began clearing the rear window but seconds later, when Jackson looked up, she had disappeared.

A series of unexplainable disappearances which occurred between 1945 and 1950 continue to baffle authorities. During that period, seven people vanished while hiking along an eight-mile stretch of a well-known Vermont trail.

Bloodhounds traced one small boy's scent for miles, then lost it in exactly the same spot where another vanishing hiker was last seen.

Only one of the hikers was ever found. Her body was located in a spot that search parties had combed thoroughly when she'd disappeared months earlier. The woman, Frieda Langer, was an experienced hiker and was familiar with the trail. No evidence of murder was ever uncovered in any of the Vermont disappearances.

"It gives rise to the chilling thought that some mysterious force took Frieda, then returned her body when it had no further need of it," Begg said.

Begg doubts that the several dozen unexplainable disappearances which occur each year involve people who are purposely hiding.

"You will be found eventually if somebody loves you or hates you enough to persist with the search," he said.

"These cases are evidence that some force is at work which defies a rational explanation."

NATIONAL ENQUIRER *1-1-80*

TAKE OUT an AD on this page in issue no. 4 !

●

NOBODY ALIVE today is a descendant of Neanderthal man.

Mystery Man Flies in Box To Seattle

10-19-79

Seattle

It looked like just another airfreight shipment until a man popped out of a box, saying, "Let me out of here," and ran away before he could be questioned, Port of Seattle police said.

According to Jim Whittom, a spokesman for the Port of Seattle police, Northwest Airlines employees were unloading a large metal container yesterday that had arrived on a DC-10 from Anchorage, Alaska.

A man carrying a small canvas bag emerged from a four-foot square plywood box inside the container and ran out of the building before the workers could stop him, Whittom said.

The man would have had to spend at least 11 hours in the box, including 4½ hours in the pressurized cargo plane, said Whittom.

"The reason for the man's actions are unknown, since the cost of the heavy box, plus the man's weight and personal possessions, ran almost double what a comfortable seat in the coach area of the aircraft would have cost," he said.

Associated Press

Lights Go Out As Carter Writes Speech

Washington

President Carter's office was hit by a power failure yesterday as he put final touches on his energy message to the nation.

The power outage affected the West Wing of the White House and several surrounding blocks at the height of the morning rush hour, knocking out traffic lights and briefly creating a traffic jam.

The West Wing, including the president's Oval Office, went dark at 8:37 a.m. and power remained off for about 15 minutes.

4-6-79 *United Press*

SHAVERTRON*

"The Only Source of Post-Deluge Shaverania"

$1.50

SUMMER 1980 ——————————————— ISSUE 4

CAUTION: THIS ZINE MAY RUIN MENTAL HEALTH!

The Queens, NY Science Fiction League and The Literary Community Have Declared that RSS, RAP, and the Shaver Mystery are Dangerous Enemies to Your Sanity !

©1980 by R. Toronto

Bernard G. Devis, then president of the Ziff-Davis Publishing Company, looked over the angry letter with the long list of signatures and began to worry. He was well aware of the pandemonium that his magazine, AMAZING STORIES was causing nationwide, but had tolerated the situation as it was selling upwards to 90,000 copies a month, when other science-fiction pulp mags were lucky to sell 50,000.

Then, in a move that stunned thousands of Shaver Mystery readers and fans, Davis announced that his company, exclusive publisher of the Shaver Mystery since 1943 and heir to the massive sales generated by the perpetrator of all this chaos, was dropping all Shaver Mystery stories from the pages of AMAZING and FANTASTIC ADVENTURES. Following his announcement, Shaver's longtime editor, Raymond A. Palmer, resigned from Ziff-Davis declaring he would found his own magazine and continue his coverage of the controversial SM.

The letter in Davis' hand was the final nail in the coffin constructed by an anti-Shaver/Palmer campaign meant to finish off the SM at any cost. Bordering on the bizarre at times, this movement was quite unique in the annals of SF literature.

Prior to the Davis Decision, RSS was headed for what appeared to be a lifelong career in SF, not only as a writer and artist, but as a phenomenon. Ray Palmer, whose days at Ziff-Davis highlighted his own career of SF writing and editing, often credited himself with "creating" the SM and RSS from the clay of that primordeal first letter to AMAZING in which RSS detailed his Mantong alphabet in 1943. RAP put alot of himself into the SM, and it paid off. The Mystery assumed greater proportions than anyone could have imagined. RSS was the bearer of "shocking truths" that were thinly veiled in SF gauze, whereas RAP hawked the Mystery from the citadel of his editor's chair like a 20th century baronial medicineman, as its most eloquent spokesman. The seismic force of these two men caused the Shaver Mystery tidal wave that inundated the SF world. RSS rode that wave for almost 5 years. It was hard on him. His stomach

Mentor Or Menace?

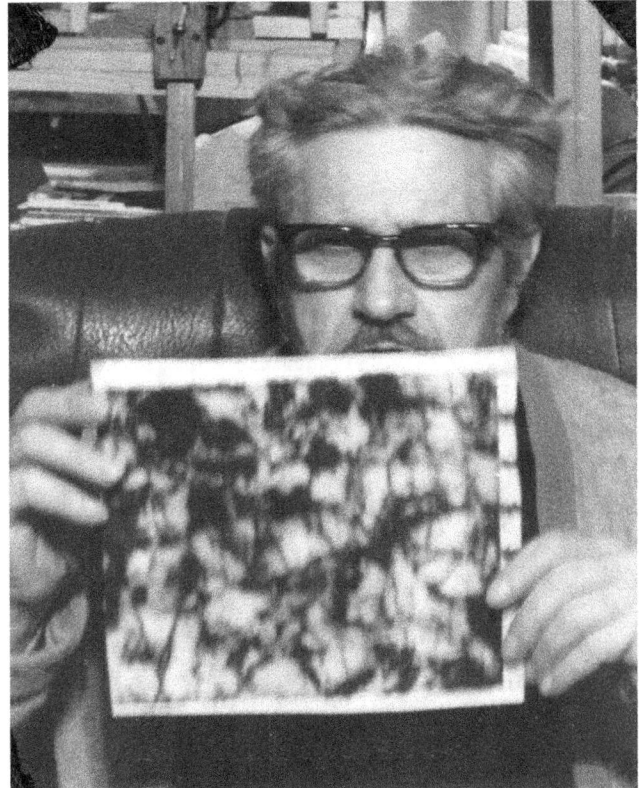

Stan Raycraft, Alexander Blade, G. H. Irwin, D. Richard Sharpe, Peter Dexter, Ruppert Carlin, Edwin Benson, Wes Amherst, Paul Lohrman — AKA Richard S. Shaver

ulcers were painful proof of that.

RAP was quick to recognize the elecromagnetic quality of the things Shaver wrote about. The dynamic energy of RSS' material kept readers' thoughts riveted to the ante-diluvian world of a Master Race, then bounced them back into the 20th century and a breed of human beings totally ignorant of their enslavement to the evil dero race. At the detonator of

*special first anniversary issue!

Go to page 5

We dont usually plug prozines because theyve got big enough advertising budgets, and dont need the likes of us. But if it has something to do with the Shaver Mystery we take exception.

While looking over the local newsstands, your editor noticed that the March,1980 issue of High Times, which bills itself as "the magazine of feeling good", has stumbled onto the controversial subject of UUI's (unseen universal images). An article by Wilson Bryan Key deals with subliminal images in American advertising. Rock book fans will be quite intrigued by this article.

« telaug talk »

by R. TORONTO

There are numerous similarities between RSS' rocfogo research,and Key's subliminal image work. They also elicit the same gnashing of teeth from their critics. Most of Mr Key's images are from Madison Avenue and deal with sex and death. The two big sellers. RSS was no stranger to either of these topics, and was well aware of the powerful tool it became in the hands of science-fiction pulp mag publishers. Look at a few of the cover illustrations on those old pulps, if you need convincing. RSS frequently alluded to the story about the martini glass resembling a D-cup bra (he meant in the minds of magazine readers).

Mr Key points to dozens of ice cube photos with weird and scary images floating around in them. The ad men deny his theories,yet use his ideas as text-book for ad-men-in-training. The public has been somewhat less than enthusiastic about his discover-ies. Why? Key explains it thusly: "We do not know a-bout subliminal phenomena because we individuals in general do not want to know...The US has a built-in need to disbelieve hypotheses that contradict the popular notions of "free will", America's fundamen-tal mythology." Just substitute the words Shaver Mystery for subliminal phenomena and youll see the similarity.

At the onset of his discovery Key wrote several researched articles on the problem..."all of which were rejected by editors of scholarly journals with comments like 'Nonsense' and 'This simply couldn't be going on.' Typical was the response of the journ-alism department chairman at UWO who, without bother-ing to look at his examples, dismissed Key from his office shouting, "You're making up all this filth. You are destroying young peoples' confidence in the press. You should be locked up as a public menace!"

Key's first book, Subliminal Seduction, a best-seller in Canada, brought equally caustic remarks from those who could not imagine that hard-to-see images of a strange, yet powerful nature peered

---

Shavertron has not only found its way into the archives of the Solano County Library, but into the "exchange" files of several zines as well. S readers are encouraged to investigate these fel-low zines for themselves, as they often contain information of interest to Shaver Mystery fans... The New Atlantian Journal: 5963 32nd Ave. No., St. Petersburg, Fla. 33710. The Blue Rose Ministry: P:O: Box 622, Joshua Tree, Ca. 92252. Infinity: David Graham Asso., Box 401-104 Washing-ton St., Decorah, Iowa 52101. Pyramid Guide: P.O.Box 30305, 741 Rosarita Ln., Santa Barbara, Ca. 93105. Polewatchers' Newsletter: Dorothy Starr, 36771-2 Third Ave.,San Diego, Ca.92103.

at us through cubes of ice or slabs of margerine. The v-p of Foote, Cone and Belding (the world's 5th largest advertising agency) labeled the book "a total crock". The v-p account supervisor of Doyle, Dane,and Bernbach noted, 'Mr Key's dissection of the Calvert Extra ad may epitomize the delusions of a disturbed personality."

The damning of what your editor calls UUI's (unseen universal images), rocfogo and subliminal phenomena is almost universal in itself. Marshall McLuhan may have hit at the core of the problem when he said, "1984 really happened around 1930, but we didn't notice." It is this vehement "anti" sentiment that has sent many an author into oblivion without so much as a second glance. Key would have long been forgotten if he wasn't making the radio and tv talk circuit both here in the US and in Canada. So who is speaking up for the SM. It lost its most ardent spokesman in 1975. Can the Shaver Mystery survive without RSS?

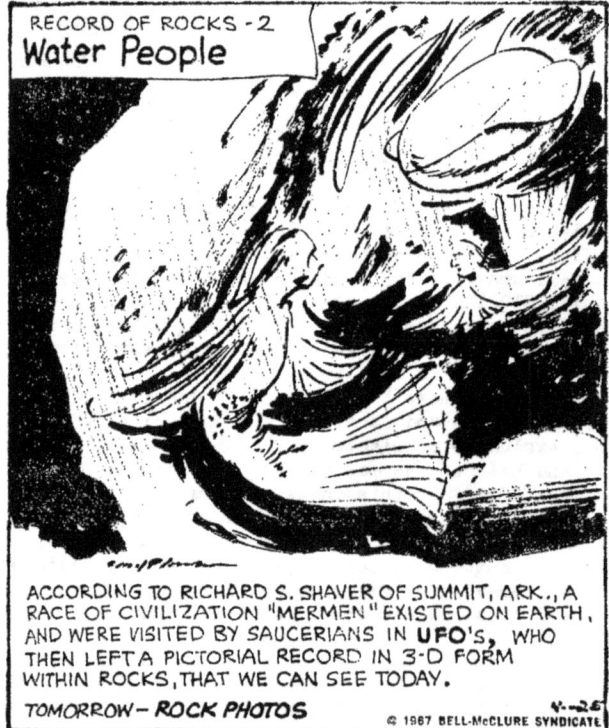

RECORD OF ROCKS - 2
Water People

ACCORDING TO RICHARD S. SHAVER OF SUMMIT, ARK., A RACE OF CIVILIZATION "MERMEN" EXISTED ON EARTH, AND WERE VISITED BY SAUCERIANS IN UFO'S, WHO THEN LEFT A PICTORIAL RECORD IN 3-D FORM WITHIN ROCKS,THAT WE CAN SEE TODAY.
TOMORROW - ROCK PHOTOS   © 1967 BELL-McCLURE SYNDICATE

Survival is the keynote as S climaxes its first year of publication. We've asked readers for suggestions as to what would help make S a better, more popular zine and the consensus appears to be that we should (1) in-crease our number of pages, and (2) that we charge a subscription fee. In the interest of the zine, we have given in to both proposals.

We hope that readers will understand the necessity of a sub fee, which will help to ensure S's continu-ing publication, and, hopefully, garner some new read-ers from the vast sea of SF afficionados who could use this material. Your editor not only invests many many hours of work in S, he also pays for its printing. We have been told that to charge no fee for S only demeans it in the eyes of some people, and that (ironically) more readers may be drawn to us if we charge for it.

This fee will then permit us to advertise in prozines for new readers, and may eventually per-mit us to expand even further. So please check out the new sub rates on page 8.

---

the invader CONSPIRACY

ARTICLE BY TAL LEVESQUE

The main problem in the study of the nature, purposes and tools of the "Alien" Conspiracy is that it is necessarily being researched in a cultural context which has already been manipulated by the conspiracy. The vast manitude of the deception is covered by layers of contradictions. It seems that there may be a number of "Hidden Cultures" based inside this planet. They have been playing several power games on our surface humanity for Ages. They may appear to be Extraterrestrials, and even lie about where they are from. But in reality this is their Planet. Races of small humanoids, Giants and those who look more or less like us, have evolved inside the Earth, with their various advanced technologies.

Surface political powers may be connected to some of the Subterranean civilizations. Our culture seems to be manipulated into developing Research Studies which, in reality, are for the conspiratorial "Invaders".

While Ufo and Occult investigators are made to spin in circles till they drop, the Saucer People are using the surface cultures as extentions of their own power pursuits. They remain elusive, but once the conspiracy is realized it becomes clear that there are hidden, powerful,cunning, Technological/Metaphysical "Beings" enjoying superiority over the rest of Mankind. The governments of the World do seek censorship and discrediting of information on this subject, because of the concerns of increasing discovery involving the traces and activities related to the "Hidden" cultures. The reason is the desire simply to preserve conditions relatively as they are, without upsetting our population.

The influence on Earth of these manipulating Invaders is not thoroughly understood, and their goals seem as varied as any could be. But, let's take another look at the fantastic enigma of the "PHANTOM PHENOMENON", and see what we do know. One of their superficial missions is the observation of Humans, the natural environment and man-made facilities. Their curiosity extends to animals, wild and domestic. This brings us to the Animal Mutilations, (done with surgical precision) which are currently taking place all over the planet. The "Mutes" are a silent yet revealing clue to the nature of the ominous Ufo Cultures.

They don't respect life, animal or human. The "Exties" are dissecting and testing animals without regard for ownership or humane concerns. These mutilations are occuring on a scale and in ways which have ruled out (for serious investigators) predators, sickle "Witchcraft" cults, and regular military research tactics. Alert observers have noted the significance of silent "Mystery Aircraft", capable of maneuvering at high speeds with hovering ability, that appear around mutilation sites. Some look like the classic "disk" shapes, usually accompanied by smaller "sphere" shaped forms. Also, many times, aero-form craft that would be easily mistaken as helicopters, but without rotary blades, are witnessed.

The Mutilation activities are quite elaborate... we are dealing with Phantom Surgeons who have "expert" technical training and scientific knowledge. All blood is drained away in an unexplained manner, too much blood than would be needed for testing purposes. Could it be a food supplement or have strong medicinal

values for a race which lacks certain nutrients in their make-up, from living Underground for generations?

The missing body parts are clearly not any that poachers would be interested in taking. But these would be the ones needed for analysis of the changes in chemical, biological and radiological conditions the animal has encountered over the past days, weeks and months. Much can be determined from examination of sections of skin, hair, eyes, genitals and internal organs.

David Perkins, director of A.M.P. (Animal Mutilations Probe) located in Faracita, Colorado, has been plotting the reports out, with color-coded pins, on a map of the U.S.A. Over the years an apparent correlation has surfaced between Mute sites and nuclear facilities. The general pattern indicates a downwind, downstream relationship.

To what extent could our government be involved,in collaboration with these Invaders from Inner Earth? Are their motives even more sinister than we currently suspect? Tom Adams and Gary Massey of Paris, TX: (P.O.Box 1094) put out a publication entitled STIGMATA, which reports on the continuing investigation into the relentless wave of animal mutilations. In issue 4 (Summer 1978) there appears a most unusual account of a woman from Berryville, Arkansas.

In 1973, Mrs L. (as we'll call her) was picking apples. She fell from a ladder, striking and seriously cutting one of her legs. As she lay on the ground too weak to rise, she saw two figures approaching. One was tall and thin, the other much shorter. As they neared, Mrs L. could see to her astonishment, that although they were humanoid, they were not human.

They began treating her badly-bleeding leg with a strange device. Within minutes all bleeding and pain had stopped and only the slightest of scars remained. The creatures then presented her with a metal Amulet with carvings on it.

She thanked them and asked if they would come to her house for something to eat. One humanoid replied that they did not eat,but only consumed "juice". When she offered fruit juice she was told they did not drink the same kind of juice that humans drank. (Note: by "juice" did they mean blood, vital fluids, brain or gland secrections from various animals, including humans, that contain elements which they need and use to replenish their "life force"?) The humanoids walked away and she returned home,with the Amulet, which she still has today. The artifact has been examined and there are markings, on both sides, some are of "pyramids" and "six-pointed stars".

Perhaps six weeks after the apple orchard incident, her dog turned up missing and she set out to search for it on foot. Coming to the edge of a clearing, she witnessed a bizarre scene. There, near two helicopters, were two "men in white coats" working on a horse that lay in the field. Also there were two men in what she thought were air force uniforms, and what appeared to be the same two humanoids that had healed her injury.

Mrs L. suddenly realized that this was something she was not supposed to see. She began to run away, but not before the "team" in the clearing spotted her. She thought she heard someone running after her for a brief while. Then, a helicopter quickly overtook her and began to descend. A blue beam of light was directed upon her, producing serious burns on her right side. For whatever reason, the aircraft suddenly retreated and she was able to seek help and hospitalization. While in the hospital she was questioned by strange visitors. She thought they were likely govern-

3

ment agents, though apparently no credentials were ever presented. After her release from the hospital, the County Sheriff persisted in maintaining that Mrs L. was "crazy" and that she was responsible for the horse mutilation, which did occur in the clearing.

The same "strange people" who questioned her at the hospital continued to visit her home, asking the same questions repeatedly. Pure harassment, she claims.

In fact, the L.'s decided to sell out and quietly move to New Mexico. But, in a short time, the same "strange people" who plagued them in Arkansas began again. At this writing, they have moved again and are in seclusion in south Texas. An investigation is underway at several levels and from different directions, in hopes of shedding more light on this and other potentially important cases, related to the "Invader Conspiracy".

Is our planet under the influence of maniacal beings who are manipulating humans on a global scale? To our detriment? Everyone is affected, in varying degrees, by strange events that they don't understand. Our minds are being played with, confusion, subliminal seduction, lies and the old 1984 "double think". The animals are being physically mutilated. But humans are being psychically mutilated. Our thinking apparatus is being destroyed by radiation, chemicals and "mind games". Thus we can observe and remember, but our powers of reason and deduction are being diminished. Manipulation of our thoughts, by the Invaders and their surface allies, is enslaving our civilization.

My friend, author Richard Shaver, with a movie contract concerning the Shaver Mystery waiting on his table at home, died suddenly, under mysterious circumstances. He had told his wife that "they" would stop him from telling, anymore, to the public about the Subteranean World and the advanced technology he had seen down there.

Author B.Ann Slate died shortly after gathering information that forced her to conclude that the "Invaders" were under the ground; had bases in the USA, and were working with an "invisible government" within this country. Every day brings revelations that equipment is being developed and used by World Governments, that only years ago was laughted at as impossible. If you didn't believe the stories of Saucer People, with amazing technology, now what do you say to goverments gaining access to the same kind of fantastic equipment? Are we being used? By who and for what, you should ask.

University of Missouri researchers have actually been able to monitor brain waves, and decode them into words. Now they are working on a remote sensor, so it will not be necessary to attach electrodes to the subjects scalp. Electro-magnetic fields, from Ufo craft, have caused skin burns (similar to sun burn) during close encounters. Another known effect

of these fields is auditory nerve induction. A way to transmit sound impressions directly into the brain bypassing the ear, using microwaves. Suitably coded, the Aliens can create voices, in your head-electronic telepathy! The Ufos have been discovered to emit microwave radiation, which is also known to have extremely potent psychological and biolgocial effects on both humans and animals. Some of the animal mutilations show signs of high-level microwave irradiation. Their internal cellular tissue was literally melted, turned to mush.

The Americans and Soviets are currently learning how to use E.L.F. (extremely low frequencies) waves, for military "electronic aggression". They can transmit frequencies that disrupt brain rhythms, heartbeat, and other biological mechanisms. What is more, it is possible, using this technology, to manipulate the earth's weather and magnetic fields, to generate earthquakes and even disrupt the thought processes of entire populations. So what's new, the Invader's have been doing this for Ages. Mind Control, via the transmission of "subliminal stimuli", was made easier when T.V. and F.M. radio became widespread. Now it is possible to monitor households and apply subliminal brainwashing over your television or radio right in the comfort of the home. Time to re-read the book, 1984!

It's shocking to ponder the question of our complicity with the Alien Invaders' drive for experimental work on atomic energy. Do they want a fusion "sun bomb", the "Shiva Nova", that will not stop when exploded, but will turn a planet into a tiny sun, as RSS predicted? When they didn't get it out of the Nazis they moved into the USA and that is one of the things we do for the Invaders now. Along with allowing their kidnapping, pirating and mining operations. When you get down to what the motives are, ultimately, of such an "Alien" intelligence, they do appear more like the "Vermin From Space" (both inner/outer) than the widely regarded Wise, Generous, Peaceloving and All-Cosmic "space brothers" from the "Xian Empire" Confederation.

It may well be that, like STAR WARS, this end of the galaxy is engaged in a war between Light and Dark forces. Too bad we are the dumb pawns in someone else's game. Who knows? Maybe they will let us play when it comes to Planetary War, with our newly developed laser guns, neutron grenades and deadly viruses. What a place to test these killer weapons, while the degenerate invaders and the elect few remain hidden in their controlled environment Subcities, deep within the planet. Has this happened before on earth? I get the strangest feeling it has. 'May the FARCE be with you."

Postscript:
The Invaders have been here from B:T:V: (before television). In fact, they want us All to have one. "Better to control you by". Yes, your tv set can be used as a monitor of all sounds around it. But better yet, a subliminal image here and there and you've got most of the viewing population intranced. So, out from our ancient

Go to page 7

TALES OF THE TUBE by Michael Fisher

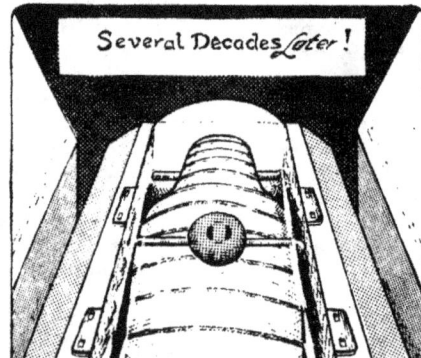

And now back to the continuing Adventures of the $15 Billion Cryogenic Man.

Several Decades Later!

Then, just before the Millenia's end ~~~

Stay Tuned for scenes from next weeks episode!

Spirit writing?—*Fossils and odd mineral forms were once believed to have been created by underground spirits. Above drawings, from Kircher's* Mundus Subterraneous, *1664, were supposed to be true representations of specimens actually found.*

--from Allan Wiseman

Mental Health con't.

this science fiction/fact bombshell was RSS, the oracle for a cosmology so bizarre that it menaced every known law of established Science. Truth, said RSS, was indeed stranger than SF fandom could imagine. "I always wonder what (sci-fi people) would do with it if they knew it was real evil underfoot and that Hell was genuine ancient city with genuine ghouls in it," he said. "Since I found out that beneath the Weird Wool there was a horrible reality much more evil than any imagined creature could be, there isn't much kick in the synthetic concoction of evil."

The energy exuded by the Mystery was its downfall. As long as SF crouched in its niche as an entertainment medium there was no need of alarm. But when two men use it to reveal what they claim in fact is a worldwide conspiracy of an alien race to destroy humanity, well, that's just too much!

A close similarity can be found in the writer/editor relationship between L. Ron Hubbard and John W. Campbell, of ASTOUNDING SCIENCE FICTION. Campbell, too, got into hot water with SF fen for tightwalking the fine line between science-fiction and fact. Nowadays, who hasn't heard of Hubbard, once a lowly SF writer along with Shaver, vying for space in the pulps, now a multimillionaire and guru of Scientology? Fans of ASTOUNDING SF complained bitterly about Campbell's absolute faith in dianetics, who went so far as to claim that his daughter's broken leg was mended in two hours by means of dianetic therapy. Hubbard survived the onslaught; RSS did not.

SM foes began to line up almost as soon as they read the first SM story in AMAZING. As the anti-Shaver movement gained steam, articles popped up in national magazines lamenting the depths to which SF had sunk, and warning of the perils of the SM. One of the earlier ones appeared in HARPERS. In the September, 1946 issue, an article by William S. Baring-Gould detailed the postwar state of American SF literature, and spoke at great lengths about the Shaver "Hoax". Baring-Gould tried not to hide his feelings when he wrote:

"...a place at the very bottom of the list should be reserved for AMAZING STORIES, the onetime "Aristocrat of Science-Fiction", now published by Ziff-Davis under the editorship of Raymond A. Palmer."

Gould quoted from an article by Thomas S. Gardner of the FANTASY COMMENTATOR, a NY based fan mag that not only lambasted Shaver and Palmer, but their fans as well:

"The crackpots, as they are usually called, number at least a million in the USA. They are, in the main, adults, and have educational levels ranging from near zero to those of Ph.D.'s engaged in technical occupations. A great many harbor serious delusions of ancient civilizations superior to ours, believe in pyramidology and the like. Indeed, there are today in this country several esoteric societies based on Lemuria, Mu, Atlantis, one numbering over 50,000 members.

"Nevertheless, these crackpots constitute a large potential buying-power for magazines...To capture these readers it is only necessary to publish issues of AMAZING STORIES containing stories which propitiate these crackpots' views in fictional guise...Palmer has instituted this very trend."

In 1946, when this article appeared, the SM still had another couple of years to run before the roof caved in from the avalanche of abusive statements by individuals and groups from all over the world. An example is found in the Spring, 1950 issue of SLANT, an Irish fanzine pubbed out of Belfast. It contains a letter signed by an English crusader against "that ghastly spectre now brooding over British fandom!" A Mr. G.C. Banks of Tankerton, Kent wrote:

"The nonsensical fantasies of Richard S. Shaver... have against all probability succeeded in lowering the stature of certain prozines. Now no one enjoys nonsensical fantasies, as such, more than I; but when they are puerile and ill-written, and interspersed with absurd 'proofs', ludicrous attempts at sex-interest, and hysterical ravings against the 'authorities' resembling the last stages of persecution mania, then I confess my patience becomes somewhat strained.

"We are told that we should reserve judgement on the Mystery, that we should study the 'proofs' offered by Mr. Shaver. Well, where are they? Usually in the 'next issue'. Is there, in the whole dreary waste of Mr. Shaver's works, even one little oasis of evidence that would justify the consideration of an hypothesis a thousand times less ridiculous than his own?

"An open mind is a good thing, but it is not the same as gullibility. Let us remember that in America, organized fandom, to its eternal credit, flatly rejected Shaver and all his works: and make it known to his would-be resurrectors by means of letters, articles in fanzines and general weight of opinion, that their attempt is nothing but an insult to the intelligence of every serious-minded lover of science-fiction in Europe...such moronic rubbish only lowers further the status of SF in the minds of the public, who already because of certain magazines and their covers, associate it with dirty back-street shops and cheap pornography."

Banks and Gardner weren't the only ones who either demeaned, threatened or tried to save the "fringe readership" of the SM. This newly labeled fringe of the sci-fi world suddenly became isolated from the "sci-fi straights". By openly claiming interst in the SM, they too became objects of "straight" hostility.

In his book, FANTASTIC SCIENCE FICTION ART (1975, Ballantine Books) Lester Del Rey, himself a frequent contributor to the pages of SF pulp mags, writes that during the SM years, "AMAZING STORIES was...appealing to a quite different audience than the one it had been slanted toward originally. The stories were often crude and frequently violent, with only the faintest concession to scientific accuracy. I've been told that Ray Palmer used to advise his writers that

Con't. Next Page

when a story lost action, they should drop an anvil out of the sky; obviously, he meant that figuratively, but some of the stories seemed to use the trick almost literally."

Mr. Del Rey equates the SM with "occultism", and says that "The regular science fiction fans dropped the magazine in shocked disgust," but were "...more than replaced by a different type of reader."

It was because of these misguided elements in SF fandom that the SF straights wanted to see the SM totally discredited. In so doing, the Mystery would not be displayed by "reputable" mags, and the sci-fi misanthropes would be deprived of the poison they constantly injected into their brains via AMAZING STORIES. They still might be worth salvaging, at least in theory. Various groups banded together to see this through. At the head of the formation was the Queens (NY) Science Fiction League. To their eternal credit, they succeeded in eliminating the SM from the public eye. At least until RAP began to pub his own mags.

When it is said that "American fandom flatly rejected Shaver and all his works", it is no doubt in reference to the Queens SFL action. Humiliating songs were hurredly composed and sung about the SM. The entire straight SF world was closing in for the kill.

Still reeling from this devastating round of vitriol, the SM found itself the subject of an article on SF in the May, 21, 1951 issue of LIFE Magazine. Usually, any kind of publicity is helpful, but in this case it only helped the SM foes by condemning it as "...the exploitation of a special type of bem (bug-eyed monster) that led...to the most celebrated rumpus that rocked the world of science-fiction--the Shaver Hoax".

LIFE crescendoed its peice on the "Shaver Hoax" to its climax:

"Finally, the fen couldn't stand it any longer. Editor Palmer, in their eyes, was debasing the ethics of science fiction in a shameless attempt to boost circulation by presenting fiction in the guise of fact. The Queens (NY) Science Fiction League passed a resolution expressing the opinion that the Shaver stories were actually endangering the sanity of their readers and brought this resolution to the attention of the Society for the Suppression of Vice. Delegates to a Philadelphia fan conference threatened to draw up a petition to get the Post Office to ban AMAZING STORIES from the mails. The fanzines bellowed for Editor Palmer's scalp. At this point somebody, according to Palmer, convinced his publisher, William B. Ziff...that the theories of Shaver and Palmer were in flat contradiction to Albert Einstein's Theory of Relativity. This, obviously, was too much. The Shaver stories were discontinued. Editor Palmer, still affirming his faith in the existence of deros, resigned his job."

It appears that SM foes couldn't decide whether to keep the SM fen isolated as an insane element, or to rehabilitate them and then welcome them back to the fold. Surely, the anti-Shaver campaign was designed to try and rehabilitate them by removing SM material from the newsstands, which would, hopefully, snap them back to reality. The question of the safety of SM readers' sanity wasn't breached again until an all-Shaver issue of FANTASTIC Magazine appeared in July of 1958. The editor, Paul Fairman, in keeping with his last name, discreetly juxtaposed a lividly anti-Shaver piece in the back of the issue by one A.J.Steichert.

In it, Steichert lashes out at the K-O'd SM by "disproving" the idea that subterranean caverns do indeed go miles into the earth; explained away such Elder mech as the telaug because there is no power source so strong as to produce the vast rays involved; granted, however, that Shaver had discussed Ufos visiting earth long before Arnold spotted his Mt. Rainier

"flying saucers" in 1947, but turned around and <u>accussed</u> RSS of creating the entire outbreak of Ufos reported by the public. The flying saucers, "a mass-hysterical phenomenon anyway", according to Steichert, "could have been due to the continuous suggestion of four years of such stories as Shaver wrote, bearing as it did on adolescent and bizarre-tending minds." He also accussed Shaver of "building a mountain of mis-meaning, piling words upon one another" to create the Mantong alphabet.

At the same time, however, he admits that he is mystified at both Palmer and Shaver's ability to "decipher" words in languages unknown to them. Confessed Steichert, "Dr. Ashly-Cock, language expert, once told me that he had interviewed both men, and was convinced that what they were doing was reading his mind." Although Palmer admitted to some esp talents, Shaver himself never made any claims to be "psychic" and in fact, frowned on the theories of "occultism", metaphysics and spiritualism.

Most menacing of all, according to Steichert, was that "The Mystery is dangerous nonsense, most dangerous because its nonsense seems to make sense." This pronouncement appears to have been the thrust of the anti-Shaver movement in a nutshell.

To those whose job it was to make sense...the scientists and writers of science fiction, Shaver became a literary leper. As the tide turned ever further against the SM, many of his contemporaries shunned his presence, his work, and theories. Rog Phillips, for an instance, got his start from a threatening letter he wrote to Ray Palmer which demanded that AMAZING cease and desist all SM material. Phillips, tongue-in-cheek, let us hope, said he would kill the AMAZING staff if it wasn't stopped. As it turned out, RAP claims he noticed Phillips 'UNUSUAL mental slant on fiction', and so another sci-fi writer was born. Long after the SM was considered by SM foes to be a dead horse (circa 1949-50) Shaver's contemporaries still found time to dredge up new epithets to toss in his direction.

Jim Pobst, an authority on RSS' literary career, describes it as a case of "...the brave-new-world'ers taking time out from their scrawlings about cosmic utopias to join hands and collectively curb stomp (RSS). It was a form of hysteria, of that I'm sure.."

To the straight sci-fi writers and fans, the SM was never "scientific" enough. Critics never seemed to tire of discrediting Shaver's theories and claims, many of which actually materialized in truth long after Shaver faded into the Arkansas hills. In the February 15, 1963 issue of SCIENCE, a letter from SF writer Poul Anderson belatedly admitted to Shaver's glimpse of the future:

"A still more inexplicably neglected field exists in the files of AMAZING STORIES for the years between about 1945 and 1950. During those years a series of narratives appeared, by one Richard S. Shaver...

"Obviously, Shaver has predicted (i) solar particle emission (ii) the aging and mutagenic effects of ionizing radiation, and (iii) recent findings as to

next pg.

BIG OLD BIRDS:

Fossilized evidence which turned up in Japan and in the state of Washington in the U.S. indicated that regions of the Earth once were populated (until about 30 million years ago) by penguin-like birds, related to pelicans and cormorants but standing, in some cases more than 6 feet tall. The previously unknown bird family, called plotopterids, was characterized by flightless fowl which swam underwater.

From Page 6:

the effect of direct electrical stimulation of various brain centers. In view of these prognostications, his other conclusions must be objectivly re-examined --unless, that is, one simply feels as I do, that while one bad apple spoils the rest, the accidental presence of one or two good apples does not redeem a spoiled barrelful." In other words, to give Shaver his due is simply Verbotten. Says Pobst, "He (Anderson) missed, for one, the correct use of the 'slingshot effect' in planetary gravitational fields (Quest of Brail, 1946), although I'd wager it wasn't thought out when Anderson wrote his letter circa 1963."

It is generally agreed by both the literary, scientific and fan communities that RSS was and still is, a menace to the sanity of good, straight-thinking people everywhere. Regardless of the veracity of anything that RSS had to say or predict, it is doubted that this type of mind-set will change within our lifetime.

Postscript:

And it is generally agreed that any "resurrector" will be equally condemned as "dangerous nonsense". It follows that Shavertron is now a threat to "serious-minded" people everywhere.

If, on the other hand, dear readers, you feel you'd like to live dangerously, let's see those subscriptions roll in!

Experiment Killed Him

Morgantown, W.Va.

John Butterick, a promising West Virginia University researcher, bled to death from a drug commonly used to kill rats, apparently in an experiment to see if he could extend his life, a state medical officer said yesterday.

Dr. James L. Frost, assistant state medical examiner, ruled out suicide in Butterick's death January 27. His body was found on his bed in his apartment, and blood was found on his clothes, mattress, a glass, the kitchen floor and in the bathroom.

Frost said the study indicates the powerful anti-coagulant warfarin caused the bleeding, and its effects were probably amplified by the use of aspirin.

Why would the 33-year-old Butterick, described by Frost as a "very intelligent young man," use himself as a guinea pig and not seek out medical help once he became seriously ill?

"He was not disinclined to try things on himself," Frost said. "One such case was documented by his ex-wife. He was a person prone to try things on himself.

"John Butterick was an independent and stubborn person who didn't have much regard for doctors. He probably didn't think doctors could do much for him.

"He was a young man whose outlook was optimistic. He told others that he might live to be 200 years old. He wanted to find the

Although his colleagues at the university weren't aware of Butterick's use of warfarin, Frost said he was known to have taken drugs independently of a doctor's advice before. When he was studying in Canada, his colleagues said, for six months he ingested BTH, a chemical used in food packaging to retard spoilage.

"There are other chemicals (other than warfarin) much more effective, much less agonizing, and much less painful," said Frost in explaining why suicide wasn't likely. "There were no notes left or letters mailed to his parents or ex-wife. There was no past history of depression."

A medical book on a night stand next to the bed where Butterick's body was found provided a clue to the nature of his peculiar death, said Frost. The book was opened to a page on the drug warfarin.

"Warfarin is thought in some small, vague, non-specific way, to result in better self-function," said Frost. More commonly, it induces bleeding and is used as a rat poison.

Butterick, whose own chemical research at the university did not include the use of warfarin, apparently ordered the drug last December. It arrived January 7, Frost said.

There was no evidence that Butterick was using other drugs or that he was suffering from any debilitating disease

From Page 4:

past (hidden below ground) come the instruments, into ou future-directed existence.

We are ALL working for the Invader, in one way or another. As we become more like them and they become more like us. It is a War of Minds played on the Battleground of Human suffering and ignorance. We must awaken and dream anew our future. Technology isn't being used enough to benefit Mankind. Instead it is developing out of a highly militaristic enterprise, that we all fall victim to. If we are to win back this planet, for pro-life pursuits, we must first realize that in the greater view, the Invader is still US. This cosmic war is a Mind Game. If we only knew how to be friends and not use one another so.

The INVADER CONSPIRACY is one of silence to our true genetic knowledge and energies. May we once again remember Who and What we are. Without this manipulative suppression being placed on the consciousness of the planet, we might All truly become "Aware". May God be with us, in the Coming Changes. To the End...or a new Beginning.

Cavers find link

Discoveries push Mammoth Cave length to 212 miles

A Cave Research Foundation explorer team of four men and one woman has discovered an 850 foot passageway that connects Mammoth Cave to Proctor Cave. Mammoth Cave was nearly 197 miles long prior to the new linkup, and was the longest cave in the world. The new discoveries and the connection add 15 miles to the total length to make Mammoth Cave 212 miles long.

Announcement of the discovery was made jointly Monday by CRF officials and the National Park Service at a press conference at Mammoth Cave.

W. Calvin Welbourn, president of the Cave Research Foundation (CRF), said the discoveries are the most significant finds in Mammoth Cave National Park since 1972. At that time a connection was found between the Flint Ridge Cave System and Mammoth Cave.

The trip was led by Roger W. Brucker, 50, an advertising executive of Yellow Springs, Ohio. It lasted 24 hours and included crawling through body-size crawlways and chimneying along projection-studded canyons for several miles. The August 11 connection trip began at the Frozen Niagara Entrance of Mammoth Cave.

The final 850 feet was explored by Dr. John Wilcox, 42, a research engineer from Coolspring, PA, and Tom

Gracanin, 23, a graduate student in geology at the Ohio State University in Columbus, OH, and a native of Cincinnati, OH.

The two explorers stripped to avoid soaking their clothing, and pushed into a low ceiling water passage that provided only four inches of air space for breathing for the first 50 feet.

"After that we squeezed through a muddy crawlway for about 200 feet to a small stream. We followed the stream to a large river passage we recognized as

Con't. Next Page

R S S

Cave Con't.

one we had found earlier in Proctor Cave," explained Tom Gracanin.

According to the two, the passage containing the stream was so small they had to crawl with one ear in the water in places. At the connection point the passage opened into a larger river from an obscure hole near the ceiling of the passage.

"Chances are we would not have found the connection from the Proctor Cave end because the ceiling lead was hidden in shadow," said John Wilcox.

Other members of the exploration party were Lynn Weller, 22, an electrical engineering student at the Ohio State University and resident of Columbus, OH. and Tom Brucker, an audio service manager from Nashville, TN.

This latest find is part of a wave of cave discoveries that began on May 27,1979, when Roger Brucker and Lynn Weller rappelled 150 feet down ropes in Proctor

Cave. They found a passage 50 feet wide by 30 feet high containing a river flowing at the rate of 25 cubic feet per second (16 million gallons per day). They named it Hawkins River after the Superintendent of Mammoth Cave National Park, Amos Hawkins.

Subsequent explorations through the summer of 1979 revealed one marvel after another. The river was followed 1000 feet to a T-intersection. The explorers used divers' wet suits and inner tubes to push the right-hand fork one-half mile to a place where the passage continues unexplored.

The leaf-hand fork leads to miles of spectacular passageways decorated with live flowstone, stalactites, and stalagmites. Some chambers are as large as 100 feet wide by 60 feet high.

The explorers left many leads unchecked as they probed the main river passage. Many of those are walking-height passages up to 20 feet wide by 10 feet high.

Roger Brucker estimated that the discoveries could easily total 30 miles of passageway by the time the leads are fully explored and the rivers pushed to their ends

Prior to the connection, the Flint Mammoth Cave System was already known as the world's longest. In 1972 the Flint Ridge Cave System in Mammoth Cave National Park was the longest listed cave at 87 miles. Mammoth Cave ranked third with 58 miles mapped. In September, 1972, John Wilcox led a team of Cave Research Foundation explorers that found the natural connection between the two caves through a stream passage. The linkup formed a single cave system about 145 miles long.

Since that time CRF survey teams have been making discoveries steadily. By the summer of 1979 they had extended the total length of the cave system to about 197 miles.

Proctor Cave, in Mammoth Cave National Park, was discovered in 1863 by Jonathan Doyle. He found about a half-mile of passageways near the entrance. Later Larkin J. Proctor, owner and operator of the cave, claimed to have found an underground river through a long crawlway.

In 1967 CRF mapping teams began to survey Proctor Cave. In 1970 they found the long crawlway and Mystic River, a quarter-mile stream that plunges into a pit. In 1973 explorers sent to check the pit found leads upward. They discovered a set of large upper-level walking passages, some of which were beautifully decorated with gypsym crystals. None of the upper levels had been entered by man before. By February, 1979, Proctor Cave was 6.8 miles long.

The Mammoth-Proctor cave connection was the result of more than 7600 hours of exploration by several dozen explorers. John Wilcox, who led many of the trips into Mammoth Cave leading toward the new river, said the 24-hour trips were some of the most rigorous known to modern cave explorers. Lynn Weller, who participated in many of the trips from the Proctor Cave end, said that the explorers had to be in top physical shape, and able to fit through 7½-inch squeezes.

•

BUTTERFLIES are cannibals

Underground Blaze Threatens Town

Philadelphia

An inferno feeding on coal reserves burning beneath the tiny town of Centralia threatens to poison its population, the Philadelphia Bulletin reported yesterday.

The fire began about 20 years ago beneath the surface of the Schuylkill County town, and continues to spread through abandoned anthracite coal tunnels, the newspaper said. Local, state and federal governments have spent $2.8 million in attempts to extinguish the blaze.

But residents believe the amounts of carbon monoxide gas and the levels of underground temperatures — which in some backyards have registered 720 degrees — are now at their highest and most lethal, the Bulletin reported.

Many of the townspeople are angry over the governments' pace in solving the problem.The newspaper quotes retired miner Anthony Gaughan, whose property is in a danger zone, as saying, "They don't give a damn for us. They didn't in the past and they still don't now."

But Earl Cunningham, assistant regional director for abandoned mine lands in the Office of Surface Mining, responds: "We're inching along because we've never done this before. We're not going to quit on them."

One possible solution, the Bulletin reported, is evacuating the entire town, rather than trying to put out the fire.

United Press

Clear Lake Earthquake — Woman Found It Devilish
2-14-80

A mild earthquake rattled the Clear Lake area of Lake County late Tuesday night. No damage was reported, but one resident thought she'd been possessed by the devil.

" 'The Exorcist' had just been on television, and this one gal grabbed her Rosary beads and started on every prayer she knew. She actually thought she'd been possessed when her bed started shaking around," said Sharon Lucich, manager of the Clear Lake

Chamber of Commerce.

Not until the woman went to work the next morning and learned there had been an earthquake, Lucich said, was she sure she hadn't had a visit from supernatural forces.

The Seismographic Station at the University of California at Berkeley said the quake struck at 11:45 p.m. with a Richter magnitude of 3.7. Its epicenter was placed about 90 miles north of Berkeley near Clear Lake.

Moving Underground

BRUSSELS — The North Atlantic Treaty Organization's European military command is going underground, according to the Associated Press.

The move will coincide with the scheduled completion in 1983 of an underground complex near Casteau, the wire service said.

Belgian Defense Ministry officials announced the move, AP reported, and said that bids for the estimated $58.5 million project are being accepted from foreign and domestic firms.

STIGMATA, an intriguing zine to be sure, by Tom Adams, P.O. Box 1094,

Shavertron Subs:

S is published quarterly at $6.00 per year. Single copies $1.50 each. Important: make all checks or money orders payable to Richard Toronto,and print "Shavertron"in the lower righthand corner. All payment must be in USA funds or international money orders. No need to send anymore SASE's!

Wanted: books/mags on witchcraft, satanism,voodoo, sacrific, multi-marriage... P. Doerr, 225 E. Utah, Fairfield, CA. 94533.

hollow earth?

by Brent Raynes

Reprinted with permission of Gary Elvers and the Universal Mutational Expedience Team.

The following "hollow earth" type story was written to me in a letter postmarked November 15, 1972 from Mr John Johnston:

"In the summer of 1966 I ran across a middle aged person who, while in the service of the armed forces, came onto, by chance, classified information that told a fantastic story.

He was my neighbor then and after telling him about my hobby of ufos, he seemed somewhat interested and told of only one bizarre story or file he came

across by <u>accident only</u>. He was in the Army in Texas and a clerk then.

He claims to have noticed a file cabinet unlocked marked "Classfied Only". Well, because of being human, (let's say curious) he decided to peek into the cabinet and came up with a diary of Captain James Cook, dated in the 1700's. This diary, in Cooks own handwriting, gave a detailed description of the events that took place in the far regions of the South Pole.

Going on what he read from the diary, he remembered what Cook had written and seen while exploration of the South was in progress.

Cook described large machines and creative men with large feet and long arms quite strong on a small trunk. Very tall--around 7 feet...slits with very little noise coming from speech, if at all, meaning telepathic communication. They were of a friendly nature and Cook's crew--some of whom died during the polar trip--and the rest with him

felt at ease in some manner with the people or aliens.

Cook told the "leader" that he needed some parts to repair his ship to get back to England. These people did help with repairs and Cook then sailed back to his homeland, but he wrote his accounts of the South Pole and as a result his diary, whether true or not, is now Army property."

(Ed. note- Cook's expedition to the pole was between 1772-1775.)

cave ritual

In the cactus dotted Guadalupe Mountains of New Mexico is a desolate area where only the coyote, deer, mountain lion and bear hold court among the sharp spines of the Spanish Dagger plant. It is an area into which few venture, and no one lives.

Beneath the upper reaches of the Guadalupe peaks, is located the largest natural cavern and cave complex in North America. Near this area is the city of Carlsbad, New Mexico, famed for its caverns and pot ash mines. Thousands of tourists flock here to see the great natural beauty of the Carlsbad Caverns.

It was in this area to the North and West of Carlsbad in a remote trading post that a strange and somewhat eerie event unfolded in the earlier years of this century.

skins and small amounts of various types of minerals taken from the ore of the mountains, stumbled one day into the post and frantically babbled out a bizarre tale.

The two had been searching for mineral deposits in the mountains when they came upon a large cavern.

Thinking that valuable ore deposits might lay within, they made some torches, lit them, and entered the inky blackness of the interior.

They had gone a ways into the cavern, according to the story, when they began to hear voices, which seemed to be chanting.

A light began to show ahead of them so they extinguished their torches and crept forward toward the voices. In time a large room opened up before them.

They hid behind a large formation

of rock and watched in great surprise, that soon changed to stark terror, as the scene unfolded before them.

In the center of the room stood robed figures in a circle around a great altar stone, and upon the altar rested a huge crystal the source of the flickering light. The crystal they saw seemed to pulsate with the rising and falling voices chanting.

Suddenly the chanting stopped and the crystal began to speak in a tongue more musical than vocal. They said it was an eerie sound, much like that of a xylophone.

Horrified, they watched until the great crystal stopped, then rose slowly until it reached the ceiling of the great room, suspended among the long, sharp hanging rocks of the cavern ceiling. Then it began to

dim, and the robed figures started a chant, and one behind the other, descended into the depths of the cavern.

Shaken by the experience, the traders made a hasty departure, not only from the cavern, but from the entire, forlorn area. They stopped only briefly at the post for some provisions for their journey to unknown places, and to babble out the bizarre story.

What was the strange crystal? Who were the robed ones? Why did they descend into the depths of the cavern? Questions that may never have answers, for it is like most of the legends of the past. No one remains to give locations and details and the ones who may remember feel it is better forgotten.

On the Importance of Writing Letters

by Henry M. Steele

This piece is best I could do because of dero interference. Headache too...thus it must be quite important for me and others. Will government action come of it? But what government? Space government?

From rotten personal experiences with US govt. and deros' ray on them, I know my own, and others' future depends 100% on how govt. gets rayed! Thus, there is no reason not to write govt. agencies and leaders. Only with a letter in a govt. leader's hands can Teros ray good feelings for one sending the letter. Otherwise, you grow old and die alone.

What do I care if govt. is rayed to muse mean and angry thoughts toward me? Attention and action is the key.

You know, I've talked with four agents now. None have the attitude the govt. would harm any of us Shaver fans! Richard was left alone for many years you'll note. Deros set him up. He had to go and climb up and grab a flag or whatever... (Ed. note: this tale will be told in a future issue). Thus we are not harmed unless they desire. The govt. realizes us plain citizens are harmless to it. Their policy to such folks: ignore them!

If you and others decide to write (sooner or later) to the CIA on harping I'm a smart citizen and not a nut--and back my discoveries as believable, etc., action could come and we'd get into a hell of a better life. (Ed. note-Mr Steele says he has the formula to an authentic de-aging mixture, which he wishes to sell for $55 billion).

The govt. fully realizes the public just can't take Shaver's information, as a CIA agent clearly explained to me, and so they never fear us and our telling such data!

I recall being taught as a child that citizens who try and contact their govt. are looked upon by the govt. as a good deal more intelligent than the masses. More upstanding.

(Final Editor's note: to date, Mr Steele has written to the President, the Pope, Billy Graham, Ralph Nader, the head of the CIA and FBI, Fred Hoyle, Melvin Beli, Nixon, Ford, the Supreme Court, numerous movie stars, and top scientists. So far, he is still waiting for an answer...except from Beli, who said there was nothing he could do. What do you readers think?)

9

Dear Richard,

In S no. 3, I was much interested in the microwave report.

Dr. Wm. Bise of Oregon has been studying these for several years now. He claims the Soviets are bombarding Eugene, Oregon, and that many people are sick and confused.

Yesterday's tv said microwaves atop the tall buildings in NYC are affecting tourists and secretaries and other office workers who are in direct line with them.

There is a paperback available that is very well done along these lines. Get a copy of OPERATION MIND CONTROL by WH Bowart, Dell Books $1.95. It is an unbelievable story...all true!

I've been deeply involved in Weather Modification for several years, studying it, and you cannot imagine what our government and the Soviets are doing with weather weapons. A real horror story.

Request a free copy of the "Federal Register" from your congressman for the March 5, 1979 issue. It tells of the U:S: Airforce's new weather-modification techniques, and what they are doing in "our" atmosphere on a daily basis. God help us!

Thanks for the newsletter-- it is great!

Regards,
George Wunder, PA.

Dear Rich,

The ANCIENT UFOS feature on page 1 was an illustrated feature in some daily papers back in the mid-1960's, and was created by Otto Binder (aka Eando Binder), the well-known science-fiction author. He was among my favorites.

Otto sent me a complete set of these features which were actual "galleys" of each week's sequence. The series was based on ufo sightings around the world.

One of my publications is called Outermost. It was a one-shot deal. In that issue, however, I have 2 stories by RSS. If some of your readers want a copy, there are still some back issues left for $1.95, each.

Sincerely,
Gene Duplantier
17 Shetland St.
Willowdale, Ont.
Canada M2M 1X5

R--Thanks, Gene, for the dope on that Shaver feature in last issue. We had one other reader who recognised the Binder ufo column.

You readers may remember Gene as the long term editor of "Saucers, Space and Science", which was a well-received and well conceived magazine. Gene has quite a listing of ufo-related books and zines for sale, so mabe you'd care to write to him.

Dear Mr Toronto,

I received the no.3 issue of S and enjoyed reading it. I do hope you can continue this effort as it is needed. Since Shaver died, there has been little said on the Shaver Mystery subject. Ray Palmer strung it along for years after HIDDEN WORLDS last issue, but never came up with anything new.

I wrote to Palmer several times a year up til his death, trying to get him to continue HIDDEN WORLDS with an annual issue. This would have been a great help to keep the fans interested and in touch. Perhaps Mrs Palmer could be persuaded to continue this publication if enough requests for it are made. I've suggested it twice, but I am only one of many that would be interested in this.

Perhaps SHAVERTRON readers should write to her and request the revival of HIDDEN WORLDS. If enough interest is shown, she may try one more issue. Science Research Publishing House, PO Box 40068, St Petersburg, FLA.33743 has just published "The Incredible Cities of Inner Earth" by David H Lewis. I haven't had a chance to read it yet. It is 50-60 pages less than advertised and at $5.95 plus $.60 postage I would say it is over priced. However, it may contain something of interest and of course would be worth it to a collector of such material.

Best Regards,
Frank Brownley
Rochester, NY

R--Your point is well taken, Frank. If enough Shavertron readers take this seriously and write to the Palmers requesting a revival of The Hidden World, no telling what might happen. As far as I know, however, Palmer Pubs. still has quite a few editions of RSS' last book, Secret World, and a fair amount of Jim Wentworth's comprehensive book Giants In The Earth. Palmer Pubs has always been interested in fast moving sales to large audiences. Since these books are not selling well at this time, it may be a chore to get them to reserect HW.

What is needed at this point in time is more Shaver Mystery fans. A new market. Then we will see more Shaver material come into print. It is almost a Catch-22 situation:

Without Shaver Mystery material in print there will be very few new fans...and without more fans, the Mystery will remain "Out-of-Print". Any suggestions???

Dear Richard,

I found the meaning of "apotheosis" (refer to page 1, issue 2 of S). Got a new dictionary a while back and it is really a good one. Websters New Collegiate Dictionary.

Apotheosis: Elevated to divine status...perfect example.

Best Wishes,
David Graham

R--Another mystery solved! Wish RSS had had one of those dictionaries when he wrote "The Apotheosis of Ballet".

Dear Richard,

The gov't. as I've been told, is into some of the mech caverns and has figured out how to work some mech. Shaver wrote once that the telemech is among easiest to figure out. Thus, gov't. would read our minds and see we are not nutty! Not years ago while Richard was writing his volumes, but today this new factor appears!

You and all fans could write the CIA and ask them to do this to show you're sane. No reply from them, perhaps, but you'd be rayed and so no harm to fans. They'd know that you knew the score. If they bothered to ray you, they'd know you're fine.

They don't care to harm the "little citizens" in the first place. The gov't. fully realizes the (dumb) masses can't take the ufo/cavern subjects...they can't believe in them. So, even if 20,000 fans joined up-no worry for us. Think how many garden clubs and organisations there are. They aren't thought about at all by the masses. Dero ray mentally controls all those in tv, papers, etc. to not get enthused about cavern data.

There was some bad ray in Summit. Your area too. Worry put in our minds.

Henry M. Steele
410 International,
Apt. 114,
Garland, Texas 75042

R--Maybe we should change our name to Shaver's Better Gardens.

SHAVERTRON

"The Only Source of Post-Deluge Shaverania"

Fall 1980

Issue 5

$1.50

SHAVER SPEAKS OUT! ON UNSEEN RUINS, GOV'T. POLICY &

THE HOLLOW HASSLE

By Richard S. Shaver...Reprinted with permission of The Universal Mutational Expedience Team...

There is really no use to one's expecting the great scientific minds of our so-great technology of pollution and putridity to do anything whatsoever about anything that requires work without pay.

One cannot, for instance, even find out for sure if Admiral Byrd did or did not fly into the Antarctic opening...or if the other account of the Swedes who sailed into the north polar opening is factual or fictional. This thing of pinning down a fact and demonstrating its actual factual content is one I've been engaged in for some 30 years, actively. And to say it is difficult is putting it mildly.

What I am getting at is to say that IF you favor the hollow earth theory as above the solid earth theory, there really is no sound reason opposing you, nor any genuinely scientific facts.

Hell, they have not even explored the interior portions of Montana! There are immense areas of these United States that have never been explored on foot.....(close-up exploration as opposed to aerial mapping) BECAUSE the area is governed by the simple matheatics of how much water a mule can carry.

That is, factually speaking, any area over 40 miles from water in the USA wilderness is apt to be an area unexplored, untrod by the human foot!

Such a fact by itself seems quite startling, but never the less is a solid and quite demonstrable fact.

Late years use of the helicopter has cut down these areas greatly, but there are still plenty of them where even a helicopter cannot land comfortably, they tell me.

The same is vastly truer of the ocean bottom, you know. One is apt to think everything is known, all frontiers explored, until one discovers for one's self it just isn't so.

What is fascinating to me about these unexplored and untouched-by-man areas is this: they contain

Cyclopean ruins undisturbed by the bulldozer and the builders who have been taking rock from the Cyclopean ruins since long before the Greeks built the Parthenon. You can see these wierd and utterly gigantic ruins in what photos are taken in these areas. These tumbled blocks of stone are the reason a helicopter or airplane hasn't been able to land and do surveying, mapping and opening of the way for the ignorant who come after and obliterate forever the last great traces of our space spanning ancestors.

"THIS IS STILL A DARK AGE"

If you think the hollow earth theory is ridiculous, these Cyclopean ruins are the most numerous of all ruins still...and while they are MENTIONED in the encyclopedias NONE has ever been dug or studied by our omniscient but apparently unindustrious and quite poverty-striken "archeology".

So do not think that if the earth were hollow, we would know. We do not know anything that "official science" does not approve of our knowing...and the only things they ever approve are things accepted for centuries...and often quite in error...the errors of the dark ages is still with us.

Did you know the Curies were refused entry to the French Academy of Science long after they discovered radium and isolated it? They were "unknowns" and their marvelous work was to the Academy not considered seriously.

The history of official science is very like the experience of Columbus with the Spanish "authorities of science" who ridiculed his ideas of a round world. They never know anything until it is forced down their throats by the ignorant workingman...like Columbus forced the round world down their throat with an actual voyage.

Today's scientists are of the same ilk...strangled in their own straitjacket of orthodoxy. They won't even look at the idea of a hollow earth until someone comes back with overwhelming evidence.

Did Byrd bring back such evidence...how does one find out for sure?

This is still a dark, dark age. We think of it as "modern" and enlightened only because our perspective is the close-up.

What is fascinating to me about the hollow earth theory is: if one could enter, one would find the vast Cyclopean dwellings still standing (BECAUSE

Continued page 5

RECORD OF ROCKS - 5
Rock Photos

WHEN STAR-PEOPLE VISITED EARTH 1000 CENTURIES AGO,
SAYS RICHARD S. SHAVER OF SUMMIT, ARK., THEY USED
A 3-D "CAMERA" TO IMPRINT PHOTOS ON SOLID ROCK
SURFACES AS A "STONE HISTORY BOOK", FOR US
TO FIND TODAY.

TOMORROW - STONE BOOKS
© 1967 BELL-McCLURE SYNDICATE

« telaug talk »

by R. TORONTO

Shavertron is now featuring a new column by Bill
Bliss, called "Pure Bliss". Mr Bliss was a longtime
correspondent with RSS, and collaborated with him on
that final installment of the SM: THE SECRET WORLD...
Bill did many of the color photos of rocks. We hope
that readers will enjoy Bill, who runs a small fixit
shop in Chillicothe, Illinois. He is proficient in
electronics and subjects occult, and may eventually do
some experimental work on an old drawing of a telaug
we've dug out of some SM Letterzines.

The fine illustrations you'll see herein are the
work of Shavertron's staff illustrator, Ralph Finley.
Unfortunately, Ralph is moving to Idaho because he
thinks California is doomed. We hope that as long
as Shavertron is above water, he will continue to
send us an occasional drawing, between shoveling
snow in the winter, and chopping wood in the summer.
Good luck, Ralph!

We're going to dedicate the rest of the editorial
this issue to John Michell's recent book, NATURAL
LIKENESS...subtitled "Faces and Figures in Nature",
(E.P. Dutton paperback, NY, 1979 $7.95). To give
you some idea of the essence of this profusely illustrated book (196 illus.) we'll quote the first line
of Mr Michell's intro: "This book is intended to re-
assure those who see faces and figures in rocks, trees,
clouds and damp stains on walls. Other people also
see such things, and always have..."

Yes, that's right, its a book on UUI's (unseen
universal images) your editor's pet subject these
days. Offering up numerous photos of giant stone
heads, animals in trees and rocks and faces in just
about everything, Michell discusses the touchy subject of UUI's in a very empathetic manner.

He writes of the concept of the "Masma" culture,
an advanced race that once traveled the earth, leaving
its trace throughout the countryside...in mammoth
rock formations (read RSS' feature article, this ish).

This Masma theory was formulated by a Peruvian traveller, Daniel Ruzo. He became aware of cyclopean ruins
of giant heads and faces, and tried to convince the
scientific world in the early 1950's that science
"...will soon find itself forced to admit that, across
the whole surface of the earth, prehistoric men, descendants of the cave painters, have sculpted in the
living stone images expressing their loftiest conceptions."

Michell relates the story of the misunderstood
poet, Antonin Artaud, who, on a trip through Mexico,
found "figures and symbols in the rocks (that were)
not random but were formed and placed together in a
significant manner. They constituted 'the signs of
a language based on the very shape of breath when released in sound'..." This may remind SM fans of RSS'
Mantong language, and lo and behold, we find 2 pages
with photos devoted to RSS in NATURAL LIKENESS!!

Unlike most writers, Michell does not condemn RSS,
but rather discusses his rock book research with an
open mind and with certain insights. He muses:

"Was Richard Shaver a man of individual genius or
a monumental crank? The answer is a matter for anyone's choice, since an idea which is recognized as
a mark of genius in one age seems merely crazy in a-
nother. A review of the myths and cosmologies of all
nations prompts the conclusion that every conceivable belief about the universe has at some time in the
past been upheld as orthodox doctrine, and may be

expected to recur at some time in the future. Shaver's
mistake, if he wanted people to give serious attention
to the prophecies and cosmic intelligence which he derived from staring at the patterns in rocks, was to be
born into the wrong age."

Rock book fans will definitely go for this opus,
which has just been given the Shavertron stamp of
approval!

More than a few fans have written in to S to in-
quire about that longtime controversy between RAP
and RSS: were the caverns really up in the sky somewhere, a la Oaspe, or down below the crust of the
earth? We guess that this arguement between the two
men was never really resolved, since neither of them
would give in to the other on it. If someone would
care to comment on this, or if someone has any new
or useful info on this aspect of the SM, please send
it along for discussion.

It has also been brought to our attention that,
after RSS' death, RAP had informed certain people
that Shaver had been delivered into the hands of the
dero! A Shavertron reader reported to us, that an
odd incident confirmed this claim to her. Do any of
you S readers have anything on this one? We confess,
it's a new one on us!!

Shavertron is pubbed quarterly at $6 per year.
Single copies and back issues, $1.50. Issue 1
is sold out. Make all m.o.'s and checks out to
Richard Toronto, not to the zine. Address:
309 Coghlan St., Vallejo, Ca. 94590. Unsolicited
mss. are encouraged, and all care will be taken
in their handling.

187-Mile Wall

Libyan strongman Colonel Moammar Khadafy
said that "fortifying Libya against any aggression
from the east" was the reason behind his $3 billion,
seven-year project to erect a 187-mile concrete wall
along part of the 675-mile border with Egypt. He
claimed the wall would be "a hundred times
stronger than the Maginot Line," the system of
fortifications built before World War II along
France's eastern border with Germany.

the Zanfretta Case... by LUCIANO BOCCONE ∎

I think I should tell you something more on the Zanfretta case. 27 years old, married, two kids, Zanfretta has actually had four close encounters of the fourth kind. By CE4K I mean his abduction and teleportation inside an alien craft by big (about 3 meters tall) drake-like aliens, who have examined his body, "spoken" with him by means of luminous-telepathic signals from their "mouth", and released him at the end of their experiments in lonely, desert areas, sometimes as far as 30 km from the abduction site. He has also had two CE3K, one CE2K and one CE1K, to a total of 8 encounters since Feb 16, 1977, of which however, he does not remember at conscious level.

An increasing number of witnesses (12 of his colleagues as of today, at least 15 policemen and watchmen working with other Genoese watching companies, countrymen, etc.) and a number of inexplicable facts (high temperature and dryness of his body in the rain in wintertime up in the mountains, strong magnetic deviation on his car, abnormal radioactivity on the ground, big alien footprints, teleportation to sites miles away from the place of his disappearance, electromagnetic interferences in the police radio network, lights of his car and his colleagues' going off and engine stopping, etc) apparently support his statements.

Psychic, physical, medical and neuropsychiatric tests have demonstrated beyond doubt that he is "mentally and physically sound". The many lie-detector, regression-controller, narco (penthotal) and hypnoanalysis treatments that have been conducted on him in my presence by internationally known specialists have shown that Zanfretta does not lie, and that he has actually experienced "something real". What this "something real" is, nobody can say as yet.

What we, as the UFO investigators of this quite unusual case, can say after 35 months is that he certainly receives luminous telepathic communications, even downtown and by day, without being aware of them. We have taken time-lapse infrared pictures of these contacts from his alien world (globes of light and mysterious glowing signs close to him, invisible to him and to us all) on Geiger-counter detection of abnormal radioactivity. Our pictures confirm his statement under hypnosis, according to which "they can find him whenever they want to, as they always know where he is, what he does, whom he meets...", and corroborate the objective reality of his encounters, unquestionably.

My theory that hypnovisualizing powers are used by these alien beings for "talking" him into the "reality" of his experience and making him believe what they want, is supported by the words he addressed to the "egg-headed" man (he had already met with on three previous occasions) at the beginning of his latest CE4K downtown, on Dec 2, 1979: "Don't look at me with those eyes, you make me suffer..."

For the time being, my personal opinion is that these plasmatic luminous etheric beings order him hypnotically (he said they know he is treated like that after each experience) to report to us only what they "hammer" into his head. Actually, not the least information on "what they really do to him" during his encounters has been revealed by Zanfretta, except the application of a sort of "electric helm" on his head to quiet him down whenever he revolted against them, or the application of "something" on his belly, or "something else" on his legs or in his eyes. Yet, we know that his story is not a fake or a hoax.

Everything, during his latest encounter for example, coincides with the times I personally recorded during the search (I was in the rescue squad) and with the sighting of lights by his colleagues and the electromagnetic interferences reported by the police. These are facts. Zanfretta does not remember practically anything of his encounters. All these encounters prove to have been taken against his will. He does not pride himself on having ridden in a ufo, nor has he to inform anybody on anything or to give any message to mankind, at least at conscious level. He has never been a ufo-literature reader: he didn't even believe in such "crazy and foolish things as ufos" two years ago...

He has a family, and wants to be left alone, by these "damned beings" too. He was wild with fear of them, at first, now, all goes quite differently.

continued next page...

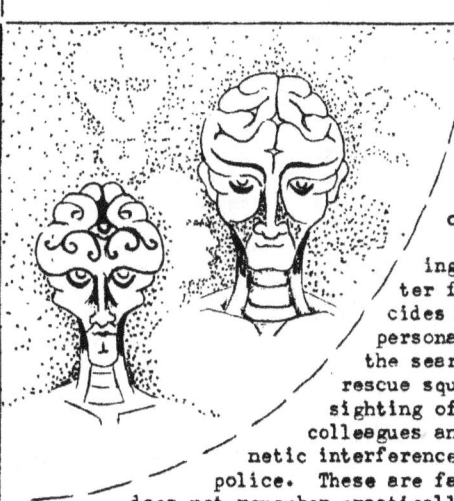

3

Those Powers That Be ✢

A poem by Allan Wiseman of Shaverian interest:
O Powers that Be--(On High)-- enthroned eternally,
Supreme Universal Twosome plus infinite, invisible T
(exd)--kindly watch over me/ That I may prevail in times
of Lawless strife, stress and/or calamitous Emergency/
Majestic, Sacred "I AM"--A to Z Ultra-dimensional lee/
Evil, god-forsaken Dero ray fight and decimate tero
guard ray day and night/The dreaded Dero might not
always be wrong--but more often their hated, age-old
enemy--the tero-- are <u>right</u>/ Both live in secluded
caves way down in the secretest, stygian deep/ Shaver's
cavern-dwelling hideous "Abandondero" at best look like
things from a bad dream when asleep/ Yes, some will
laugh, ridicule and scoff, till these dummies preview
"hell" with the lid yanked off! / Don't let the "druks"
get to you my folly-ridden friend/ Uncontrite reader,
if they zero in it may well spell your quite ignom-
inious <u>literal</u> end!
PS--In case you are not enamored by the male (and/or
female) charms of the ghastly-mutated and minified
gnarled and murderous Abandondero (No! No! No!)--
Cheer up (Ho! Ho! Ho!) there be always the rollic-
some and scintillating (Oh! Oh! Oh!) CHARO (Go!
Go! Go!) End

SHAVERTRON Needs Help!

At long last, Shavertron can offer a set of 10
Kodak photo-postcards with an RSS sketch on each one.
These cards are suitable for mailing. They are sketches
and doodlings that RSS had tacked around his desk in
his studio. They reveal the many sides of RSS! Set
of 10 cards...$6 plus 25 cents postage...or 5 cards..
$3.50 plus 25 cents post.
All monies from this Shaver Mystery

project will be used to keep Shavertron afloat.

Shavertron also is offering the complete set
of the Otto Binder feature, "Ancient Ufos", now
displayed in Shavertron. The complete set of 6
Shaver "Record of Rocks" installments...$6. Each
one is an original from the origi nal plates. An
unusual bit of SM memorabilia. Use ordering instructions as above. All goes to publication of our
Shaverzine!

Policeman bitten by weird dog-man
3-5 1980

Police in Roanoke, Virginia,
will never forget the bizarre
night of the howling dog-man.

Answering a disturbance call,
police found a naked man wearing a dog collar, standing on the
roof of a shed howling and shouting.

Trying to put cuffs on the man,
officer E.L. Mills was bitten on
the hand.

Neighbors said the man and a
group of dogs had been chasing
cars and digging up gardens.

Residents were either laughing
or terrified.

"It wasn't just the man who
thought he was a dog," said Mills,
"the dogs seemed to think he was
a dog too. It was uncanny."

NEXT ISH — Dero Deluxe

SONOMA CO. STUMP
April 23-30 1980

April 19 - In Forestville, a
deputy returned two female
juveniles back to their mother after they sneaked out and
attempted to hitchhike to a
Monte Rio party. ... A
group of youths led a deputy
to Goat Rock Beach where
they told them they saw a
meteorite hit. The deputy
reported finding remains of
the meteorite covering a 15-
20 foot circumference. Most
of these meteorite fragments
could not be touched because
they were still extremely
hot.... A felony vandalism
report was made to deputies
by a Forestville man who
told them someone exploded
some type of device on his
water tank. The explosion
completely destroyed the
tank. An investigation is
being conducted.

Zanfretta Case con't.

During his latest experience for example, he revolted against them when one of them called him "pic-
colino" (this is at least what he reports under hypnosis), he criticizes their ugliness and scolds them for
their bad manners...The fact that he threw at them the
mysterious "object" he was instead to hand over to us
already in July (a crystal sphere containing a pyramid
of unknown bright metal, which should prove to the terrestrians "their existence"), thus making us believe
that it was his fault if he didn't bring the ball to
us, is in my opinion only a trick, an invention of such
beings to justify their failure to keep a previous
promise. At least, so we are led to believe...

The day following his close encounters on July 31
and December 2-3, 1979, Zanfretta urinated black
(initially). No physician has ever in the least been
able as yet to account for this fact (black urines of
witnesses of CE were reported for the first time as
early as 1947 in Finland). Nor have ufologists been
able to supply any rational explanation hitherto..
Today, we can see in it the possible elimination of
Zanfretta's latent T-bacilli, I.E. the effect of the
action of a high orgonotic charge on his organism during
his stay inside the "glowing hot alien craft"...some-
thing similar to Wilhelm Reich's treatment of cancer
in an orgone energy accumulator and consequent expul-
sion of tumour debris (black in color as the T-bacilli) with the urines of cancerous patients.

There is also the "silhouette" of the "boss"
Zanfretta usually sees in a panel inside the alien
craft, and the "shape" of the "object" he used to dream
of recurrently: "silhouette" and "shape" are very similar to George Van Tassel's "light motor", whatever UFO
investigators and researchers may think of it, and to
Blumrich's reconstruction of Ezekiels visions in 593-
563 BC.

It is still difficult to say how true or how false
was the message released to Van Tassel by the Sumerian/
Accadian entity Ashtar, who explained to him how their
"shan" vehicles work. The fact is that, in Sumerian,
"shem" or "sham" or "shan" means "The Gods' Chariots",
and the derived word "chan-chan" is the Civilization
of the Drake, all over the world.

Still in Sumerian, "LAHMU" means the planet Mars.
In a report drawn up by him because "he felt the need
to do so", Zanfretta writes that "if the terrestrians
are not prepared to accept them and cohabit with them
they shall be obliged to turn to "LAVUX", which is
closer to their own cold planet..." Now, the orbit of
Mars (Lahmu or Lamux) is actually closer to the Planet
of Crossing (the symbol of which is a "cross" or a
"winged disc", the Sumerian civilization refers to as
the 12th Celestial Body of our solar system (they already knew of Uranus, Neptune and Pluto). The Planet
of Crossing is many times greater than our planet,
and re-enters our system every 3600 years according to
the Sumerian Tablets. And, under hypnosis, Zanfretta
reported that "they live on a cold planet, four times
greater than the Earth, about 4000 years away from us.
Is it exaggerated to consider all these linguistic,
geographic astronomic, archaelogic, clypeologic inter-
connections and interrelations? I think they are as
worthy of consideration as the facts reported by
Zanfretta under hypnosis and by all witnesses of his
many encounters...."this is how they tune in".

Ed. note: Mr Boccone is a leader in the Italy-
based ufo study/research group, the GRCU (Gruppo
di Ricerche Clipeologiche ed Ufologiche.) This
organization has pioneered many new research techniques for ufology. We are pleased to be honored
with Mr Boccone's presence in Shavertron.

SUPPORT YOUR LOCAL

From Page 1:

the moon falling upon the earth seven times has fairly well destroyed their original LOOK in most places). BUT in the interior, they may have been protected enough from the awful shock and tidal waves of the moon falls to have survived in a way that would allow genuinely complete reconstruction...at least on paper artistically...of their wonder and their might and their vast vitality and vigor.

One might even find some space ships lying about ...in unrusted usefulness. Reconstruction of their space drives might be possible without having to force the Rock Books down their pureblind mouths. It is this possibility of the space drive being once again man's own that makes me talk Rock Books, for the pictures and plans of sphere ships and saucer ships are quite frequent in Rock Books. How to get our scientists to look at them seriously with their million dollar equipment is the only real problem to again entering space and space commerce.

It is this sort of thing that leads me to consider the hollow earth as a possibility. There are certain appearances in astronomical photos that support the idea that ALL planets are growths that form around a magnetic field, and magnetic fields are doughnut-shaped. That is, space dust...in a doughnut shape. This leaves polar openings in the age-old growth that we call planets.

Certain photos of the transit of Mercury across the sun's face show that light from the sun passes THROUGH Mercury, and the only way this can be explained is that Mercury has a hole all the way through which shows only when it passes between earth and the sun.

Certain photos of polar regions show that the polar regions MAY be regions of constant FOG. The Polaris expedition under the ice to the pole brought back film movies of their upward plunge through the ice to the polar area. Now in those movies, which were on tv networks at the time, the fog was so dense one could see only six feet or so. The ice then broke through as they came up appeared to be only some six inches thick.

You have two phenomena supporting the polar opening theory right there. On film, too. Fog only forms at certain temperatures which are not at all "polar" temps, rather warm air is necessary. And ice only six inches thick supports this warmth deduction. That is, everything points to a foggy polar condition and a steady warmth of most peculiar high temps for that supposed frigid area.

Photos of Mars show a similar rather wierd fog condition, so near as one can make out. How you can have gog on a world supposed as arid and airless as Mars, I don't know. It may be dry ice, but one can only guess. And that is just about all they can do as yet...guess.

Just what they do know and find out about this polar opening theory one can only guess they would keep secret, anyway.

If we knew just what secrets "official" military files keep from the public, we would be mighty angry.. ...that is the only fact in the whole mess of guess work.

So the hollow earth is just as tenable a theory as any other theory. All theories are guesswork, awaiting positive determination by a "qualified" scientist. If you ever meet a qualified scientific body, I will show you a corpse that needs embalming.

It is a curse built up in my mind over 30 years of trying to make some sense with once of them or another. There is no way I have ever found of making such a contact short of holding them at gun point to discuss any off-trail subjects.

They are plain scared of unorthodoxy for their livelyhood depends on being accepted as oh-so-certified-pure, it seems.

Nothing frightens the average scientist like the breath of the whack, the off-trail, the "ufologist" or the hollow earth sort of theorist.

Just as nothing frightened the scientists of Spain when called upon to back up Columbus in his search for funds to sail around the round world. They ridiculed him, no matter what they privately thought, because their University jobs depended utterly upon being accepted as orthodox, Christian, dependable, unwhacky, and quite unthinking servants of things as they are.

So don't think the hollow earth isn't possible. It is very possible, as no "scientific" body anywhere ever had the guts to investigate the idea honestly.

The inaccesability of the polar regions protects the theorists, they can have polar openings if they wish. As the prime source of ufo, it isn't really needed, because the flying saucers are, in fact, sub-

mersible and have been observed diving into the sea and even into lakes frequently enough to convince anyone who can read. They don't really NEED a polar hole to run into or to come out of, there is the ocean itself. There are said to be water-traps into the underworld by which they can enter the endless caverns and pre-deluge cavern cities. A saucer that came to earth in the night, dove into the ocean and entered the underworld by way of the water trap is about as unobservable as a ship entering or leaving the fog-shrouded polar openings.

The only way anyone can prove or disprove the theory is to set out with millions of dollars in equipment, helicopters and cargo planes, and really explore that fog-bound pole. It is perfectly possible that a helicopter could lower itself in the center of the fog and never hit water, but lower on and on into the central opening of earth. I don't know personally, but I'd like to know.

You can collect all the aerial photos of the polar area ever taken, I suspect, by a judicious pesteration of the larger library authorities. I once found a whole library of rare and expensive art books in the Detroit Museum, which was never opened to the public (to protect the books). If you knew the right people you could get a permit card to study the books. But the poor average tax-payer never found out about the library, he only paid for it. Most governmental agencies of the more expensive and luxurious sort are like that...reserved.

continued next page...

If they knew all about the polar openings they would "protect" the data from any public knowledge, one suspects. It is the way they do things. The "secret" of the underworld is like that, no secret really, It just isn't possible to get round the official fear of the subject with any genuine publicity.

Secrets of this kind have a way of keeping themselves. The average guy just doesn't have any way of saying anything, even if he knows about it.

That is really what all Ufology publications are about, you know. They are private people trying to get round the "official" scientific habits of secrecy, reserved fo scientists, redundant security, and general stupidity about what is best for Mankind. We know, you and I who have read a large number of ufo publications, that there must be a fire to make all the smoke. BUT just what the "official" secrecy is hiding we can't find out. In fact, one can learn more about Russian space plans than one can learn about the secret files of the US government on ufo.

The turth is, they are scared to death of the very word, and would like to sweep it under the carpet forever. Reason: they KNOW something you and I aren't permitted to find out...they KNOW what official collected files have to say about persecutions, mental obliterations, deaths, MIB murders, etc. They know enough to be afraid to know more and to be afraid to let the public know more. There is always the old saw: "to prevent public panic", you know.

There is, in fact, whole worlds of data on tel-augment devices and telaug work...mental subversion.. ..call it by some name, you know what I mean, I hope ...which is never publicised, and which those who KNOW about are afraid to even talk about. Such files are automatically kept away from the inquiring public for their own good...or out of fear of personal consequences...one can't help wondering how all this really stacks up.

The Hollow Earth data exists somewhere in this mass of secret files and security protected data, no doubt. But about all we can do about it is talk, wonder, and conjecture. Which is what I am doing, since I can't do more.

We commoners are always angry when we run into this fact of life. But it is the same fact of life you run into when the headwaiter at a posh eatery puts up the red rope and won't let you enter. You just don't belong to the world of influential people...and if you did, you would find out that those people who can pass the red rope and get a table are living in fear and wonder and speculating at the same blind alley of inaccessibility of all the real information on earth.

I live in this sort of anger perpetually. With me, it is a habitual state of mind. All the real info that is needed to set the world right is denied to anyone who could or would do anything with it. They have done the same thing with the Rock Book library I discovered...pushed it under the rug of ignorance they keep the minds of the world under. I can't fight

HOLLOW EARTH A FACT

it to get the Rock Books recognised as the source of encyclopedic information on such needed subjects as pre-deluge space travel and space drives.

The hollow earth theory is probably no theory, but a fact. But how to get the data out from under the rug and look at it is the same problem as breaking down the security of the Secret Bureaus. It is a problem a lot of spies are paid alot of money to solve.

With my Rock Books, you have the total library, quite available, of races of people who travelled space for millions of years! To publicise and make

available the contents such Rock Books, I find, is just as difficult as proving the hollow earth is actually hollow. One feels the same way Galileo felt when they locked him up for insisting his telescope didn't exactly fulfill the Eclesiastical prognosis of what the skies contained.

Galileo died in jail for insisting his telescope was more truthful than the priests who insisted the angels didn't want men watching them in any telescope.

Columbus only missed the same fate with the flat world pedants by proving his point...and it took a Queen's jewels and some capable seamen to do it.

We live in the same sort of dark age of mental incompetency today, because one can't be heard above all the shouting of the mad meat peddlers...(what do you call the mad world of unthinking words forever dinned in our ears on tv and radio and publications?) It is certainly no place to look for things like information on polar openings. Or it is no place to peddle a pre-deluge Rock Book, they are too busy spending millions to peddle more soap.

So, you can have your hollow earth, if you can hear yourself think long enough.

One of the greatest corroborations for the hollow earth theory came when the Apollo 12 mission dropped it's drouge, and the sound of it striking the moon's surface rang and rang like a bell into the instruments they had set up on the moon to detect quakes The sound indicated a hollow moon, and was stated over the networks at the time it happened. I really don't understand why such a simple bit of data wasn't smothered in official dunderheadedness, can you?

I suspect that if someone were determined enough, as determined as the people who probe sonically for oil bearing hollows in the underlying strata, were to make a sonic survey of the whole world that perfect maps of hollow parts of the earth would not be difficult to create.

I know a fellow who maps caverns with nothing but a waterwitch wand. His maps are used too, by perfectly sane and stable groups of speleologists for underground explorations. They check out, compared to actual maps of the caverns so witchwanded. They check out on scales of about one foot error in 12, which is pretty blamed good for standing on top of them.

So it would not be impossible to develope apparatus for deciding just exactly what cavities exist inside the earth, instead of speculating interminably. Sonic echoes are not impossible to create in rock strata. Something of the kind done with penetrative radio waves might be worked out too, as a check on the other.

So, instead of talking about it, why not map the cavities yourself? That would be a job, wouldn't it?

There are maps of all kinds in 3-di in Rock Books. First you have to get them recognised as manmade maps of earth's strata, and of ocean currents and so on, before they would do you much good. There are really lots of maps of earth's cavities already in existence, lying about ignored as rocks. How to get our so-wise organised science to pick them up and look at them and understand them and decipher them, that is the problem. How do you lead a mule to water? How do you make him drink?

This is always your real problem in life, a mental one, not a material one. And considering my own experience, I suspect that is a literal statement... there is no material there. There only seems to be. They do not think, they reflect.

They reflect, they mirror the thoughts of others they have read in their texts, they do not reason or decide or deduct or analyze. They just reflect the
conclusion next page

worn-out opinions they inherited from a dry-as-dust drowned-in-error educational institution dedicated to the perpetuation of all errors and all statue-quo.

How to get anything NEW and different decided upon and implemented and actively put into effective action is something they never dare really think about.

I have spent sixteen years (is it?) trying to get a few of them just to LOOK at a few rock pictures, with a record of total failure. They already KNOW all rock pictures are accidental in origin, and there isn't any use in looking at any of them. Not one of them can even think of "sticking his neck out" even so far as to look at a rock seriously as a creation of pre-deluge man.

You want to know if the earth is hollow? They don't think it is, and though there are a dozen available ways of finding out, they won't make the effort because they know it is unnecessary, irrelevant and quite foolish.

The theory is still held that earth is all molten under the surface crust, you know. Quite, quite molten, still, even though there are any number of worn out oil wells spewing out salt water so cold it frosts the pipes and freezes it's immediate surroundings. There is plenty of data that the earth is NOT molten in the depths, and may indeed be all very, very cold like the frozen tundras. But, officially, earth is still a molten mass in the center. Since they are twice wrong about everything, it may turn out to be molten by a kind of double mistake.

There is evidence that gas and oil we use was NOT the product of lavish nature, but was instead stored in the earth by the great ancient races for the purpose of fueling their space voyages, and for heating their domed cities during the ice ages. That all of it was produced over immense periods of time by man himself, in the past. Produced and pumped into underground storage by mankind...us...our ancestors.

With that kind of fact, not even considered as a fact, although one would think they could figure out whether that oil and gas was stored or produced by nature...don't expect "them"...official science, to ever determine if the earth has polar openings or in fact is a hollow ball like a doughnut. They won't decide or accept until some Marco Polo comes back with the goods of trade. Then they will jump on the bandwagon with plenty of reflections about it all.

There is no organised science,with muscles and mind. There are only little individuals afraid to have an opinion, incapable of action for the same reason you and I are incapable of organised action and thought about anything.

When you try to contact an organised scientific group, you can never manage to contact anyone other than a secretary...a person with a business college diploma, who has no interest in, or knowledge of science, nor any curiousity about it, either.

We do not have a society of active minds. We have a bureaucracy of inactive minds, lead bottoms, no head and lots of fancy words all ready for the purpose of brushing off any bother or work.

There is only one remedy for all this, you know. You have to start over, organise your own scientific body, finance your own excursions into research, create all anew every bit of your world of active mentality. For most of us, just getting two people agree about anything at all is quite impossible.

So whether the world is hollow or solid, molten or frozen, is something we just can't afford to find out by ourselves. And there isn't really anyone else to want to bother to find out.

Photos of the moon's polar areas show a suspiciously round pole that could be fogbound polar hole too, with all the atmosphere of the moon inside and a cloud layer hiding it. But how to decide that when all the sites of landing are elsewhere, I don't know.

One might as well be a snail with no arms, no legs no eyes to speak of, and not much to go on but a nose. (As to be a man of today's race of men). It's quite impossible to really learn anything. And its no use asking the professor snails, either. They can't even use their nose without asking permission of the board of alumni.

So, in a blind world, if you have one eye, keep quiet about it. They might find out you don't see things with your nose!

Soviet Disease Story

The Soviet Foreign Office in Moscow provided what it termed "a serious" explanation of the story that an epidemic of anthrax in the Sverdlovsk region last year — reportedly responsible for hundreds of civilian deaths — had come about as a result of a mishap involving development of biological warfare. The offices said that the outbreak had resulted from improper handling of meat products, not "lethal agents" for warfare.

Thurs., Apr. 24, 1980   ★   San Francisco Chronicle 9

Lab Union Seeking Skin-Cancer Probe

The major state employees' union announced yesterday that it is asking federal health and safety officials to conduct an independent study of the puzzlingly high incidence of skin cancer at the Lawrence Livermore Laboratory nuclear weapons research center.

A promised "in-house" investigation by the U.S. Department of Energy would always be suspect, said Keith Hearn, spokesman for the California State Employees Association (CSEA).

"We want an outside investigation to analyze this situation," Hearn said, adding that the U.S. Occupational Safety and Health Administration (OSHA) is in the best position, technically and politically, to conduct such a probe.

State health department officials released a report Tuesday that said workers at the Livermore lab have an incidence of malignant melanoma — a virulent skin cancer — five times that of the general population in their Alameda and Contra Costa county communities.

The disease generally is associated with heavy exposure to ultra-violet radiation — most commonly too much sun — rather than the radiation associated with plutonium and other radioactive materials used at the Livermore laboratory.

"We're concerned about the melanoma situation," said U.S. Department of Energy spokesman Hank Bowden. He said the department would consider any request by any individual or group "on the next step" in identifying the problem.

He added, however, that he knew of no precedent for letting OSHA or any other outside agency conduct an independent investigation of health hazards at a nuclear facility.

The Livermore laboratories, federal facilities operated by the University of California, are exempt from both state and federal OSHA laws.

CSEA represents about 1000 blue-collar, white-collar and scientific personnel among the 7000 workers at Livermore. Hearn said two of the three workers who died of melanoma were members of the union.

7

PURE BLISS

by Bill Bliss

THROW OUT YOUR TV, QUICK! I've been trying to convince a fellow independent soul (the local giant) that the boob tube subverts the attic of the brain. It only gets to him a little bit and that finally gets rejected. To illustrate the point, I sounded out a male customer aged about 22. In about 10 minutes it became evident that he was unable to think of not having a TV. Actually unable to have the thought consciously. He did some fascinating side stepping mentally. Looks like being your own man is for the fortunate few who have independent mentalities. Almost everybody deals with systems on the terms of the systems.

Another Shaver mystery--- how come he never used any of my technical advances in rokfogo? Come to think of it, though, I still haven't gotten around to trying powder negative infra-red rokfogos...

I've had alot of people actually <u>knocking</u> at the shop door lately...a few always have. I often ask them if they also knock at filling stations, laundromats and banks, and so far no answer. I've asked other local businessmen, and they say they haven't had any knocking.

I wonder--maybe crossovers (from other parallel worlds or where ever) have an empathy for me. And they actually <u>do</u> knock at businesses where they come from. I'm not a common model in this world, so maybe they think I'm a crossover too. Maybe some of the fixits I get are way far out. A very intelligent male of around 45 was by this morning buying resistors (he was hep to electronics, but not hep on stock resistor sizes) (???????) because he was building a testing device to measure weak air currents...for wot purpose he didn't know. Or is the Military/Industrial Komplex out getting el cheapo R&D in the boondocks? (They must have to when the big domes and big labs bomb out).

The "Did I Mention It Before" department...I keep having an inkling that often a rock book itself is the mechanism, or a mechanism. Found a good image of a solid state (an amplifier) chip, about 1/32", in some galena. Is it an actual working artifact? Would that account for some of the occasional unusual efficiency of some early crystal detectors?????

I would say, yes, definitely, the Shaver Mystery is durable. It is part of a bigger mystery I call THE COSMIC SNOW JOB. I have an impression that somewhere in ve management of the cosmos (or at least part of this galaxy) a decision was made a long time ago to populate inferior planets like this one. So... logically, the inhabitants could not be hep to the big scene for lots of obvious reasons. And it figures that the most efficient way of keeping them on the naive side would be to make some of their mentality limited. Was just reading the last Velikovsky interview in FATE zine. It really shows up there. Most significant thing about the whole V. scene is the utter lack of komment/criticism of the chapter he did in WORLDS IN COLLISION about post major disaster general psychology.

On hearing voices, there is a strange thing that was (still is?) in my branch of the Bliss clan. A few days before someone died, a loud clear voice was heard from above--always in houses and nowhere else--calling the person's name. I heard it twice as a youngster.

Somewhere in the stacks of paperbacks here is an account of some mysterious coins and jewelry that were found by a well digger before the turn of the century here 40 feet deep in the gravel. Chillicothe sits on old river bottom and the gravel is as deep as 120 ft. I asked quite a few local old timers, and they had never heard of it. Some of the ancient machines could simply be buried as well in caves. There is some good evidence that an advanced civilization once was in this area.

I found some statue fragments in a gravel pit--from their proportions they would have been at least 30 ft. high and showed a good competency in sculpting. Most were of grey granite, and unfortunately were in too poor condition for any possible restoration. I found a small 3" stone-reddish brown and extremely hard and dense. It has had flats and radii cut on it. To me, it looks like it was roughed out for something, and never finished. It has had a bit of wear, so the work on it had to have been a very long time ago. It is hard enough to require a diamond saw-it could be worked with abrasives (as diamonds have to be) of near or the same hardness, but that would probably be impractical for most common purposes. Opinions from people I have shown it to are that it might have been a loom weight, a peg of some sort--it is a lot like pegs used by carpenters to push against when planning boards or a cam. I found one good rock pic on it by dusting it with common talcum powder and rubbing the excess off carefully.

There is the unusual account in a Churchward book of Niven's diggings near Mexico City where he found a city where modern concrete had been used for construction (in one room of a goldsmith's house) and they had electric lights. That should have been big news and roused great enthuiasm but evidently not. Many

PURE BLISS

such things are found in obscure places. Mysteries of time and space by Brad Steiger has a photo of a rather common looking spark plug in solid rock. So that and many other things (steel cubes, gold chains, nails, etc.) found in coal and rock leaves practically no doubt that quite a few technologically advanced civilizations existed in the past. One doubt could be that the past was not (somehow) structured as we would think by our own observations of the recent past.

How about people who mysteriously <u>appear</u> from thin air? I almost got (good thing I can move fast even tho middle aged) clobbered by one a few years ago, while crossing the street in front of the shop. The street was empty of traffic and all of a sudden an old man in a Pontiac-looking sedan appeared and it was doing about 20 mph, and he stood on the brake pedal and I moved my carcass in high gear. He went on around the corner and headed south. His tires left marks on the pavement, so if that was a phantom, it weighed a couple of tons.

The propieter of the pool hall (now the Kingdom Hall of the Jehovahs Witnesses) was standing out front shooting the bull with some friends and they saw it. He said later that he had seen a few such appearances, but he never told anybody since they might think he was a nut.

Richard, you got rayed to not mention those agent's names in the last issue, thus my believability doesn't appear too good for fans and others: Major Wayne Aho, (ex-Army Intelligence) P.O. Box 867, Eatonville, Wash. 98328, and Mr. Dick Williams (ex-CIA), and a Rickey Gillespie, CIA.

You're rayed to remember wrong, dero thoughts on brain cells. I told you three times in different letters that I didn't know the de-aging native mixture but a man did who desires keeping it quiet. I harped I have specific information that certainly can track him down, in time, using CIA/FBI men or agents hired by a large corporation. You "forgot" (via dero) to state the reason my price appeared so high. Same amount the bureaucrats give away each year! Without this reason it sounds a bit nutty. (Dero know-how).

Also, I harped anytime you put statements by me which are about the government, to say I think we have basically a good government, but it's mentally rayed, and that I've tried to help it in the past but that it's no use. Oh well, due to ray on their agents and bosses perhaps it doesn't matter too much anyhow. I'll get what deros want. Good ray will get me what they want too. Personal messages from both sides show this factor clearly!

MILLION $ $ Cave Entrance Revealed By Steele— NO Charge
An Open Letter from Henry M Steele

Since the deros prevent me from getting a lot of money from the govt. on certain information (I asked a million) I'll reveal the secret below. The deal was included in that long letter to Turner (head of CIA). We don't have a govt. "for the people"! Why?

From years of checking into things I know the governments take their orders from Space Travellers, dero ray, and maybe Tero-"Eaves" ray.

I hope you will put the above in the next issue. And the following: Here is something backing up Shaver as much as anything could in a society of government-run suppression of cavern data and related subjects. Here is what Shaver-fans have been looking for. But it takes money and time (small expeditions) to get there.

Deros want this info kept quiet. They also harp to me that a govt. man will read your newsletter-- probably one of those pretending to be a good fan. And they can mech-read my mind on everything and just keep quiet about it. So--I've decided to tell how fans can get together and track down a mech-cavern staffed by Indians. As some may question how I got this data, let me explain to them:

There are two places one can easily talk to people: Florida beaches and Texas parks. In a Dallas park one day, I talked to an Indian. To make this to the point, I knew of Shaver's "Red Legion" piece, so I just up and asked the fellow if he knew any stories pertaining to old Indian caves. He (I can't remember his name) started telling me a story he overheard as a child. His old grandmother was telling the story to some elder Indians, thinking that the Indian child was sleeping. The boy woke up in time to hear interesting details...first, know this:

Along some Texas river is a mech cavern entrance!! Instead of having to look all over the planet we now have the specific state and the specific type of place. There arent many Texas rivers, are there?! Just follow one after another and in some months (perhaps only a few) we'll spot the large entrance. A large hole faces the river. His tribe in the olden days used this large opening to live in. At least it seemed large to these Indians. This data is the best we can

ever hope for it seems--and is something we can put to use providing money and time can be had away from jobs. A collection taken and strong boatmen/hikers appointed from us Shaver fans?

Details: The tribe lived only in the front part of the cave. They fished and shot deer. On occasion, they would have encountered "The Old Ones", who came from deep within the cave. These never talked or associated with the tribe. They came out for deer and fish. They lived much longer than his tribe members (via mech stim we now know) and so their specific title. At times the entrance--Indians could hear a hum from way back in the cave. One time a few decided to see where these "old ones" came from. They walked very, very far back. They got in far enough to hear a hum (mech). Finally they saw the tunnel start to become dimly lighted in the distance. They became frightened at this and returned. Never did they go that far again.

This fellow didn't hear from his grandmother where their old cave was. The tribe moved from it while she was just a child. She died while he was a child.

How correct can Shaver get?? He and Palmer have stated lots of people know something of mech caverns, but are scarred to speak out. While living in Dallas I ran into a few who knew a little of mech caverns, their people, dero tricks, etc. You bring up the matter by just mentioning caves or people living in caverns. You get in return a Shaver type tale. Thus, no need to be just an intellectual. No need to simply believe...you know. If you Shaver fans would ask folks like I did sooner or later you'd get results. See how valuable you Shaver fans are for each other? Keep together, get addresses and write each other. make new fans. Henry.

Elephant Refuses to Talk
4/9/80

Moscow

The Karaganda zoo claims to have a talking elephant, although the local correspondent of the Moscow daily Komsomolskaya Pravda has his doubts.

Reporter V. Ryzhkov went along to interview Batyr, the 10-year-old Indian elephant, but came away disappointed, he reported yesterday.

"Batyr doesn't like giving interviews," Ryzhkov reported. "He gets nervous at the sight of a microphone or a camera lens."

Still, Boris Pavlovich Kosinsky, the director of Karaganda zoo in the Soviet Central Asian republic of Kazakhstan, insists that his elephant can talk.

"You know, I didn't believe it myself at first," Kosinsky told the newspaper.

"But later, I was a witness more than once to the 'chats' of the little elephant."

Asked what words the elephant had mastered, Kosinsky said:

"The elephant's vocabulary is filling out fairly quickly. Batyr is already saying a whole sentence — 'Batyr is good' — he knows the verbs 'drink' and 'give'..."

On one occasion, when Batyr was being moved from one cage to another and refused at first to budge, the elephant was heard to repeat his keeper's injunction, "move, Batyr," Kosinsky said.

United Press

LETTERS

Dear Rich Toronto,
"RAP never (quote) dug out anything new..." (SM) What? Howabout his Atmospherea theory (Ufo's come from cavernworld-in-the-sky)? Palmer Vs Shaver skirmishes over interveining years...RAP favored OAHSPE, you know. RSS stuck to his guns, very interesting. TRUTH somewhere, "in between"! (Bit of both, ie. in perfect balance, trik-ee!)
"Cave Ritual" (issue 4) recalls to mind the robed and cowled figure in a rock I found which featured a great Satanlike figure as well. "Invader Conspiracy" got to me. Pg. 3, the blood drained cattle overloaded with body poisons (even the Bible warns against this "food" source.) But such blood could be used asa great soil nutrient. Much animal by-products are used thusly by us surfacers, being "inedible".

The MOON is a best supra-source of good bio (life-giving) soil in our entire solar system, (even lavaflows pale by comparison!) Point is, sub-earth soil is easily depleted, lacking contact with any ORGANIC matter en-masse such as the surfaceworld has. Minerals alone cannot sustain life. Subvital nutrients found in cows' blood for the no longer readily available lunar topsoil (enriched)!! Why? Dincha ever raise mushrooms, for example? God, they eat up the soil like crazy!
If you read certain scripture you'll find where outcasts from the "holy land" area found refuge in caves.. hence the cavernworld route, right? Along with "kosher" food laws (favoring cattle and sheep above swine). Small clues, but significant? The ufo invaders are raiders in a strict meaning of language--they are silent, hit-and-go Vikings of the space age. Note the vital clues: "6-pointed star" on the amulet, (Star of David?)...the pyramid, indicative of the Exodus from Egypt, land of the pyramid? Is this a symbolism of the 10 lost tribes of Isreal?? Also, the "Kosher"-like approach to the Mutes. Why center on cattle, a clean animal? Swine, for example, are "de"-filled. Well, why not "fly" to Luna for the fertilizer? OK--could it be the moon is watched too much nowadays by us??
Allan Wiseman,
LA, California

•

SUNSETS in Antarctica frequently apear green.

•

Dear Rich,
The "illustrated" stones from Kircher's MUNDUS SUBTERRANEUS (furnished by Allan Wiseman) were certainly intriguing. Kircher was apparently the Charles Fort of his day, as I've run across references to him in connection with all kinds of "occult" topics. He also claimed to have been taken to other planets by a "genius". There is a new biography of him, ATHANASIUS KIRCHER, by Joscelyn Godwin, available from Shambala Books for $6.95. I have not seen it as yet.
What is your source for the "Cave Ritual" article on page 9? Don't recall having seen it anywhere previously.
Hadn't thought about Frank Brownley's suggestion that readers contact Marjorie Palmer and urge the publication of an annual issue of THE HIDDEN WORLD. It's a good idea. Also, some people may not realize that several of the previous THW issues are still available from Palmer Publications, and at considerably more decent prices than are normally charged by the various rip-off artists who masquerade as booksellers.
Lou Farish, Ark.
R--As usual, Lou is full of useful info to SM fans and ufo buffs alike. His UFO Newsclipping Service (UFONS) is the same: full of all the info you would ever want to know about ufos. Published monthly, Lou's service is one of the most comprehensive in the business. Write to him at Rt.1--Box 220, Plumerville, Ark. 72127 for more info.

Dear Richard--
I think you're being duped on the Ziff-RAP-Shaver thing. Hell's Bells, every interplanetary yarn of the 1940's violated Einstein's Theory, so why would Ziff care if a few fans protested at that? The theory isn't a law that one can be punished for breaking, like murder or robbery. It's something that remains a supposition (though there's alot of confirmative data now, years later.
PS- Glad to see the Shaver drawings and illustrations. More, please!
Eldon Everett
R-- That's what makes the SM so fascinating, Eldon! There are so many things that happened in RSS' lifetime that don't seem to make "sense" to us. Dero tamper? As yet, no one has materialized the fabled "Einstein" letter. RAP claimed its existence in the May 21, 1951 issue of LIFE, so shall we believe him?

ANOTHER peculiarity about the South Pole: You can get a sunburn there and freeze to death at the same time.

•

Dear Richard,
I am sure you have heard of a popular weekly publication called THE NATIONAL ENQUIRER. I buy a copy occasionally, and in the March 4, 1980 issue, a few seers made some predictions that they claim will occur during this decade. Only two will be mentioned, as they tie in with what Shaver has siad. To quote: (1) "Scientists will develop a special treatment for clothes which will repel dirt and perspiration. This will make garments self-cleaning--you'll hang up dirty clothes at night and by morning they'll be clean." (Predicted by Shawn Robbins) (2) "A new planet will be discovered in 1985..." (Predicted by Fred Davies)
It seems to me that Shaver once described such self-cleaning clothes were worn by the Elder Race. And he claimed, also, that our solar system was made up of TEN planets, not 9, with the tenth one yet to be discovered.
Another matter, Shaver wrote about the Elders traversing space in craft that EXCEEDED light-speed many times over. Yet the brilliant Albert Einstein would have shook his head vigorously at this "mad" utterance because, to him, nothing in the universe--NOTHING--moves faster than the speed of light. Yet FATE Magazine (to which I have subscribed since it first came out over 30 years ago!) had the following item in the January, 1980 issue--page 20:
"Was Einstein wrong in his basic conclusion that nothing could fly faster than light? According to Walter Sullivan in the New York Times, at least four celestial objects have been observed that appear to be traveling four to eight times faster than light!
"In recent years, a number of 'super-luminous' objects have been tracked as they flew away from three quasars. One distant galaxy, noted for its explosive behavior, has appeared to eject two such objects-- one at five times the speed of light and the other at eight times the speed of light.
"Some astronomers attempt to explain the contradiction by saying that the quasars are not as distant as has been believed and therefore the speed of the ejected object is exaggerated."
Interesting, wouldn't you say? Certainly something to think about and mull over.
Jim Wentworth

SHAVERTRON

"The Only Source of Post-Deluge Shaverania"

Winter 1980   Issue 6
                     $1.50

DERO DELUXE

When Shavertron's editor asked Rich Shaver how he'd managed to elude the clutches of the dero for all those years (this was in 1972), the Master of Mystery explained

"I get this question frequently. The whole answer is a very complex one, you know. The question arises from a totally false concept of the how and why of deros.

"Everyone on earth suffers from dero, not this one or that one. It is as universal a plague as commercials on the radio.

"Telaug fields are wider-spread than radio, more all-permeating...and once, the whole earth was ruled firmly and well by their use. These ancient built-ins are like a telephone central for the whole world built into bed-rock and then sealed forever...today we call that sort of "radio" transistorized, solid state...they had solid state telaug for perhaps a million years before the moon hit earth and wiped out the surface buildings... left the underworld largely untouched.

"This world wide radio-telepho-ne-telemach, which rules men's minds still operates, but with the degen-erate dero infiltrating the old ser-vice chambers and changing all men's internal frame of reference... changing everything that they do and say and think constantly...cut-ting them into stupidity...searing off neurons...giving them delusions and neuroses...making them think themselves mad...there is no end to their deviltry..unnoticed BECAUSE they USE fast-thought...which is a jacket that speeds up the thought in the mind as well as the body's reactions...by removing the natur-al resistance of the nerves in the mind and body.

"Fast thought rules earth to its detriment...operates our Hitlers & our Chamberlains and Czars and Em-perors...to destroy us all so near-ly as is most painful.

"To ask Shaver how he fares with them is rather like a fish asking another fish if the water is wet.

"The water is wet for all of them. Some get it quick, like JFK and his brothers. It doesn't al-ways manage to kill first crack..

as witness the living Kennedy brother...who has been very close to dead twice at least...once in an airplane crash and last time driving off a bridge and killing his secretary.

"Some people they keep alive as ploys...toys..bait.. part of their plots. Read 'Clytemnestra', and other Greek tragedies in which their strings on the puppets show right in the plays.

"One of the best descriptions of a dero is in 'Perelandra' by Lewis...which is very much available in libraries, I believe. He calls it the Un-man, or the bent eldil. Perelandra has a companion novel, not about the same world but I forget the name it with the same characters.

"Anyway, what the un-man does to the mind of Eve is very educational as it is precisely how it sounds and how the results work out when the un-man gets into the mind...and they do get into all minds everywhere to produce the mess our world is fast becoming.

"I mention 'Perelandra' because it does help to get the dero into perspective the way he paints the un-man and how his mind works BUT .in fact the picture can be even more simplified.

"A dero goes backward is fact. The thought is the opposite of our own...and "Evil" is "Live" spelled backwards.

"This is a fact. Our thought has an inward drawn particle or ion

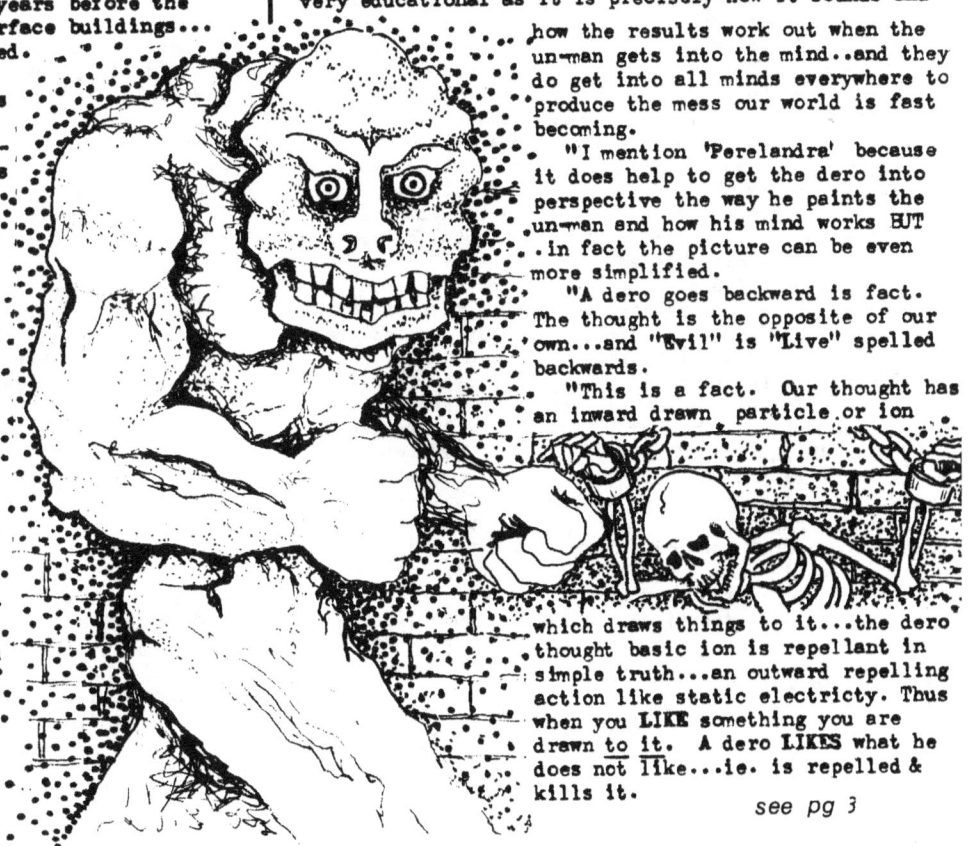

which draws things to it...the dero thought basic ion is repellant in simple truth...an outward repelling action like static electricty. Thus when you LIKE something you are drawn to it. A dero LIKES what he does not like...ie. is repelled & kills it.

see pg 3

RECORD OF ROCKS - 4
Stone Books

RICHARD S. SHAVER OF SUMMIT, ARK., HAS FOUND 3-D IMAGES ON MANY SPLIT ROCKS, WHICH HE CLAIMS ARE A **HISTORICAL RECORD** OF AGES AGO WHEN SAUCERIANS VISITED AN EARTHLY AMPHIBIAN CIVILIZATION.

TOMORROW - PETRIFIED LIBRARY
© 1967 BELL-McCLURE SYNDICATE

telaug central

As promised, this issue will be devoted to understanding the ins and outs of deroism. Maybe you dont think of deros as being an "ism", but according to RSS it is a worldwide movement, limited not only to the knarled, ugly-looking demons underground. Deroism fills all strata of society, in all parts of the world. As with Communism, Deroism's goal is total control of everyone and everything. To become an enemy of the Dero isnt pleasant, but its better than being one.

Since its inception, Shavertron has spoken out on various dero-run subjects, and (heaven forbid) has kept the memory and writings of Richard Sharpe Shaver alive. This would qualify us as a "resistence element" to worldwide Deroism, and we're proud of that. We are also proud of the fact that we're still here! When S started out as a 4-page zine financed out of extra pocket change, we had no idea what would come of us. Well, evidently other people have already figured that out, and have forwarded us about it.

Since last issue, we've received letters from well-intentioned friends, making it very clear that we are playing with fire. From Trevor J. Constable (author of THEY LIVE IN THE SKY, COSMIC PULSE OF LIFE etc.) we hear: "I feel quite sure that if you persist with Shaver material and digging into his activities, you will almost certainly get a sharp introduction to occult forces you cannot control. You would find this unpleasant, and depending on the circumstances, you may not be able to extricate yourself from the toils of the forces Shaver described. Focusing your mind and energy for long periods on any subject brings its astral correspondences and connections down on you. BE YE THEREFORE WARNED.

In regard to the article on Zanfretta in issue 5, Constable remarked: "The Zanfretta case is an ongoing and interesting example of obsessive abuse of a human being by low grade astral forces with advanced technology".

From the Borderland Sciences Research Foundation, headed by Riley Crabb, we ordered and received in good shape a copy of RETRO ME or Psychic Self Defense, which, as Mr Crabb pointed out to your humble editor: "As you continue to probe the borderland seeking illumination on life and its problems, you'll attract the malevolent attention of certain creatures. Since you choose not to leave them alone, they will not leave you alone, unless you command their respect by proving that you know how to behave yourself, and how to defend yourself. They only know, and respect, power--power under control and handled intelligently". Needless to say, Shavertron headquarters is now being reinforced for the onslaught. Mr Crabb has given us permission to reprint some excerpts from a recent Round Robin, the informative organ of the BSRF (PO Box 549, Vista, California 92083). We want to thank him for this privilege.

Are we being overly paranoid? Or is there good reason for us to watch our step? Of course there is! And we have just the bit of evidence that would point to a real reason for being paranoid. Photographic evidence. During a partial solar eclipse in California last year, your editor, using infrared film, (some of you readers may know of my work in the field of invisible Ufos) captured two sinister objects hovering directly over Shavertron headquarters. From the looks of them, they aint friendly, and so we must assume that this place is being watched. Infrared film only picks up anomalies in the heat range, invisible to the human eye, so we are being observed by invisible beings... creatures, whatever you want to call them.

This is why we need the support of our reedership. Your humble editor cant carry the banner alone. As you may well imagine, Deroism is dedicated to the destruction of this zine. Without your help, it may go down in flames. We do appreciate, in every way, the help and enthusiasm of all those fans who have written in, with money, subs, clips and the like. Please keep it coming. If any of you have old letters from RSS sitting in a bottom drawer, why not xerox it and send it to S for publication? We need any and all SM material. Your editor is still working on the biography of RSS, so any and all leads to any Shaver material is needed.

The "What a Coincidence Dept":
It may interest some Shaver Mystery scholars that today your humble editor received that 57-page FBI file on Ray Palmer under the Freedom of Info Act. This "Act" (and that's exactly what it is, folks) seems to be a waste of time. Out of the 57 pages released, 27 were "missing in action", unfit for publik reading. And the other 30 pages were so heavily censored that not one incident described therein can be deciphered. Why they even bothered to send this to me is a good question. Oh, I forgot: we have a right to know.

Well, at any rate, here is the coincidence: Mr Joseph Seigeldorf, a fan from New Jersey, sent in a copy of a letter written by RAP, originally sent to Gray Barker. Since much of the heavily edited pages of RAP's file related to the Maury Island affair, and to Ufos, it might be well to reprint RAP's letter in its entirety:

"Dear Gray,
The Fred Crisman summoned to testify in the Clay Shaw trial was the same Fred Crisman who was involved in the Tacoma Maury Island Affair, and the same Crisman who claimed to have shot his way out of a cave in Burma, receiving a hole the size of a dime in his arm from a "ray gun" wielded, he said, by the dero. His exact words to me: 'For God's sake, drop the Shaver cave stories! You don't know what you are dealing with here!' He is the same Fred Crisman who offered to go into a cave in Texas and bring out some of the ancient machinery if I would send him $500 expense money.

2

"It was not Clay Shaw who was ruined financially, personally and physically, it was Jim Garrison who was ruined. He was (as I told him in a letter) subjected to IRS audit, finally won the case in court but at tremendous financial cost-- which was the IRS goal in the first place. He was also libeled, framed in a drug ring, and hounded from office, finally losing out in a re-election bid.

"I have Garrison's letter stating that they were one and the same man. I also have my answer to Garrison, predicting that Crisman could not be subpeoned, that he was CIA and tremendously powerful.

"There is a definite link between flying saucers, the Shaver Mystery, the Kennedy(s) assasinations, Watergate and Fred Crisman. There is one common denominator for everything that is happening in the world today. That common denominator is right where Shaver said it was-- no matter whether you prefer caverns or the lower astral or another dimension". RAP.

Next issue: Alternative 003, the CIA and the SM.

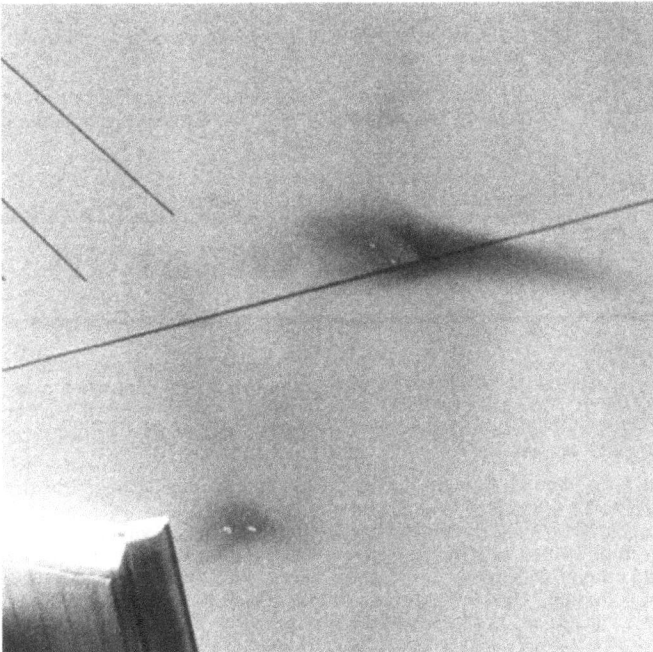
These strange, dark objects were spotted with infra-red film as they hovered over Shavertron headquarters. Note two white "eyes" in each.

Ashtar and the Dero :

Trevor J. Constable got into the Shaver Mystery briefly while investigating Ufos for his book, "They Live in the Sky", published in 1958 and now out-of-print. He asked his chief source of information, Ashtar, Guardian commander of many space ships, about the reality of Richard Shaver's Deros-- the Abandondero.

"At the core of your planet, there dwells a great degenerated race, an astral race, which is degenerate not so much in science, but in every moral respect as you know and understand. They are capable of space flight within the astral regions around the earth but are earth-bound. They are the forces of Eramus, whom you call Satan. They emerge at the South Pole. On your surface they have allies who are without morals and without mercy (the assasins of the Kennedys and Martin Luther King, for instance). I give you this information that you may be aware of their existence. I enjoin you to forever close any researches into this astral activity in the interests of your own safety."

TJC to Ashtar: "Is there any broad general method by which the etheric or friendly craft can be distinguised from the astral machines from the center of the earth?"

Ashtar: "As a general rule, you may conclude that all cigar-shaped craft are potentially hostile to your people. These are craft from the center of the earth which have carried out and are carrying out acts...Our craft are for the most part heel-shap-ed, or disc-shaped. This is a rule of thumb as you term it..."

TJC: "Are there any basic rules...by which the various craft can be identified when they appear solely as light manifestations?"

Ashtar: "There is a broad general rule...It is not exact. The true interplanetary craft, the ventlas of our forces will appear to your optics with a manifestation of colored lights, usually green, red and white. They will sometimes appear constantly red and green, other times they will appear to be flashing. Those of the Satanic forces seldom exhibit color, but come with white or bluish white manifestations. This should aid you in selecting the ships with which you might have contact."

Note from Riley Crabb: Last year, in the July-August Journal, we ran J.R. Jochman's article on "The Clones of Enki". The message there was that an ancient Sumerian civilization was so advanced that their biologists deliberately created a race of sub-humans to work the mines of South Africa. I posed the question, were these humanoids able to reproduce themselves as do ordinary humans? And if so, what became of their descendants? I believe the answer to both these questions is in Richard Shaver's Cavern World Deros. These are the descendants of the slave workers of a great Atlantean civilization which were abandoned-- abandondero-- when an all-out atomic war of that time made the surface of the earth uninhabitable. The elite escaped in space ships. The slaves had no choice but to adapt themselves to their underground environment-- if they wished to live!

Shaver from Page 1 -

Once you get this basic difference through your mind you realize that all life has one basic ingredient... normal attraction for other life..we admire a deer... we dont kill it unless we have to for food.

The dero kills everything he can for the same admiration is reverse in him to the opposite emotion like hate.

A dero is a magnetic phenomenon, but so is a man. He just dont know it is all. Neither does a dero..he is that way and thinks its natural. A man can become "cafard" from the sun after a few days desert exposure. Some men come in from the desert and kill everyone they see...cafard. A dero is that way all the time.

A cafard victim can be cured by a cold pack of wet ice blankets for a week...BUT a dero can never be cured. He is permanently flipped into sun-polared magnetism. A normal man's magnetic flows are earth polared, not sun polared.

Deros talk contradictions. Normal people talk normally, and laugh at contradictions, thinking they are jokes. You can spot a dero b y his use of cliche's and contradictions, and we have some in our so called normal life up here. People who talk cliches, and bore you with contradictory concepts turn out to be murderers at the first opportunity.

They actually cant think of anything else to do... but destroy. People do flip into deroism occasionally, as witness the sniper who got into the tower and shot everybody in Austin...was a "normal" but rather dull young man...til he flipped."

3

-9-80 By Jack Hopkins Wash.

James Monroe Thorne, charged with robbing the same Seattle bank two days in a row in January, was on the witness stand yesterday, telling a strange tale of being bombarded by light rays and hearing a mysterious voice that ordered him to commit the holdups.

Thorne, his arms and legs shaking uncontrollably at times, told King County Superior Court jurors at his second-degree robbery trial that he had been plagued by "hallucinations and visions" since taking LSD while in prison more than a decade ago.

The 37-year-old defendant told of seeing "great balls of light" in the sky and feeling tremendous surges of energy "come up through the ground, enter my feet and go through my body."

He said he was sitting in a downtown Seattle cocktail lounge a little more than three months ago when "a voice appeared out of thin air and said: 'You are going to go to 4th and Union and rob a bank.'"

He said the command was irresistible and he went to the Seattle Trust & Savings Bank at that location and did as he was told.

"The voice was overpowering," he said. "It had authority over me. And there were rays of light that would come down and hit me in the head. I couldn't block it off. I had to do what it said."

Thorne told jurors in the courtroom of Judge Shannon Wetherall that the voice returned the next day and ordered him to go back to the bank and rob it again.

He admitted both holdups, but said he wouldn't have hurt anyone if he had been denied money in the robberies. "I would have just walked out of the bank," he said.

Thorne's testimony came late in the trial stemming from robberies at the bank on Jan. 23 and 24.

Gunman Seizes Masonic Hall

Manchester, Mass.

An armed, 33-year-old unemployed physical therapist who wanted to tell the world that "Masons kill people," was seized by the police yesterday after he took over a Masonic hall for more than three hours.

The man, identified by authorities as Ernie Lassen of Fort Lauderdale, Fla., was grabbed by state police Lieutenant Robert Dunn as he delivered a long, rambling diatribe to television cameras some 50 feet away from the hall. The police said Lassen, armed with a .22-caliber rifle, took two Masons hostage at the beginning of the siege, but they escaped after about ten minutes.

12-26-79 *Associated Press*

A Description of The Nimitz Gunman

S.F. 2-1-80

Fremont police said yesterday they have a description of the gunman who fired an automatic weapon at two motorists Tuesday on the Nimitz freeway.

They said one of the two persons fired upon in the incident was able, under close questioning, to describe her assailant as a white man with long dark hair, a dark beard and a mustache.

Tuesday morning, drivers Willie King, 44, of Oakland, and Maria Moreland, 21, of Fremont, were shot at by an unknown assailant who riddled their cars with large caliber slugs.

Fremont police said Moreland gave her description of the gunman to police after she saw him stop his car on an overpass and assume a firing position. Seconds later, she said, heavy caliber slugs ripped into her late model Toyota.

King was fired upon while on the Nimitz by a passing car — possibly a black Camero or a Pontiac Firebird.

The car also matches the description of the gunman's vehicle offered by Moreland.

A Berserk Tenderloin Gunman

S.F. 11-24-79

One person was killed and two others wounded last night in the Tenderloin by an unknown gunman who, a witness said, "just walked up ... and went nuts."

The assailant fled the corner of Turk and Mason Streets on foot leaving behind him an 18-year-old boy and a 14-year-old girl with gunshot wounds in their legs, and Roy Ledford, a street-person known as "Judo," with a bullet lodged near his heart.

Ledford, whose address was unknown, died minutes later in surgery at Mission Emergency Hospital. He was 24.

The wounded were identified as Thomas "KC" Owens and Angela Wise. Like Ledford, they were described as street persons and their addresses were not immediately known. They were both listed as being in stable condition.

Witnesses said the incident occurred at 8:30 p.m. when a tall man dressed in a black leather jacket approached a crowd waiting at the corner.

Ben Schafer, a friend of the dead man's, said the gunman "just walked up and pulled out this big gun. He started shooting everywhere, just shooting at people and in the air. The guy went nuts!"

GIANTS IN THE EARTH - *revised*

by JIM WENTWORTH

If my GIANTS IN THE EARTH book is ever reprinted, I hope it can be revised with additional data related to the Shever Mystery. To strengthen it and give it more clarity. This data of news items, book and article quotations, etc., I have been gathering steadily for the past several years. One item I have enclosed with this letter: Jim Wentworth.

The following to be inserted on page 22- first column-between 2nd and 3rd paragraphs...

Two possible explanations of such important data giving are to be found in BREAKTHROUGH INTO THE THIRD MILLENIUM by Louis Pauwels and Jacques Bergier. And note that the data was supplied during sleeping periods.

Danish physicist, Niels Bohr, who won the Nobel Prize for his work in laying the foundation for present-day understanding of the atom, "related how the idea of the atom model he had sought for many years occurred to him. He dreamt he was sitting on a sun of burning gas. Planets rushed past him, hissing and spitting, and all the planets seemed to be connected by fine thread to the sun around which they revolved. Suddenly the gas solidified, sun and planets shrivelled up and became motionless. Niels Bohr said that he woke up at this moment. He realized at once that what he had seen in his dream was the atom model. In 1922, he won the Nobel Prize for his discovery his "dream".

An engineer of the Bell Telephone Company in the USA read reports of the bombing of London in 1940. They upset him badly. One autumn night he dreamt he was dreaming the design of an apparatus that could train anti-aircraft guns on the previously worked out path of an aircraft and ensure that their shells would hit the aircraft in a specific point regardless of its speed. The next morning the Bell engineer made a sketch of what he had already drawn in his dream. He finally built a set in which radar was used for the first time. The celebrated American mathematician, Norbert Weiner, was in charge of the project for manufacturing it commercially.

4

PURE BLISS

I wonder if the location of Dero caves can be determined from the character of towns and cities. This town
and those in a 20 mile radius are mediocre. But those
further out are good to excellent. To the south of here
(including Peoria) the quality ranges to nil. It's not
just the buildings, but also the people. Us money-grub-
bing businessmen aren't a guide though—we thrive anywhere.

I had a thought on telaug receivers last week. One
of the circuits that was supposed to work used a special
tube-- no other would work. I've given Jurgenson's and
Raudive's observations on the reception of mystery signals (sometimes purporting to be from spirits of the
dead) alot of thought. They were extremely weak signals which were first detected with tape recorders.
And later very simple receivers-- even on the AM radio
band-- and were local in origin...the immediate vicinity.

Evidently, standard electronic equipment was almost
unsuited to the signal. I got to wondering if that tube
was actually working like a microphone in the supersonic
range (about 18,000 to 40,000 cycles per second).

All tubes are sensitive to vibration which can be
a problem. Since no amplifier is absolutely linear in
response, chances are the amplifiers on the tape recorders Raudive used were making like very inefficient
detectors. So, since condenser microphones respond to
extremely high frequencies, one connected to a common
grid leak detector (obsolete except for use as sync

signal separators on tv sets) might work fairly well.
Haven't built it yet. Condenser microphones
were used in the 1920's and 30's until other types of
microphones became practical. For common audio they
have a very low output and are difficult to design for
good fidelity. Likely, the best source for a common
condenser mike is one used for tv remote control
(Zenith). Otherwise just a piece of then metal foil
stretched close to a metal plate (less than 1/16"), and
about an inch across should work OK. Could it be that
Telaug and those J&R signals are acoustic high frequency and modulated the same as common AM radio?

The tuning coil (necessary??) can be a common 15Kc
tv oscillator coil if it does not go to a high enough
frequency, turns can be removed. Since there are no
broadcast signals below 100 Kc, the receiver needs to
be in a well shielded metal cabinet. A higher gain
triode or pentode can be used, but the fidelity would
be poorer. And too, amplification could be used before the detector, and the detector can be any of the
regenerative circuits. If a great deal of amplification is used after the detector, DC may be needed for
the filaments, since grid leak detectors are prone to
being hum sensitive.

Something hairy about 7.8 Kcycles occured to me
instantly: The second harmonic, 15.6Kc is right close
to the common horizontal scan frequency of tv's---
15.575. Aha! That's one thing that has been keeping
all of those eyeballs glued to the boob tube screens.
No doubt as you know, various systems can lock onto
or "syncronize" harmonics. I looked up the musical
scale in THE RECORDING AND REPRODUCTION OF SOUND by
Cliver Read. It shows the piano scale and 7800 cycles
is off the end of it. The frequencies for A and F
notes are not given(?)

The dielectic constant of water is 81 (it is chem-
ically pure and hard to keep it that way).

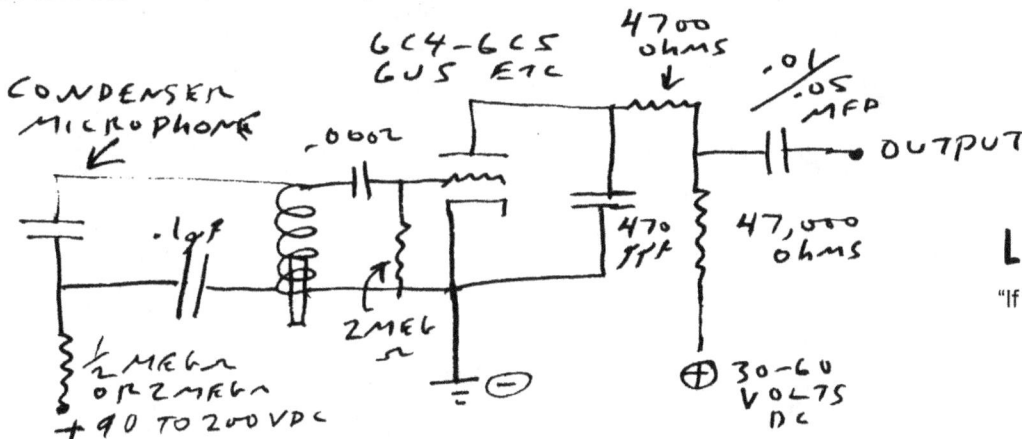

THE BLISS
☆ TELAUG
from

Bliss
Laboratories

"If it's impossible
we're doing it !"

5

One in 20 die each year 'with no known cause'

12-11-79

A STARTLING one in 20 people die without the medical cause of death ever being known, leading pathologists have claimed. That's an astonishing 100,000 mystery deaths each year.

These shocking figures were revealed after the bizarre death of 28-year-old Mary Koch, who died while sniffing a bouquet of roses sent by her husband to celebrate their eighth wedding anniversary.

Dr. William J. Bauman, a noted pathologist from the University of Wisconsin in Madison, said: "I investigate dozens of these mystery deaths each year, and I have to mark the cause of death as 'unknown.'

"We simply have no idea why some perfectly normal and healthy people suddenly die.

"The death-by-roses case is very typical of these rather bizarre deaths."

Bauman and Dr. Craig Bolles, a colleague, conducted exhaustive tests on Koch, but failed to determine any cause for her death. "Miss Koch had no allergic reaction to roses and even if she did she would not drop dead like that," Bauman said.

Bauman and Bolles said these unexplained deaths occurred about 100,000 times a year in this country out of the two million that die.

"It's very scary," said Bolles. "It is not outlandish to say that some people could actually die of fright.

The recent cases investigated by Dr. Bauman include: a boy who died suddenly while waiting to catch a pop fly during a softball game; a woman who promptly died after a television set fell near her creating a loud crash; a woman who died suddenly on a street corner while waiting for the light to change.

"They don't have to have had heart attacks. Some people just fall into this instant death category."

A strange and incurable affliction of the brain

3-30-80

By Karren Mills
Associated Press

MINNEAPOLIS — Dave Byrne worked in a bank. He knew numbers the way most people know words.

But in early 1977 he began making mistakes when figuring the balance in the family checkbook.

A year later Byrne, his wife and their two children took a trip to Colorado. Byrne remembers nothing of the vacation.

Byrne, 43, has Alzheimer's disease, an irreversible and progressive degeneration of the brain that impairs the intellect of an estimated 500,000 to 1.5 million adults in the United States.

Alzheimer's is the most common of a group of similar diseases often lumped together under the terms presenile dementia, organic brain syndrome, brain atrophy and arteriosclerosis of the brain.

Researchers have not determined what causes the disease, which can strike as early as the 30s and in older persons often is written off as senility. The earlier the disease strikes, the faster it progresses. Researchers have found no way to slow the progression.

They do know that the brains of Alzheimer's victims have an accumulation of abnormal fibers that look like tangled filaments. In addition, groups of nerve endings degenerate and disrupt the passage of signals between the brain cells.

Outward signs of the disease begin with memory loss. Patients gradually begin losing other functions until they reach a state requiring total care.

Byrne's wife, Madelon, a registered nurse, says she thought her husband was having a nervous breakdown when he began displaying symptoms of Alzheimer's disease. "He was with us physically and that was all," she says.

Doctors diagnosed Byrne's problem in late 1978, telling the family to "live with it," because nothing could be done, Mrs. Byrne says. "Your marriage is in jeopardy. Then you are hit with this diagnosis and your whole world falls apart.

"They didn't tell me what was ahead of me. He would get obsessions. He'd shave non-stop for two or three hours. The house had to be neat and clean but he wouldn't remember to bathe. I had to be a 24-hour policeman.

"What really threw me was the loss of judgment and reasoning."

She also says it was hard for the children to understand what was happening to their father.

Such feelings of isolation and frustration plague Alzheimer's disease victims and their families.

"Counseling for the patient is a very significant unmet need," says Dr. Leonard Heston, a University of Minnesota psychiatric researcher who is studying the disease.

The Alzheimer's and Related Diseases Association was formed to meet such needs. The organization's Bay Area chapter is in San Francisco. It's called the Family Survival Project, and is a special project of the Mental Health Association of San Francisco. (Its phone number is 921-4404.)

Most researchers believe there is a genetic factor involved in Alzheimer's disease.

In some very unusual families where onset of the disease in the parent has been at an unusually early age (20s or 30s), about half of the first-generation offspring are likely to develop Alzheimer's disease, Heston says.

That proportion decreases rapidly with increasing age so that relatives of later onset patients have a very small risk, Heston says.

"The risk of developing Alzheimer's disease at an early age is extremely small if you don't have any known affected relatives," adds Heston.

The residents of the town of Xucurus, some 90 miles from Buenos Aires, Argentina, claim that men nine feet tall, green, with antennaes on their heads, and square legs, are seen daily leaving a cave. The cave was found last February, when agriculturalist Gerardo Cordeiro dreamed he would find treasure if he went to a certain place. Not uncovering gold or jewels, Cordeiro found a cave with nine connecting tunnels with strange inscriptions on the walls. The place is now being by 100's of people from the town and nearby locals, who expect to find "treasure" or see the "Martians who, according to witnesses, resemble enormous "portable radios". (Hustler? '79).

Washington

The Pentagon says its experts believe they have fixed the U.S. missile alarm system to prevent false alerts like the one that recently sent ten U.S. and Canadian jet interceptors scrambling to meet a nonexistent bomber attack.

President Carter and Congress were advised Tuesday of the corrections.

Defense Secretary Harold Brown ordered the investigation that led to those corrections after an apparent computer malfunction was blamed for the false November 9 alarm of a Soviet missile attack.

Officials said at the time that a test tape simulating such an attack was fed into a computer at North American Air Defense Command headquarters in Colorado Springs, Colo.

Due to an apparent mechanical malfunction, the tape was transmitted to other military commands and federal agencies, the Pentagon said.

The error was corrected within six minutes, and word of the alert did not reach the president or Brown, according to the Pentagon.

Pentagon officials said senior government leaders were not notified because within about a minute of the alert, NORAD had advised the National Military Command Center in the Pentagon that "it was evidently a false alarm."

Dero Joke?

11-29-79

Associated Press

No Fun at the con
BY MIKE COHEN
CON Unrest Turns Violent - JOHN KEELS OVER !

On June 21, 1980 I attended the first UFO convention to be held in New York in 13 years. One of the guest speakers was John Keel and I had a chance to speak to him privately before he gave his speech to the convention. Mr Keel is a brilliant speaker and appears very rational when he talks about UFO's and other topics dealing with the occult.

In my private conversation with him, however, he became very irrational when I brought up Richard Shaver's name. He started screaming that Shaver was a liar and a fraud, that he had a very bad effect on him in his youth. Keel claimed he was into science-fiction in the 1940's and Shaver's writings distorted reality and confused him. I asked him why Shaver was so popular if his theories were based on lies. He answered that in New York City, there are thousands of mentally ill people who constantly call the police to report that "rays" and "voices" were affecting their minds. In other words, he was trying to imply that anybody who believed in Shaver was mentally ill. After I explained to him that New Yorkers aren't the only people who hear "voices" in this world, he had to admit that it goes on elsewhere.

He also had no answer when I told him that psychologists still do not know the exact causes of "auditory hallucinations"-- 35 years after Shaver published his writings on the subject.

Mr Keel appeared ill to me when I was speaking to him. His skin was extremely white. As he became very agitated while talking about Shaver, his skin color became even whiter. Of course, this could have been caused by the tense atmosphere of the conference. People were losing their tempers over small incidents. Violent arguments frequently broke out.

Mrs Hill was one of the guest speakers and she was speaking about UFO's and her famous kidnapping when she was denounced by people in the audience as a fraud. Perhaps Keel was also caught up in this madness, but he seemed very rational when he discussed every other topic except Shaver.

I have attended science-fiction conventions and I noticed that sci-fi writers hate occult writers because they believe that the occult is a distorted version of sci-fi. Many of these writers really believe that the occult is based on lies and can hurt the public (as well as the sci-fi field). In the 1940's, there were several articles in the press attacking Shaver on the same grounds-- claiming that Shaver's writings were hurting people's minds. Keel, being a teenager at the time, apparently was impressed by this logic and he still believes this propaganda.

On the other hand, Keel could have reacted to my questions about Shaver in such an irrational manner because there is a conspiracy on the part of the establishment to destroy Shaver's ideas and writings. At any rate, my conversation with Keel showed that Richard Shaver is still alive and well in the minds of the people who make up the establishment (and Keel is definitely part of the establishment).

Deros *do make You disbelieve!*

BY HENRY STEELE

From visiting Richard Shaver for a few weeks, I learned that cur-deros had been raying me since childhood. As it's a degenerate pastime of theirs to do this to surface people, I perchance got the ray harm. From years of trying to get folks to trust and believe in cavern data, I know this mental ray action of theirs is "the stop". May-Day, May-Day...you'll get rayed to reason not to put this idea in Shavertron, standard dero way. (Ed. note-- the dero must have fallen asleep on that one!) As Shaver told me, don't trust such negative thoughts. When one gets a good progressive idea, do it at once, he said.

The aspect of letting everyone know about that Texas river cavern entrance (revealed by me in issue no. 5), seems like the best proof we've got to progress this cavern subject. Note how no reaction came to me on it. A need to state why to fans. They don't think that THEY can get rayed. Deros hate the original-thinker and one who appreciates beautiful things. Deros see Tero ray and follow it. Anything or anyone Teros like, Deros try to harm, Shaver stated. "Good guys die young", an old saying, but (via ray) all too true. I have noticed that anyone in the public eye who comes up with a brand new idea that is meant to help people and might get pushed through, always seem to d-i-e prior to his intended action. Take the case of Felix Frankenfurter, the onetime Supreme Court judge.

Frankenfurter came out in the news media regarding some general concepts he greatly desired to advance. When I read them, I "knew" he would die soon. And he did, shortly thereafter...via ray, as most Shaver fans can guess.

This judge was alive during the Warren years, and was very well-known back then. His ideas were just filed away somewhere, never to be heard of again, since the rest of the Supreme Court is only interested in "running things", not improving them. Shaver wrote that the government is under firm and steady dero mental ray control so no one notices the normal thinking they'd otherwise get at times. No contrast allowed. Can you fans who have all his 16 volumes remember this?

Our leaders harp they are following the guiding hand of Providence. Along with Shaver's data, I have read in a non-Shaver source that this is all they can tell citizens. That they follow occult-type advice: dreams, voices, super strong feelings, etc. They can't conceive they are rayed just as any plain citizens can be. Ego? "I follow the hand of Providence-- I have a mission," said President Johnson on tv shortly prior to dieing (via ray, I know-- BIG dero joke!) I know other leaders have harped the same thing: Uncle Winnie, Uncle Adolf, a few senators and others.

Hey-- if they are getting holy orders, how come there have been so many wars throughout history via their "guidance"?

Editor's note: Henry Steele has alot more to say on topics such as the Masons, George Adamski's burial plot, his "mech dreams" and the fake mystical con game that space people are playing on us. This will appear in future issues.

A Hole Is Eating San Jose

By Rick Carroll

1-12-79

Yvonne Crosby stood on the brink of a big, gaping hole in her front yard yesterday and shook her head.

"I wish it would go away," the San Jose housewife said.

The hole, 20 feet in diameter, appeared mysteriously last week not ten feet from the front door of her Willow Glen home on Pine avenue.

Her life hasn't been quite the same since.

Each day the hole grows in size and is now threatening to undermine the curving sidewalk that leads to her door. New cracks opened up around the edges after yesterday's rainstorm.

What used to be surface level turf has sunk up to ten feet, and nobody knows the depth of the cavern beneath it.

Beyond roping off the hole and posting a danger sign, Crosby isn't sure what to do.

Meanwhile, the strange hole is becoming a major attraction.

At first only worried neighbors came; but they were followed by concerned city engineers, a puzzled geologist, and curious sightseers by the hundreds.

"I never thought so many people would be interested in a damned old hole in my front yard," she said. "But they are.

"The other day," she said, "the city bus even stopped so everybody could get a good look at the hole.

"Everybody walks up to it, looks down in it, and then walks away, shaking their head," she said.

Even as she talked, a small crowd gathered to peer into the yawning crater.

"Don't get too close," she admonished a mother with a small child who stood dangerously near the crumbling edge.

What caused the hole to suddenly appear remains open to speculation. She said it could be an old septic tank, or a well, or maybe a bomb shelter — who knows?

Some thought it might be an old irrigation well that connects an underground river but, according to city records, there's no evidence of such a water system or even a storm drain.

The city sent out engineers and a geologist.

"They were very nice," Crosby said, "but they don't know why this is happening. They said they were looking into it."

From the original owners of the house, which was built 42 years ago, Crosby learned that the hole made four equally strange appearances during the late 1930s and early 1940s.

"They put old bedsprings in it and dumped truckloads of concrete chunks and all kinds of things down it, but the hole swallowed it up," she said she was told.

"Then they put steel beams across the top and topped it with twelve yards of cement, but even that's gone now."

She disconsolately pointed out a chunk of concrete — the last remains of the 1940s fill — slowly disappearing down the hole.

"I sometimes wonder why this is happening to me," she said, as another carload of sightseers jumped out and looked down the hole.

They just stood there speechless and shook their heads.

"It's strange," one young man finally said.

Why Nudes Ran Wild In Mustard

Lansing, Mich.

One of three sisters, naked and smeared with mustard when they were arrested in a stolen truck, says they were "high on sunshine and the Holy Spirit," and trying to get back to the Garden of Eden.

"We were reading the Bible and got filled with the Holy Spirit," said Doshaline McCuin, 30, Tuesday in a telephone interview from her Ingham County Jail cell.

McCuin, and her sisters, Charlene Roper, 27, and Sandra Lewis, 25, have been jailed since their arrest last Thursday, unable to post $1000 bond each on charges of joyriding and indecent exposure.

Police were summoned to their Lansing Township home on a report that three naked women were running around outside in the sunshine. The officers said they found the three in a delivery truck being chased by a uniformed truck driver.

Police said all three women, who share a house, were smeared with supermarket-variety mustard.

McCuin said mustard is in Chapter 13 of the Bible's Book of Matthew, which states:

"The kingdom of heaven is like to a grain of mustard seed ... which indeed is the least of all seeds: but when it is grown, it is the greatest among herbs, and becometh a tree ..."

She added, "We went out naked because the Bible said we had to get back to the Garden of Eden."

And the delivery truck?

"It was just a spur-of-the-moment thing," she said. "It was just sitting there with the keys in it.

"We just don't understand why we took the truck," she added.

In jail, the sisters continue to read the Bible while awaiting a preliminary hearing.

"We are certainly not members of a cult," McCuin said. "We caused a lot of commotion. But we were brought up with the Bible, and this is God's way to get us back.

"We were lost and had to find our way back to the garden," she concluded. "With God sustaining us, we are on the right track."

Associated Press

SHAVERTRON

"The Only Source of Post-Deluge Shaverania" $1.50

SPRING 1981 ━━━━━━━━━━━━━━━ ISSUE 7

Notice any changes? Right off the bat, you probably checked out the cover, which is just one of many never-before-published sketches by Rich Shaver that will appear from time to time on the front page of Shavertron. We have Dottie Shaver to thank for them. Dot is still working away on the Arkansas end of Shavertron, as she did with the original SM Magazine. She has helped to make S a worthwhile zine, and we hope she won't lose interest in us or this project.

Some of you may remember that we said that this issue would deal with the controversial book, Alternative 003. We were going to go ahead with it, but so much NEW Shaver Mystery material has come our way here at S headquarters that we just couldn't let it stew on that proverbial back burner for another 3 or 4 months. We hope that this issue will speak for itself in defense of this last minute change.

notes from the under ground

By R. Teronto

We are delighted to have a new contributor on board: Ray Archer (a classic SM name if ever was one), has written an article concerning his studies into Mantong. Mr. Archer also has some intriguing experiences to relate to S readers concerning an ancient Roman mine he has explored in England. But this will have to wait for a future ish.

For the first time in this issue, Jim Pobst, our Canadian historian/researcher on literary aspects of the SM, has put together a piece about RSS' "mystery manuscripts", with a special request of S readers. Another Jim...Jim Wentworth, has come back with his usual SM bravado in a short article detailing his impressions of derelict ships and ufos...along with his semi-regular feature, "Revisions for Giants in the Earth".

Mike Cohen has an interesting book to review, and if readers are inclined to do so, please write to Mike at 215 E. Gunhill Rd-6A, Bronx, NY.10467, and he will arrange to send you a copy of this unusual book. Mike has made arrangements with the British publisher to make this book available to S readers. Drop him a line!

Another Shaver Mystery fan and inner earth explorer you might like to get in touch with is Mary LeVesque, editor of the newly reserrected HOLLOW HASSLE. The HH met an untimely demise about 7 years ago. Those of you lucky enough to have a set of the original HH in your files, will be happy to learn that you can now continue your collection. Mary decided that the time was right for a NEW HH, to help hollow earthers in their quest as we roll into the 1980's. Your humble editor is on the board of consultants, so you'll be seeing a new era of co-operation between our two zines..............Please

write to Mary at P.O. Box 255, Santa Fe, NM. 87501 for your sub @ $6 per year, quarterly.

This might be a good spot to mention future contributors. Charles Marcoux, a long-time SM follower and leader in the field in his own right, will have articles in future issues. His new book, I Search for the Portals, is a must for any SM fan. He has pubbed it himself, in a xeroxed 8½ by 11 inch format, with B&W and color xeroxes of his cavern and "psychic" photos. The book has maps of the Superstition Mts., where he did extensive researches into cavern entrances. Some of the material is reprinted from articles in the BSRA Round Robin and there are repro's of the covers of every one of the original Shaver Mystery Magazines. Readers who are interested can contact Mr Marcoux at: 931 W. Pierson, Phoenix, Arizona 85013..cost of the book is $8.20 ppd.

One final book we'd like to tell S readers about is Vaughn Green's "Astronuats of Ancient Japan". Now, this might not appear to relate to Shaver or the SM, but wait! On page 74, we find a chapter called The Caves of Shaver! In it, Green relates some of his correspondence with RSS, and rounds out the SM controversy. The book is full of odd occurrances throughout history, Forteans will like this, and other chapters read: Goblins of the Sea, Gods Underground and other Legends, Docks in the Sky, Drowned Gods...and much more. You can buy a copy of this softbound book from the author himself (maybe even get him to autograph it for you) by writing to Vaughn Green, 548 Elm Ave., San Bruno, CA. 94066.

You will also note that you are getting 4 extra pages this issue. These are donated by Henry M. Steele, who paid for their printing himself, since he deemed the information vital to Shavertron readers. See what he has to say, and then make up your own mind about his revelations. We'd like your input.

It may seem like this ish has been a long time in coming to some of you. But because our Winter 1980 issue came out last summer, you can see that we were way way ahead of schedule. We decided to bide some time, and fall in line with regular, quarterly publishing dates. So expect to see your issue of Shavertron in your mailbox around the solstices and equinoxes now.

Remember, if you like what you see, tell your friends to sub!

Shavertron is published quarterly at $6 per year, or $7 for foreign subscriptions. And that's by surface mail. We invite contributions that relate somehow to Richard S. Shaver...manuscripts, letters, or bits of information anyone might have concerning RSS or the Shaver Mystery.

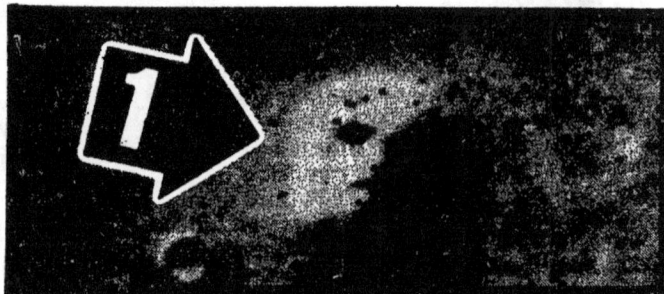

● This amazing photograph was taken in the northern latitudes of Mars.

MORE on MANTONG

By Ray Archer

One of the most fascinating aspects of the famous Shaver Mystery, I find, is the Mantong Alphabet.

After looking closely at the formation of English words, I have come to the conclusion that the underlying foundation of some words contain clues to an existence in the past of a civilization more advanced than our own.

In this old culture--which may have been the fabled MU-- they appear to have utilized RA or power from the sun, to drive their machines.

Interestingly enough, our own names for transport systems today still retain a trace element within them from that former time.

Now words such as "traffic", "train", and "trailer" take on new significance, each containing the old name RA label.

It could be that because of the dim memories stemming from that solar age, the later cultures, particularly the sun kingdoms of South America, came to look on the Sun as their god.
An apparent symbol of sun power is the ruler's crown or tiara. This suggests an obvious connection between both RA and RO.

The latter word according to Richard Shaver means "controlled"...such words signifying a monarch or ruler either contain RA or RO in them, it seems, as do the following: Royal, Emperor, Pharoah, and Tyrant.

Take the word R-O-T-A. This is a combination of two Mantong words, RO and TA. The former we already know. The latter appears to mean a slave and sounds similar to Tar, an old word for an early sailor.

We also tag or tab our possessions. Rota means then, "controlled slave" or RO's, RULERS, TA. Today's meanings of the word is a wheel or a roster, a table of duties, or turns for workers.

There is an indication that crossing of various animals and men may have been achieved, ie. MU-TANTS, in the distant past. Perhaps, here is a clue, a connection, with MU. As well as being used for work purposes, to "amuse" (freak shows) seems to have been one other of their tasks. This may explain the word MU-SEE-UM (them). This agrees in part with Shaver's explanation concerning the mythological beings, Centaurs etc. of the Greeks.

These ancient people appear to have known of the wave form generated by the human voice. This might account for such words as "row", "whistle" and "wail". Now, the W is the common denominator in these three words, and for good reason as we shall see.

Take, first of all, the form of the W (like the flapping of wings). When put alongside one another like this: WWWWW.....as you see we get a wave shape.

The old words for(possibly) their oceans and seas, seems to have been WA and SA. More of our words today, for instance, "water", "swan" "wash", "sap", "sad" and "say" now reveal their likely source. We now have some idea of the way our words came down to us from the old tongue. I now have discovered that the letters of the alphabet must have a pictographic symbol as their origin. In other words, letters depict real observations of things...taken from everyday life. The "S" is obviously an Asp or snake symbol and means to h/issue--ESCAPE, a sound-word.

O is a very important (source)symbol which stands for a mouth or hole. It has links to the Universal Egg of life traditions of the early cultures concerning the beginning (B-EGG-IN-G)? of the world.

The M can be connected with the snake shape as well, as these two words: "Maggot" and "Worm" seem to indicate. This letter also, denotes a wavy motion (the inverted W) whe n coupled with any of the 5 vowels, you get a Mother concept,...such words as "follow", "now", need little explanation. Moth, mole, mute, omit, mouse etc. all appear to be assocaited with either an orifice or entrance.

The Q seems to originate from an old circle-bar symbol (SPO). This is where the following words have their source: Spoke, Spool and Spoon. This sign Q became the modern Q and the familiar ?-mark of interrogation as well.

It takes little imagination when studying this symbol above, to see how it resembles the objects in actuality. Take for instance, WASP...(winged sting?). SP here means penetrate as Spear and spike do taken in this context. Last, but certainly not least, another bar added to the circle-bar sign meant a Dispute or Argument. These words probably refer to the change in the Sun mentioned in Shaver's stories...when "D" particles rained-- Disc-spit from (RA) upon the earth.

The second word comes from RA-GU...Sun mouth, where Rage also originated. We now understand the reason why the underground cities were hollowed out below the earth.

The Ancients' surface dwellings were called T-IONs. This means growing cells--the T of course stands for healthy growth, if we slightly alter T-ION we get TI-ONE, a little more, ONE being (ON-OWN) we end up with TI-OWN, much like today's word Town. The old word T-ION changed down through the years to TEN or TENE as in the two words Tent and Tenement. The connection with buildings is again quite evident.

Another old word-meaning, the same as TI (to join with) is NE. These two antique words are often found together in presentday words, although in some cases, NE is altered to NA. This explains the following below: --Nation...this comes from NE-TI-ON. The significance of NET is obvious from this.

There are many myths and legends throughout the world telling of a time in the past when people escaped disasters by dwelling underground in vast ancient tunnels. These tales are especially numerous among the American Indian tribes, being traditions passed down to them from their ancestors.

The name given to these subterranean abodes seems to be D-IONs, and this word altered, came to us as DEN. Both the old word and the new mean an Hiding Place or Hid-den, and comes from a longer one..Dungion, our Dungeon, an underground cell.

I myself now suspect, that the sun was not the only reason why these people became RA-CLOSED or Recluses. RA-CELL-US in the D-IONs could very well have been fallout shelters for nuclear attack.

This appears to be supported by such words as Engdangered, the universal color of warning: Red for Danger is present here, and today we ourselves have got the term "Red Alert" perhaps the old word for this is RED-A-T-ION, our Radiation or nuclear contamination.

So just what are we to make of all this? Unfortunately, the two most controversial persons involved in the Shaver Mystery, Richard S. Shaver and Ray Palmer are no longer with us. Perhaps the answer is that there is nothing new under the Sun. The underground D-IONs are being built again, ready for the next conflict. Maybe the Bigfoots and other weird creatures reported from time to time are the remnants of the last nuclear war.

It certainly looks as though Shaver was right. The answer to the whole riddle is beneath our feet.

THE MANTONG ALPHABET

A—Animal. (Used AN for short).

B—Be. To exist. (Often used as a "command").

C—Con. To see. (C-on; to understand).

D—De. Detrimental, disintegrant energy. (The second most important symbol in the alphabet).

E—Energy. (An all-pervading concept including the idea of motion).

F—Fecund. (Used "fe," as in fe-male—fecund man).

G—Generate. (Used "gen").

H—Human. (A very metaphysical concept here, not fully understood, but used in the sense "H-you-man": a human is an H-Man).

I—Self. Ego. (Same as our English I).

J—Generate. (A duplication of G, but with a delicate difference in shade of meaning. Actually Ja, in contrast to Ge is a very important distinction. G is the generating energy, while J is animal generation per se.)

K—Kinetic. (The force of motion).

L—Life.

M—Man.

N—Seed. Spore. (Child, as "ninny").

O—Orifice. (A source concept).

P—Power.

Q—Quest. (As "quest-ion").

R—Horror. Danger. (Used AR, symbol of a dangerous quantity of disintegrant force in the object.)

S—Sun. (Used "sis"; an important symbol, always referring to a "sun" whose energy is given off through atomic disintegration.)

T—Integration, Growth. (Used TE; the most important symbol of the alphabet; the true origin of the cross symbol. It signifies the integrative force of growth; as, all matter is growing—the intake of gravity is the cause. The force is T. TIC means the science of growth. Integration-I-Con (understand).

U—You.

V—Vital. (Used as VI; the stuff Mesmer called "animal magnetism").

W—Will.

X—Conflict. (Force lines crossing each other).

Y—Why.

Z—Zero. Nothing. Neutralization. (A quantity of energy of T neutralized by an equal quantity of D. Futility.)

HUNDREDS of balls found deep below the earth have got scientists in a spin. For they could have been made by prehistoric man—which would mean there was intelligent life on the planet almost 3,000 million years ago.

The balls, from one to four inches across, were found in mineral deposits at the Wonderstone Mine in the Transvaal, South Africa.

An official who cracked several open found that one kind contained a sponge-like substance which quickly powdered when it was touched.

The other type was solid metal, blue with a reddish tint and containing specks of white fibre.

By PETER ELLIS

Three neat grooves—like the seam on a cricket ball—ran around the centre of each ball.

They had no irregularities and no known geological process could have formed them, says Roelf Marx, curator of South Africa's Klerksdorp Museum.

He was amazed when he displayed one of the balls with samples of other rocks.

After some months he found that the ball had turned itself round.

Marx couldn't believe it and kept watch. Sure enough, the ball was able to revolve on its axis.

"I have no explanation," Marx says. "The sphere baffles everybody. It looks man-made, as though cast in a mould."

Geologist Professor Andries Bisschoff says: "From the position in which these things were found, it is likely that they are 2,8000 million years old.

"I don't know why they revolve on their own axis —nothing in nature could make them do that."

The balls were all found in the same layer of the mineral pyrophyllite. They all fit perfectly in the hand, as if they were designed that way.

One theory is that they were primeval missiles. Now scientists are puzzling over why they were needed.

WEEKEND, July 2-8, 1980

URBANA, Ill. (UPI) — Police are trying to determine why hundreds of dollars were torn into one-inch squares and scattered to the wind.

Police answered a report at the Lincoln Trailer Home park late Wednesday and found about 10 children and adults furiously trying to recover pieces of torn $10, $20 and $50 bills being tossed about by the wind.

"It was just blowing around on the ground ...," Lt. Charles Gordon said. "If they (trailer home residents) found enough one-inch square pieces to piece together a $50 bill, it would make it worth putting the jigsaw puzzle together."

Gordon said the incident was the third time this month shredded cash had been reported in the area.

Someone Is Tearing Up Quite A Bit Of Money

Napa Register, 10/10/80

RICHARD S. SHAVER'S MYSTERY TITLES

By Jim Pobst

Not the least of the many mysteries which surround the puzzling career of Richard Sharpe Shaver is the fate of some thousands (even hundreds of thousands) of words by his pen. Begun and perhaps never finished, or completed but never published, these "mystery manuscripts" continue to perplex & entice the student of the Shaver Saga. When, to them are added companion volumes by other hands, (some announced by Shaver's own Aldebaran Press), a sizeable library of material is seen to be missing from the official record of the Shaver Mystery. It is hoped that if any reader has any further information about the following items, they will write to SHAVERTRON, and through its columns share their knowledge with the rest of us.

A) WARNING TO FUTURE MAN: Paris Flammonde in his book, UFO EXIST states that this manuscript "of sorts" was scrawled on the backs of envelopes, laundry bills, paper bags and other scraps receptive to a pencil". Ray Palmer, however, claimed it was in the form of a 10,000 word letter sent to the Ziff-Davis Publishing Company offices, typed with "ultimate non-ability" on a "toy typewriter with several keys missing". It was with this letter as a base, Palmer stated, that he produced the 31,000 word ms. "I Remember Lemuria". (AMAZING STORIES, March 1945). In the quarterly book THE HIDDEN WORLD no.2 Palmer reveals that he added "expansive dialogue", "local colour" "bits of action" and "battle scenes". The actual "letter manuscript" that Shaver had written was, Palmer said, filed away in accordance with Ziff-Davis policy, in company with the other manuscripts relating to that issue, all destined to be destroyed after the passage of six years. Palmer "lifted" it for his personal Shaver file but by 1961 claimed to have lost track of it. There is another theory current among sf fans to the effect that the whole Shaver Mystery was orchestrated at

least a year in advance of the initial publication and that therefore the WARNING TO FUTURE MAN ms. never existed. Only if and when this most valuable piece of Shaverania is produced can this rumour be quashed.

B) THE ELDER WORLD: By all accounts, this was to be Shaver's super-novel--a story of the caverns "replete with documentation and proof". But, says Palmer, the loss of Ziff-Davis income broke Shaver's spirit temporarily, and Shaver handed the portfolio to Palmer with the words, "You finish this book--- it has me licked". Palmer describes it as a "helter skelter collection of individual and unrelated chapters, and various conglomerations of notes". Parts of this appeared in THE HIDDEN WORLD (1961-1964), but there may have been other unedited chapters not published. Shaver was said to have begun writing this in 1949. It was advertised for future sale as early as 1948 in Vol. II, no. 4 of the Shaver Mystery Magazine as "A big lavishly illustrated and handsomely bound volume... a proper exhaustive study on the whole subject of the prediluvian culture". Though it was never to appear in finished form, it was to have cost $6, be illustrated by the author, and would include for free, a "Letters To Shaver" folio. If a more complete description of the contents exists, other than that in THE HIDDEN WORLD's pages, the readers of SHAVERTRON would no doubt like to hear about it.

C) THE ALDEBARAN LEAFLET: In 1948, subscribers to the Shaver Mystery Magazine and selected others received a list of proposed publications from Aldebaran Press. Comments on the books projected were given, as were prices. As well as the Elder World, they included: "Grey Lord of Death" by G. Archette..$3, (this saw print as "We Dance for the Dom" by RSS in AS 1/50); "The Magic That Was" by RSS...$2.50; "Letters to Shaver"... $1.50;

"Shaver Mystery Digest"...$1.50; "Forever is Too Long" by Chester Geier...$2.50 (this appeared in FANTASTIC ADVENTURES for March 1947); "The Shaver Omnibus"...$7; "The Wizard Kingdom by Morganstern...$2.50; "Witches Heroes and Mysteries"by P. Cognini...$3.50; 'Mandark" by RSS...$4.00.

D) THE ROGER BACON MANUSCRIPT: In the Editor's Page feature of the last issue of the Ziff-Davis pulp magazine Mammoth Adventures, Ray Palmer announced that to hand was a new Shaver story dealing with Roger Bacon, the Franciscan monk (A.D. 1214-1294), natural philosopher and mathematician. Had it appeared it would have been the fifth Shaver tale in this magazine, the previous ones having dealt with such diverse locales as Babylon after the death of Sennacherib, Yucatan in the time of Cortez, and the Incan and Aztec civilizations. Mammoth Adventures failed to sell enough copies, folded after the eighth issue, and presumably the manuscript was either returned to Shaver or destroyed at Ziff-Davis.

E) KINGDOM OF THE GODS: The first and second issues of the science-fiction magazine Other Worlds on sale in the latter half of 1949, promised in the back cover feature for "Your Reading Pleasure", "a tremendous new tale from the thought records of the dead race who once inhabited the lost caverns of the earth. Beginning a brand new series of the world's most imaginative and stimulating stories". Nothing under this title did appear and it is not known if this mention was merely a 'teaser' or the working title for the four-part serial BEYOND THE BARRIER which did run in Other Worlds (November 1952- February 1953). Mutan Mion and his Arl re-appear in this long novel which ranks with the DREAM MAKERS as Shaver's best work.

F) THE SHAVER MYSTERY: In the May 1957 issue of Search, there appeared a small boxed advertisement: "Coming next September-the hard cover book, THE SHAVER MYSTERY". Ray Palmer announced in the June 1957 issue that University Books would publish this book in the fall. He claimed authorship and revealed that it "will explain the Shaver Mystery quite completely-- and it won't cost a fortune, either!" I have no information that the book ever saw print, or in fact even existed in manuscript, although it is possible that parts of it were incorporated in Palmer's contributions to THE HIDDEN WORLD and THE SECRET WORLD.

As would be expected from such a prolific writer as Richard Shaver, there were title changes in the transition from ms. to published story. Working titles such as THE LIMPING HAG and MULTI-MIND saw print as CULT OF THE WITCH QUEEN (Amazing Stories, July 1946) and QUEST OF BRAIL (AS: December '45). In a letter to Richard Toronto, Shavertron editor, Shaver mentioned that GREEN MAN'S GRIEF (Future: January 1951) was first called WHY GREEN PEOPLE ARE UNPOPULAR. But the above mentioned titles cannot be so easily traced as this. I think they represent separate and distinct pieces in the Shaver jig-saw puzzle-- pieces which for many and varied reasons we are unable to read, judge and assess.

Somewhere, perhaps in the Shaver File at Palmer Publications, or with the numerous and scattered Shaver collections of his old and new fans, there rest the above 'Mystery Titles'. Possibly even more.

Book Review: WAR IN THE AIR

Richard S. Shaver blamed all wars and other human tragedies on dero and their ray machines. Is there a master plan to destroy our civilization? If such a plan exists, has it been published in books or in other literature in the past? There is some evidence that the great British writer, H.G. Wells had access to the dero's master plan to destroy Western Civilization.

Wells liked to predict the future in his famous sci-fi novels. When he wrote THE TIME MACHINE in 1895, he informed the public in an indirect way that the dero were killing and eating humans. By having the main character travel 70,000 years into the future, he shows why civilization was destroyed and why the Morlocks were eating the Eloi. Of course, Shaver claimed that this existed at the present time and has existed for thousands of years. At any rate, Wells did seem to have knowledge of dero activities at the turn of the century.

H.G. Wells was able to foresee the serious problems of the 20th century including overpopulation, air pollution and the World Wars decades before they became evident. The American people are not aware of these prophecies because the two novels which contain most of them have not been published in the USA. These novels are THE WAR IN THE AIR (1908) and THE WORLD SET FREE (1914). In this book review, the WAR IN THE AIR will be discussed and a future article will review THE WORLD SET FREE, the world's first book to predict the coming of the a-

tomic age including a description of anuclear war and nuclear-powered rockets travelling to the stars.

THE WAR IN THE AIR is one of the most incredible books written in the past 100 years, and it is a great crime that the book publishers have refused to sell it to the American people. When Mr. Wells wrote it in 1907, conditions in the world were not as bad as they are today. Western civilization was at its height in culture and civilized behavior and there was a universally accepted belief that Man was improving as a species. Wells was one of the few people living before World War I who was able to see through this dream world and he was able to accurately predict how the dero would destroy our civilization by forcing human beings to slaughter each other.

THE WAR IN THE AIR more accurately predicted the events of World War II than WWI. Wells claimed that the USA was to be attacked by German, Chinese, and Japanese aircraft in the 1930's. Although this prediction was not completely accuarate, because he believed that all the major US cities would be destroyed by air power (to take place in WWIII), it is a fact that Alaska and Pearl Harbor were attacked by enemy aircraft. He also predicted that all the world's major cities would be destroyed by aircraft in WWII.

The attack on Pearl Harbor by the Japanese on December 7, 1941, which resulted in the destruction of most of the US Fleet fulfills another prediction he made in Chapter 5: "The Battle of the North Atlantic". This chapter is one of the most frightening in the book, because Wells describes how a German air fleet annihilated the US Fleet. It is a fact that the Germans came very close to destroying both the US and British Fleets in both world wars by using subs and aircraft in the North Atlantic. The only problem with this prediction was that the Japanese succeeded in destroying most of the US Fleet, not the Germans. This is a minor consideration, however, since the military dared not believe that aircraft could destroy large warships until the 1920's and the concept of air power destroying an entire fleet was not proven until the attack on Pearl Harbor.

How did the British people look at this book? On Nobember 5, 1908, THE TIMES of London, one of the world's greatest newspapers, reviewed this novel and the paper attacked Wells for predicting a terrible future for the 20th century. The British critic who wrote the review attacked Wells on a number of predictions which he and most of the world believed would never come true. Among the predictions which disturbed him included Well's description of the world wars, the use of aircraft to destroy cities and the collapse of civilization after these wars took place. He was also very upset by Wells' prediction that a World War could begin over a minor incident. Six years later, however, WWI began when one man was assasinated! Summing up his review, the critic accused Wells, one of the greatest writers of our time, of being a poor writer and THE WAR IN THE AIR as a poor piece of fiction!

Of course, Wells had the last laugh. In the 1941 edition of THE WAR IN THE AIR, he expressed his true feelings:

"Here in 1941 THE WAR IN THE AIR is being reprinted once again. It was written in 1907 and first published in 1908. It was reprinted in 1921, and then I wrote a preface which also I am reprinting. Again I ask the reader to note the warning I gave in that year, 20 years ago. Is there anything to add to that preface now? Nothing except my epitaph. This, when the time comes, will manifestly have to be: 'I told you so, you damned fools.'"

Why are humans damned fools?? Did Wells know that the human race was being controlled by the dero? Or was he a real psychic and could see accuarately into the future? Nobody knows the truth about this matter, but it seems that THE WAR IN THE AIR could be classified as a real dero nightmare.

Editors note: Mike Cohen is a writer/researcher in the ufological field, having had many articles published in Beyond Reality and other zines of this area of study.

Derelict Ships and UFOs

By Jim Wentworth

Derelicts have been discovered on still waters-- intact and seaworthy-- not once, but many times. Here are a few examples:

A deserted, two-masted ship called John and Mary was found adrift 50 miles south of Bermuda. Time: April, 1932.

The yacht, Gloria Colite, was found abandoned two hundred miles souuth of Mobile, Alabama in February of 1940.

So, too, in September, 1955 was another yacht, Connerama IV, found 400 miles south-west of Bermuda.

The date of the discovery of the 60-foot Maple Bank, devoid of life, north of Bermuda, was June 30, 1969.

And, on October 31, 1971, the U.S. Coast Guard came across the lifeless Lucky Edur, a fishing vessel of 25-foot length.

Let us now put our imaginations to use and picture a cargo ship plying the calm waters of the Pacific. Everything is peaceful. Of the 15 crew members, some are eating in the galley, one is mopping the deck, two others are painting a lower corridor. The remainder are all dutifully busy.

Suddenly, the one mopping the deck lets out a yell and points a shaky finger to the cloudless sky. Some 2000 feet above is a silvery UFO, circular in shape, about 60 feet in diameter.

The piercing yell brings all personnel dashing on deck to stare fearfully at the strange object, dropping rapidly and silently toward them. When about 200 feet above, the UFO stops its descent, but keeps pace with the swiftly moving ship.

Sensing its alieness, those aboard begin to experience increasing fear and terror. This reaches a pioat where they go berserk. Senselessly, they hurl themselves overboard, uncaring that they are in shark-infested waters.

Soon after, the UFO streaks upward, and disappears from sight within seconds. Meanwhile, the 15 men in the water realize a new menace is upon them. A fleet of sharks begin to close in. Before long it is over. All men have been killed and eaten.

The next day the derelict is discovered by a passing ship and boarded by several sailors. They notice a number of strange things-- a half-eaten meal in the galley with chairs overturned, a scattered mop by a bucket of soapy water on deck, two brushes near a paint can below. From all this it is obvious that there had been stark panic aboard the abandoned ship. But what happened? Theories are voiced breathlessly.

One imaginative theorist says that a UFO might have been involved. Unknowingly, he was correct. He further theorizes that the alien occupants kidnapped the entire crew of the cargo ship. Here, of course, he is dead wrong.

There are UFOlogists who hold to the idea that the crews (and passengers) of all derelict ships are the kidnapped victims of aliens. Not necessarily so. Not in all cases. Perhaps some crew members were indeed whisked aboard a UFO as captives, but it could also be true that other crew members that are missing from abandoned ships suffered the same watery fate as just described in the fictional story above.

This theory is upheld by Charles Berlitz, for in his book, <u>Without a Trace</u>, he writes on page 155: "During the 1972 period of frequent sightings over Puerto Rico, some minor incidents concerning small boats occurred which, although receiving comparatively little attention, may have some bearing on the mystery of the many craft found over the years in the Bermuda Triangle, afloat and seaworthy but without their crews. For while more striking occurrances were being watched in the sky by thousands of observers, several abandoned boats were found in Puerto Rico waters off Mayaguez and Carbo Rojo. Occupants of these craft were known to have been aboard when the boats left port. About the time of the crew's disappearance, the crew of another craft, a yacht, were startled to observe, in the early evening, a UFO approacing them at a slow rate of speed and at an altitude of less than 200 feet. As it came closer, before suddenly disappearing, the crew experienced a common sense of terror and several of them attempted to jump overboard before being dissuaded by their comrades. This little-noted incident might possibly furnish one indication why so many boats are found abandoned within the Bermuda Triangle, in that unreasoning panic might suggest that escaping, even into the unfriendly but familiar sea, would be preferred to staying on board and facing the approaching unknown."

News helicopter lost

MIAMI (UPI) — A Coast Guard cutter searched the Bermuda Triangle today for a television news team helicopter with four men aboard, missing since Wednesday night.

The 210-foot Vigorous looked all night for the missing Bell Ranger aircraft, and planes and helicopters, which rejoin the search at daybreak, crisscrossed the Florida Straits until 10:30 p.m. Thursday, a Coast Guard spokesman said.

The spokesman said the unusual after-dark air search was ordered because "we were told the helicopter had a life raft aboard and we assume the raft was equipped with flares."

Aboard the missing helicopter were pilot George Snow, 45, of Boca Raton, Fla.; NBC cameraman Randy Fairbairn, 31; Dan Cefalo, a free lancer working for NBC, and Joseph Dalisera, 52, a video technician for ABC. *11-14-80*

'Ghost Voices' Threaten Flight Safety of Airlines

HILLIARD, Fla. (AP) — Mysterious male voices that have radioed false instructions to jet pilots could create "a very dangerous situation," although routine safeguards are designed to guard against such hoaxes, federal officials said Tuesday.

The latest "ghost voice" broadcast a false order to the pilot of a Delta Airlines jet when it was near Gainesville, Fla., on a flight from Tampa to Indianapolis on Saturday.

Five fake transmissions were radioed to pilots at Tampa International Airport in a three-day period in May, then stopped.

"It has got to be somebody on the lunatic fringe to do this — he's creating the potential for a very dangerous situation. Fortunately, these were caught in time," said Federal Aviation Administration spokesman Jack Barker in Atlanta.

The false flight instructions were countermanded before they caused any accidents or near-misses.

"Fortunately there are enough safeguards to catch the fake calls," said an FAA supervisor at the Jacksonville, Fla., tower. "It's routine for the pilot and the controller to repeat instructions to make sure they're understood. They acknowledge transmissions."

Barker said he had never before encountered someone trying to interfere with radio instructions to airline pilots. It is a federal crime punishable by five years in prison. The FAA, Federal Communications Commission and FBI are investigating.

Delta spokesman Dick Jones at the airline's Atlanta headquarters said the pilots were aware of the trouble. "Obviously, we are concerned about this thing. It could have an impact on the whole industry," Jones said.

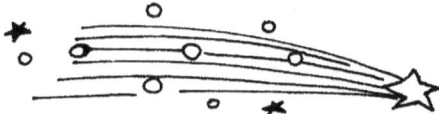

HERB CAEN

YOU'VE READ about ships found adrift and deserted. Among the most mysterious of these was a schooner discovered in the mid-Atlantic in 1881 by the Ellen Austin, an American vessel. All was in order. Nothing was missing. The Ellen Austin's master put a crew aboard the abandoned ship and headed for port. A squall came up and separated them. The Ellen Austin finally found the ship again, only to see it was once more deserted, the crewmen missing. Another crew was persuaded to take her in. Another squall came up. This time the schooner simply disappeared. Nothing was ever heard again either from that final crew or the ship.

★ ★ ★

Once upon a time I found some beautiful and perfect scroll rocks in a gravel pit. They were heavy and black and dense and had fine yellow scroll/ornamental stuff on them. I gave them to Shaver...packed them carefully and they made one extraordinarilly heavy small package. Took them to the post office and ran into a female hardcase (she kept telling me for five years that there was no such thing as special book mss. rates...she also told me a few times they didn't stock foreign exchange postage cupons since nobody wanted them...told her I did).

She plunked the box on the counter scales and it was too heavy for them. Offered to set it on the big floor scale for her and wuz informed that postal patrons were not allowed behind the counter--even though I usta be a mail orderly on a Navy LST. She huved and grunted mightily and got it weighed. Told her it went first class and she said parcel post insured. About 20 minutes later, I won and it went 1st class. "What IS in that box??" she inquired peevishly. Of course, since you are also a writer, you know that when the mind has the writing habit, one comes up with things more often right when you need them instead of a month later. I had a juicy thought in a flash ..."It's a war surplus atom bomb trigger", I said informatively and casually. "We don't have to know what is in 1st class mail", she said with a frozen puss.

Quite a bit later, the rocks still hadn't arrived in Arkansas. Were they being held up as evidence in a workman's compensation case when a mail sorter got a hernia hefting them??? I got on the phone to DC--pushed a few panic buttons (atom is a magic push button word with ye establishment) and got ahold of ye postal inspektorr. I had had some business with them a few years before over a phantom mail bag key. How to get through their input filter in a jiffy was easy--I just said they had

an atomic incident fomenting somewhere between Chillicothe and Summit. When I got ahold of ye inner office, I explained wot had happend and offered th the insight that atom bombs have detonators and no triggers, they had the opinion that the parcel was being held in Dallas. A couple of days later, it arrived in good shape at Shaver's pondee. Forget how much of all that I related to him. He had had a big rumble years before with ye Post Office, about publishing health food advice. All of which is inadvisable to pub--it could afflict things like a 2nd class mailing permit. So, it is a rare event in my corry--a DNQ (Ed. note--- Bill has since given in and let me pub this story). (Also, your bumbling editor made a slip of the keys in Bill's last col: There definitely ARE broadcast signals below 100KC).

by BILL BLISS

Got the book, Alternative 003 the other day, and everything came to a screeching halt and I read the first half of it. There is alot in it that is variance with wot passes for common knowledge... (including ye encyclopedia). Somebody Else is On The Moon, by George Leonard...He made a long study of NASA and observatory photos and saw constructions and immense machines on the moon. Gads, I just overheated a moccasin by getting my foot too close to the electric heater under the desk. Time out while I cool off my ingrown toenail....Got as far as page 229 in Alt3 last night. Wotta tale. Owell, if the planet does go shot, it will get restocked by the extra-terrys anyhoo eventually. I have an inkling that zoologists andscads of other oligists will always find that idea highly unacceptable...

THE PROBLEM OF BACK ISSUES: The problem is that very few are left due to a recent ad campaign which chomped up most of them.....#'s 2,3,5 and 6 still available in short supply..@$1.50.

GIANTS IN THE EARTH - *revised*

By Jim Wentworth

"Revisions for the possible second printing of the book, "Giants in the Earth", available from Palmer Publications, Amherst, Wisconsin."

The following to be inserted on page 117, second column, between 1st and 2nd paragraph:

This was at the Ypsilanti State Hospital in Michigan as a paranoid schizophrenic. The following quotes were taken from Search, Summer 1977, it is Palmer speaking:

"I had it first hand from the nurse who attended him, and was furnished hospital documents to substantiate it. Later, I found printed hospital stationery used by inmates to write letters, among Shaver's files which he opened to me. I never said anything to him about it, because I had made a sensational discovery, and didn't want him to clam up on me. He was providing me with great masses of scientific material which were not in any current textbook, and which I was comparing with another source (Oahspe) I had come across."

"I learned then that Shaver's condition in

Ypsilanti had been catatonic. According to psychiatrists, he had removed himself from reality, living in a shadowy imaginary world in his own mind. He even had to be fed. All his adventures in the caves were in his own mind. So they said.

"He, Shaver, KNEW that the 8 years of his cavern experiences coincided with the 8 years of his incarceration at Ypsilanti. Even the hospital psychiatrists state that he was 'out of his mind' (that his body was there, but the personality was not)--it was somewhere in a different world which they could only call imaginary."

Editor note: Rich Shaver contested this claim of Palmer's. In an interview rebuttal in Caveat Emptor, claimed to have spent only 2 weeks in the hospital for treatment of sunstroke. He said that RAP was being conned by the dero to discredit his material. We hope to reprint both the RAP interview, and RSS' rebuttal to it in a future issue...RRT.

9

LETTERS

Dear Rich,

I found Shavertron mag. a very good read. It's interesting how bitterly the sci-fi people oppose "amazing facts", Fortean, Shaverian science, etc. My own books (2 of them) were handled by Mrs Del Rey of Ballantine's, who told me she disliked the kind of books such as mine which she called "anti-scientific". Then I got a poor deal. My book, Natural Likeness...(reviewed in issue 4, Shavertron)... was withdrawn within a few days of publication, copies were sold to waste-paper dealer. I hope you will be able to do a book on Shaver and UUI's. It's an intriguing subject. Mary LeVesque sent me a wonderful Indian head from Wyoming, but I had no space to include it in the book. It was good to see your reproduction of Berringer's stones. Do you know that good book, "The Lying Stones of Dr. Berringer" by John Work? There are many anomalies in the modern explanation of fossils, also of rocking stones, erratic boulders, stone piles, etc. Fashions in geology change easily, so perhaps Shaver will be taken seriously one day.

Sincerely, John Michell
London

R-- I am dismayed, John, to find that the one book in recent years that gave Shaver a break (Natural Likeness) got tossed into the paper-shreder. I personally feel that it is a great book, on a most-ignored subject which should be important to every thinking person on this planet. The illustrations alone should have saved them from becoming particle board, but NO. You did a good job...more could not be asked of you. RSS was well acquainted with your problem...RRT.

~~~~~~~~~~

Good Heavens-- It's hard to believe that a Shaver-theory oriented zine actually exists-- I do hope you keep it in the black-- its very hard to put such things out, as I can well appreciate.

To understand the problem of malific identies and their control requires some background in how the human being functions in relationship to other life forms around them. Most persons have the false assumption that other life forms think in a similar way to themselves. This is simply not true and causes great misunderstanding when trying to unravel some of the more exotic mysteries of this planet.

Exorcism and defense against any identity is very simple and complete when you can challenge them correctly. If your freedom of choice is being a-bridged you have the right of defense. The fact is, of course, that factions of domination on all dimensions have done a good job of keeping this fact with held. Without proper comprehension, people want to depend on others--whether ideologies, leaders or systems.

I send the Modern Humans Comp Courses all over the globe, and once the first two courses are comprehended, it answers about 80% of the questions pertaining to such mysteries as exist... you have bits and pieces of the truth in Shaver

and others, but I haven't seen it all in one lump sum outside of the Comps.

Please enter me for 6 future issues of Shavertron.
Later, Al Fry

R--It's good to have a Modern Human on the S sub list, Al. If your Comp courses can answer the problem of the Shaver Mystery, it might be worth investigating. (Al has quite a book list of unique works, and other things of interest.) Here is his ad:

Dear Richard, Thank you for the sample copy of S. Overall, I was very impressed. Enclosed is a money order to cover back issues 2,3,4, 5.

The Ashtar and the Dero article was the most valuable bit of information in your newsletter. The Bible backs Ashtar's statements. When seen in this light, the Deros are the earthbound demons who fell from grace and torment man. The torments of Hell described by the Bible exist underneath our feet. RSS described them in his writings. The benevolent disc-flying saucer beings are the angels of the Bible. Their struggle with the malific forces are also described in Oahspe.

The annotated Allende Letters, many of HP Lovecraft's stories, HG Wells' Time Machine, the Bhagavad-Gita, Blavatsky's The Secret Doctrine, books I and II and Isis Unveiled, also detail this eternal struggle. Another aspect of the Bible which is hotly being disputed is the idea of "rapture" where God's chosen vanish from the Earth. I maintain this "rapture" has been going on for centuries and the annotations in the Allende Letters back me up. This might also be the answer behind the Bermuda and Devil's Triangle.

Ashtar is also on the mark about hollow earth entrances at the poles. Cigar shaped UFO's

10

have been frequently sighted in both vicinities. UFO researchers like Bender and John Stuart, who have made this connection have been silenced or murdered, as have those who have experimented with anti-gravity and electro-magnetism. They are too close to the truth...but this is where UFO investigators must channel their efforts if they are to arrive at the truth. Not only do they face danger from Deros and MIB, but run the risk of being silenced by organizations on the surface whose heads have directly allied themselves with the forces of Eranus in return for power and wealth. Groups like the Tri-Lateral Commission are proof.

Jason Royale, KS.

Dear Richard, On your (or someone's) piece about some author and "Ashtar"; ray caused the mind to estimate this subject was good for the newsletter. NO, because "Ashtar" runs down Shaver's information "disproves it" to his fans, and makes the readers get to thinking Ashtar is good and Shaver then not too right, etc. Richard told me that this Ashtar bozo is a dero. From being a past expert of Spiritualists, I KNOW Ashtar is trusted 100% by these seance-suckers. He's a big-wig in such circles, and we know from Shaver that this faith is dero-run. Even the books on space contactees say to keep away from seances as they are negative. Take it from one who knows.

Yours, Henry Steele

R-- George Van Tassel would have disagreed with you, Henry, on the "seance" bit, but then again, Van Tassel was Ashtar's chief medium for years. Will any of you readers bear Henry out on this?? Did your humble editor goof again?..RRT

Dear Rich, In 1975, I heard a newscast about a plane crash near Mt. Weather, VA. Some newscaster that was broadcasting from the scene made the statement that he could not understand what all the govt.

men were doing at the crash site. He later came on the air again and stated that he had found out that the plane crashed right near the President's bomb shelter, under Mt. Weather. Needless to say, I never saw that newscaster again, but it stood to reason that there would be a tunnel extending from Washington, DC to Mt. Weather.

To add further to this adventure, it seems that our govt. is seriously considering moving the White House to Hutchinson, Kansas. Now Hutchinson is built over an area of large quantities of salt and already vast caverns have been dug out of the salt and are used for storage vaults to preserve a number of things for a number of people. The movie industry stores a great deal of film there, as salt keeps things dry and preserves them. It seems strange that this is the place where they are considering putting the new White House. I also heard from a couple of sources that there are tunnels leading from NORAD in Colorado to Kansas and perhaps all the way to Wash. DC at this time, as I heard the story quite some time ago and their ultimate objective was from Norad to DC. The PLOT THICKENS!!

Mary LeVesque

Dear Mr Toronto, I'm sorry to say that I threw away an interesting item I would have liked to see pubbed in Shavertron. It was from the Purdue University Exponent and sounds like there is a static variety of Deros in Lafayette, Indiana. They pubbed a letter from a student who said "There are men who walk the tunnels beneath Purdue"...and maintained that certain forms of activity were spreading across campus.

I was immediately reminded of the Shaver Mystery, but had no one at the time to communicate it with. This was 3 years ago. Dero activity would be even more advanced now...only yesterday the power went off over the city and they attributed it to a bird landing on a fuse box. I think some people here call them "Disorgs". You can publish this news item if you want, or use it in the letter column, but without my name. I hope you do. I think Lafayette should be known for its Deros.

R-- Phew! Shades of Shaver! "Disorgs" is a very descriptive word for deros. I'll have to remember that one. Thanks. Readers near Layfayette, take notice...RRT.

Dear Richard, In your Winter, 1980 issue, page two, you mentioned your experiments with infrared film, and photographing the invisible. Why not tell us readers more about this subject, as it appears to be timely.

The Philadelphia Experiment: Project Invisibility, is a book about a ship that disappeared (became invisible) in the Phila. Navy yard in WWII, during tests to make it radar-proof.

This past week, ABC-tv news told of a new US plane that will be coated with a substance that will make the plane invisible to enemy radar.

Unlike the Navy ship which became totally invisible the plane will be seen with the naked eye, but not by radar.

There are many who believe the US Navy continued the 1943 experiments (in which Dr Einstein was involved) and have perfected just such a technique that can be used in time of war. Perhaps there are others out there who can shed some light on the Invisible factor?

Regardless, we'd like to hear of the Toronto experiments. How about it?

Best, Geo. Wunder PA.

R--Aw gee- whiz, George, you wanna see those weird little pix I took out behind the cemetery... (doing my Jimmy Stewart imitation here).

No, actually, there are plans in the works here at S headquarters for pubbing a collaborative article by myself and Charles Marcoux...I supply the pix, and Charles will interpret them. Mr. Marcoux has been photographing the invisible for almost 40 years...(make note of his address in the editorial). His book is full of his work. Don't know how well these pix will half-tone, though. We'll have to experiment at the printer's.

11

This Hoax A Bare Fact

OKLAHOMA CITY (UPI) — A woman who stripped down to her underwear and walked through a shopping mall told authorities she was following instructions from a man identifying himself as a local disc jockey.

Police said Tuesday the unidentified woman, who had been promised prizes she thought were worth the embarrassment, was the victim of a hoax.

The woman, wearing only a bra and panties and pushing a stroller with a baby in it, was stopped by a security guard as she walked through the mall Monday.

The woman was told by a male caller posing as a disc jockey, if she would wear only her underwear while walking through the shopping mall, she would win a $16,000-a-year job at the station, $10,000 in cash, a car, a moped bike and $1,000 for each of her children, officers said.

New Pyramid Found

CAIRO, Egypt (UPI) — Archeologists have discovered a new pyramid buried beneath the sands of the Saqqara desert south of Cairo dating back to the year 2560 B.C., the newspaper Al Akhbar said today.

The newspaper said diggers have uncovered 65 feet of the pyramid, which appears to have been constructed on a 60-square-yard base. The discovery was made by a Czech archeological mission, but confirmation was not available from Egyptian authorities.

The newly-discovered pyramid was said to date to the Egyptian fifth dynasty, which would make it younger than the famous Step Pyramid of the third century Pharaoh Zoser, also located in the antiquity-rich Saqqara desert 15 miles southwest of Cairo.

The Step Pyramid is considered by archeologists to be the first important stone structure in Egypt and the forerunner of the great pyramids at Giza.

The substructure of the Step Pyramid has an elaborate system of underground passages and rooms, with a burial chamber 81 feet below ground reachable only by way of a slanting shaft carved out of rock.

There was no indication whether the archeologists suspected the new pyramid covered underground vaults, nor whether the structure was built for a king or lesser royalty. *11-13-80*

«THEY»   By Al Wiseman

Know a rhyme that cheers and amuses? In time,
you'll come to one which fools and amuses. Here
is a Mystery to solve-- so what can you deduce,
my friend, what can you evolve?

They dance on my shoulder, they dance on my head,
when I grow older, They grow younger instead.
Noisy as a fife and drum, from out of nowhere they
come/ What are they, can I be so dumb?

They dance on my shoulder, they dance on my head,
when I grow older, They grow younger instead.
Strange appealing phantoms these, They steal into
my room with ease-- can They be real entities?

They dance on my shoulder, They dance on my head,
when I grow older, They grow younger instead.
At the end of my wits, They fairly give me fits--
when one stands, the other one sits.

They dance on my shoulder, They dance on my head,
when I grow older, They grow younger instead.

A Mysterious 'Dinosaur' Lurks In Congo Swamp

Chicago

An elephant-sized animal with claws, a long neck and tail seen in the swampy jungles of western Africa may be a dinosaur, an expert on "hidden animals" said yesterday.

Scientist Roy Mackal of the University of Chicago said inhabitants of a remote section of the Congo call the swamp-dwelling beast "Mokele-Mbembe." They describe it as 15 to 30 feet long with large, clawed feet and lengthy neck and tail.

"We don't know exactly what it is we're talking about," Mackal said. "A small dinosaur fits the picture. But we hesitate to claim that. You can make an equally good case for a large monitor lizard."

Mackal, author of a book on "hidden animals," has spent more than a decade searching for Scotland's legendary Loch Ness monster.

He and James Powell, a herpetologist living in Plainview, Texas, spent February traveling through swampy jungles in a largely unmapped area asking the inhabitants about "Mokele-Mbembe." They plan to return next August.

Mackal and Powell did not see any of the creatures, but the natives told them the animals have smooth, brownish-gray skin, a long and flexible neck, a very long tail and three-clawed feet as big as frying pans.

"We would show them picture books of normal animals — buffalo, elephants — and they would identify them. We would also show them pictures of reconstructions of extinct animals. When they saw a picture of the brontosaurus, or of any of the sauropods, they pointed at it and called it 'Mokele-Mbembe.'

"The response cut across all ethnic, geographic, cultural and educational lines. We admit we're biased by the consistency of the description — we think it's a real animal rather than a bogey man type of thing."

The brontosaurus and other dinosaurs are believed to have died out 70 million years ago.

Science 80 Magazine, published by the American Association for the Advancement of Science, said in an article printed yesterday that the creatures reportedly feed on the nutlike fruit of a riverbank plant and keep to deep pools and submerged caves in the area.

Mackal said there have been reports on the creatures for two centuries and the best came in 1959, when pygmies allegedly killed one that was disturbing their fishing on Lake Tele. He and Powell have offered a reward for any bones from that animal.

The two researchers hope to return to the Congo next August 1, at the start of the rainy season, and take their equipment into the remote area in dugouts to set up a base camp for the search.

United Press

Deros Con History

BY HENRY M. STEELE

I shall write this article as if the reader knows just as much about the deros as I. All statements are not opinions but _factual_. Mr. Shaver told me I could comprehend the truth of his stories better than anyone; that I understood the dero set-up all too well -- their mental ray control on surface people also. From personal experience before & since I visited Mr. Shaver for afew weeks at Summit, Ark. I KNOW the mech cavern culture & related aspects are VERY true. Other articles by me gave some sources backing up myself & Mr. Shaver. No need to restate them -- agents Major Wayne Aho, Dick Williams, Rickey Gillispie, & non-govt. Leo Didway, the Indian...

DERO-HISTORY via their mental ray control is still going on. Anyone who has truths to advance surface-man is harmed socially by dero ray on others he contacts with letters, meetings, articles, books, etc. Degenerate-ray is causing this same deal for me & has done so for over ten years now. Ray causes you to be ignored _so_ no action is taken by various leaders to advance civilization. Mr. Shaver explained how the dero communication system worked in a volume. You know details -- similar to action taken by a ganster organization up here as far as expertise goes. They phone quickly to various cities to inform members about someone who is to be "stopped" when he shows up. Another mental ray approch _done thru history_ is to put thoughts into the minds of those leaders who can assist the fellow, to consider him just abit nutty, & his specific discoveries impossible for anyone to come across! The type of people who can get action in this kind of society we have are called "The Professional Class". Such "folks" are those having some sort of title before their names: Senator, President, Lawyer, Professor, Rev., Bishop, Mayor, City-Father & Fuhrer (opps, sorry about that). Leading businessmen are a part of this set-up too. All have an averson toward entirely new science -- my dad's only defect.

ALL THROUGH HISTORY dero cavern mental ray on The Professional Class has assisted them to disregard almost all inventions & discoveries. Such discoveries are lost to civilization by these non-experts! This historical fact is known to scholars -- has been for generations but without knowing the cause mainly is degenerate-ray thoughts & not their own. We were taught this negative-reaction to _new_ science in grade school in the 1930s -- from an university-study. Our sweetie-teacher explained that the great majority of citizens having inventions or discoveries they came across were ignored & thought little-of by the above type of people. The experts grew old, staying poor, & died with everyone loosing out! A low percentage of these fine self-made experts were paid attention to, she said, but not until many yrs. passed & they became old. All _their_ science proved out factual in all cases Mr. Shaver gave the explanation (the main one): The deros, _in time, get_ tired of their vile "trick" on all concerned & just stop the ray. Both the scatter-ray & specific-ray thoughts are used. Used on the-know-it-alls.

In my case, however, as I know of the deros, they will never let up; I'm, in dero's eyes, liable to talk to leaders about them. Also liable to relate certain truths to govt. & church taught me by The Space Travelers when a wee child in the 1930s. Deros & these Space Travelers don't _ever_ want such people to even start considering my data just might be true & theirs wrong! No, I'm not a public-type contactee who's conned into the faked mystical!

I didn't experience anything awake. Mr. Shaver said I received communication-ray from their ship. When its done while you're asleep it seems like a type of dream. After my last mech-"dream" I had a quick impulse to look skyward & saw what we call today a scout craft zip along & bank. I was near a golf course our mother had taken us to. A silver dollar size; it banked & I saw part of its dome. A beautiful yellow-gold craft. I knew the score. Never said a word to anyone, knowing they were too stupid to trust me about such a thing, & my mech-"dreams" thru space-on planets, & the teachings. Years later I read of some of the same teachings in Mr. Shaver's volumes! "Ol' Sol" is in the worst catagory of all sun-star types -- its bad old yellow color denotes this. It throws out bad energies causing aging far too soon, etc. just as Mr. Shaver explained. My Space Travelers treated me as one of them pretty much. We'd con leaders of lower-evolved populations (& their masses) with our - their - act about the mystical being true -- best & only way (only?) to control their minds & actions. Ray from our craft on their heads helped alot. Earth leaders got this act too. People here have real weak brains - brain-power - they taught & showed me. Their prophets also are actors. The gods of ancient times were actors & this con-game goes on. They know people here can't reason thru anything correctly--- & always arrive at the opposite conclusion from the normal-way they would. Remember, schools still teach most of us nowadays are part Neanderthal; this ALSO "helps". Note: While there is a clear MOTIVE to lie about the mystical being factual to some political leaders, & church "rulers", there is NO motive to BOTHER lieing to a wee child!!! Why would they BOTHER?? They are busy doing things all the time. Via science they never age & don't need any religious moral rules to think or act by. NOTE: Bible states some Earth leader wanted his tribal-God to make up moral rules for Earth-man to abide by. This kind of request was a complete surprise to his God! He & his angels never needed any rule-book of morals; brains different. No crimes.

Remember Mr. Shaver writing a dero coned Samson with the strength-thru-long-hair story? Well, in some paperback buried someplace that's on ancient astronauts, it states Jewish-Hebrew history says Samson's tribe was backed by Yawah, the Mt. Sini Tribal-God & that Samson's tribe was an OUT-LAW tribe!! These degenerates would come out of the hills, rob the camel carivans of silver, gold & coinage, kill the guards & carry off women!! This tribe's religious leader put down how great (to them) the tribe was & how great their specific-God was -- on his say-so!! That all the good Jews & Gentiles living in cities & having caravans (no big trucks back then) were really the Bad Sinful Jews & Gentiles! I'm for the non-bigoted Jewish-Hebrew city historians! We reside today in such city-cultures plus the tech nical advancements called science. (So, we're all going to Hell, eh?). Sad.

MECH-MADE HISTORY: It runs religions; all faiths started as mystical cults T V harped. If you Shaver fans really desire my cancer & de-aging cure & information you'll have to go against ray-thoughts, feelings etc. & contact govt.-church leaders. I've tried for years but ray runs their minds just as Mr. Shaver wrote, & also told me. Ego helps too. Helps make them consider we're all dull-witted. A nation of dull-wits, eh? Why do these Professional Class People desire ruling such dull citizens?? Ray control does it. Some get told that if they lead a life of alot of public-action in governing others, it leads to their next life (reincarnation) being among Earth's Hollow Earth people as a plain citizen. They follow their "dreams"; such non-scientific brains CAN'T figure its mental ray control on their heads & that lies are put in they can't check out!! They mentally are fit for just The Stone Age level; none can invent or discover anymore than an ape (no science-desires either -- to start off). But they can carry a spear for a tribal leader while condeming their opposites in brain-functions! $$- back guarintees mean nothing to them! Nothing wrong with the stone age cultures if you don't mind missing science. Scientists hate the stone age I was school-taught in the '30s, & know they're alot smarter than govt.

The first place my Space Travelers flew me was ----- over the ice of the so-called south pole & into the gigantic hole to the earth's "Inner Lands". I was amazed to see a small sun, hills, farms, small cities, etc. They showed me how they coned the cities' leaders & people with the mystical faith; pretending they were the ancient gods (a-la Greek type) worked just great! What an act! Ship (mech) ray beamed on their heads helped even better. I was considered one of the ship-people too; we didn't really care to be thought of as gods as this wasn't our real nature. Later we flew into other globe's "Inner Lands"; such populations were always trusting this con-deal. I was with the two highest evolved types of Space People; these possessed the strongest brain-functions -- much better in brain development too, & different sometimes in their thought-process. I was sure glad to observe this type of thought was a peaceful thought-process, per chance! The only thing about us they are very discussed about is the ultra-stupid way

we reason thru anything; not only is it done wrong but conclusions are the OPPOSITE from the right way!!! This too is no lie. Getting a high-paying posission comes from having high grades, right? But one uses the memorizing & memory parts of the brain for this -- not the reasoning-area! Would you like a tie-in here? Well, we were taught in that grade school from a university study that almost all people have fine retention & think fast but don't possess good reasoning. On very rare occasion someone has trouble retaining data (so lower school grades a-la Thomas Edison) & thinks slower . But this type reasons very good. On super-rare occasion comes along a person who can do both ways great she said. Space Travelers told me I could reason fine; correctly thru subjects. The only earth person doing so. I couldn't believe this & I asked them did they really mean it; they assured me they did. It was this factor, they explained, that I was selected for such trips & teachings. Also my mind (brain) was a good bit closer to theirs in likeness, in evolvement, than anyone else here, thus I could take their lessons.NOTE: The con-artist won't say such things as they are extreamly hard to believe. I know there are other correct-reasoning people here.But maybe they couldn't take the specific lessons given me?? I was shown a mech cavern with good people attending the large devices; back then I wasn't told the words Mr. Shaver used -- only vital stuff for lessons. They sure knew how to teach! I sent a long manuscript to our editor detailing everything I was shown, taught & experienced in these extreamly vivid, colorful & clear mech-"dreams" which he'll put into future issues of your newsletter. I mentioned the above here as it shows the fact we have Our History ray-controled by these ship ones too! Oh yes, for you fans I wish

to say that the Tero-cavern I was shown was a Tero-"have" one: plenty of strange very large devices. Guess what color they were? --- PINK! This color caused the cave to look brighter for the people I saw.Note: Our experts harp pink makes the mind relaxed, peaceful & contented & happy. How smart can Teros get? These Teros were alot stronger in their brain-function than surface people. "My" Teros shown were about half-way up to the Space Traveler's brain-power, fans. The Travelers give them (not us) help when its vital! Evolution the factor. You shall learn all about this & the other things. NOTE: I was not told to go out & "preach" my anti-mystical information, & other data like those coned-contactees were & are! They are firmly instructed to spread the word of the mystical. They are selected for their gullibility, as explained in my full story. Sad: Listen to this fans:
Over a year ago I caught the end of a T V news clip. Some Wash., D.C. senator was being interviewed - rayed to not recall his name - well-known in Texas. Right at the film's end he harps, "God told me to become a senator."!! You've no idea just how GULLIBLE this fellow acted-sounded; I did not know he was a senator until I heard this about him. Note how easy for businessmen to fool this type senator! God telling him? Its deros, right fans? Mr. Shaver said so. Listen, this means all important elections are ray-controlled; folks made to "feel", "muse" & whatever, that certain senators - anyone - well, you know. Also, he appoints via mental ray! Mr. Sha-

ver clearly stated in his writings the deros greatly desire money to be
kept in the hands of the few, to make the masses' life hard & to control the money. Note there is only so much mech for specific mind-control,
& thus it can just handle a relatively few leaders. Notice the papers say
the real wealthy are pulling away from plain citizens in wealth; they make
even higher profits while the masses make less & the govt. thinks "everything's fine". My dad was a wealthy Chicago businessman decades ago & asso-
siated with other businessmen for many years. At least twice when a child
dad told me that next-to-all of them were coniving, cheating, lieing, etc.
all the time. That the people never catch on! Who comes from the people?
Why, the top elected officials who consider these con-artists as " real
good businessmen -- upstanding!" I've read this as well; a wee bit gets
out . As a little child I'd over-hear them talking. They consider elected

fellows stupid. Prices get raised on purpose by them -- slow enough so no
one catches on; it started in the '30s when a doz. of eggs cost 6¢. They
just lie to news men, harping they can't figure out how to stop the price
rise. Easy for them, as they realize everyone trusts them like good little
commies! I heard them talk about all this anti-citizen stuff. Deros harp
they like such brain-types & ray them nice.Some of these businessmen are
deros Mr. Shaver said, & wrote it too. Deros come from space also -- all
together for collecting money & power; their mental-ray protects their operations,legally -- making judges think the ray-way, & others.Seen this!!
My mech-"dreams" showed black space ships waring with "my people" so I
know Mr. Shaver's correct on this aspect also, & he realized I got it
right. "Ancient Astronauts" & "Official UFO" (same pub.) long ago had two
~~articles on top gansters being seen by witnesses, on record, coming down~~
                                    to
RIGHT HERE deros cause the typer ~~to~~ goof up & from personal experience I
know its hopeless to try to do anything over, fans! NOTE I was typing on
gansters!! To make this typer print out well for you to read it I have to
type over each line & you see how the ray moved the paper on this subject.
Then they make you miss a line to take up space needed. And they know you
will use up space to explain the whole thing for fans who can't believe too
well ALL ray can do! ~~Ty~~ Trying to re-type the page is hopeless as ray ~~cause~~
will cause more goof ups & a nite will pass & nothing gets done for you! I
shall try again: GANSTERS -- articles on top gansters, on record, coming
down at nite in some city vacent lot via egg-shaped craft!! The rayed re-
portors couldn't think much of their witnesses statements. No one paid any
attention to these named witnesses! THEY saw the ships & men get out in
ganster-suits! Note my discoveries get ignored too. Nobody helps via ray.
NAMED IN TWO ARTICLES WERE "DOUCH SCHOLTS" (spl.?) & "LEGGS DIMOND"!!! Note
this second leader was always bragging he could never get shot; when the
deros got tired of watching & filming him(Mr. Shaver's data) they stopped
the ray & then the minds of opponents wern't "confused" about shooting him
anymore. Cur-deros showed me, via scenes & entire thought-patterns that the
same thing was done on the govt's. man, Eliot Ness. Very clear "moving pictures" depecting the "hero" as the actor we've seen on that T V series yrs.
back .... Robert Stack, so I'd know what the deal was. Ray protected Ness
via same "confusion" so films could be made by deros; then ray gets tired,
turns off (scatter-ray on his area) & thus gansters get to think of killing
him, & do in real life, as some of us have read. Deros desired him going
around killing gansters for awhile -- the crazies. Later gansters were
allowed clear thoughts about getting him & so they soon did. Mr. Shaver
wrote deros love to film REAL wars & view them as we moo over Hollywood-
made wars, so real-wars get created & stupid govts.never get wise. SAD.
Recently deros harped they approve of the coniving businessman-brain workings, & crime brains too & stem them up to do fine, & con govt. elected
leaders. I've seen just how everyone "jumps up & minds" real rich bozos as
a child. Real artificial to a child's mind! Kids arn't rayed mentally, fans.
Mr. Shaver's data explaines fully.

ALTERNATIVE 3...Avon Books, 959 Eighth Ave.,
New York, NY 10019 $2.25 by Leslie Watkins...

Alternative 3 would make a great movie...and
that's its main problem. Originally broadcast on
April 1st as a British tv documentary, Alt3 is just
too wild a tale for some people to swallow. Some
even compare it to the famous Orson Welles Hallo-
ween radio broadcast of 1938. And not all of these
skeptics are perpetual "debunkers". For example:
Riley Crabb, successor to Meade Layne's Borderland
Sciences Research Foundation and editor of the
well-known journal, Round Robin, explained it to
your humble editor this way:

"We have a copy of Leslie Watkins' fanciful
"Alt3" here. To your editor, it's an interesting
piece of science fiction. True, Watkins bases his
tale on factual quotes from the daily newspapers,
but the wild extrapolations are nothing but fiction as far as I am concerned...such as the claim
of a joint Russian-American base on Mars. For me
to believe that Watkins will have to present more
solid evidence than his "interviews" with scientists
and government officials no one ever heard of."

NOTES!

But, like other "wild tales" throughout history,
there is something about the book that keeps echo-
ing in the back of peoples' minds ...they just
can't toss if off, regardless of the fact that
they know there isn't really an American astro-
naut named Bob Grodin, as the book claims. It was
one of these people who finally prodded your lazy
editor into reading Alt3 in the first place: Henry
Steele. He sent me my copy, he had an extra, as
they are darn hard to come by. Ever seen it in
your local bookstore? Then I sent my copy to Bill
Bliss. Seems it's one way to get it circulated

Evidently, the book had been banned in the USA
for a time, as well as the tv documentary. I don't
think the tv documentary has hit USA airwaves to
this date. I have tried to contact the author,
Watkins by mail...but no reply. Even told him we
were going to run this issue and would he mind
saying something (anything) to you readers...si-
lence. This negative result seems to be common.
It also happened to Mike Cohen, who wrote an article
for Beyond Reality Mag on Alt3. Is there a Leslie
Watkins? Well, even if there isn't we're going a-
head with this special issue.

We have two choices to make here: either Watkins
wove a fanciful story out of real and unexplainable
(at least for now) news stories OR: he tried to reveal something of real importance to us in slightly
fictionalized form.

Here is the story in a nutshell: during the
mid 1970's, a British news team began a story on
the so-called "brain drain" to find out why so many
top-notch scientists were leaving the country to
find work in other lands. What they found was that
many of the departed scientists had simply vanished,
with clever "covers" fabricated to throw suspecting families and friends off the track. Where were
these people going?

At any rate, the book unwinds a story that e-
ventually uncovers a plot by the super powers (the
USA and USSR) to establish a base on Mars for the
best human minds to flourish. To build these pro-

digious "new Territories" they kidnapped (and still
do, according to Watkins) myriads of John Does from
Anywhere USA as slaves to do their dirty work.
Tagged as "designated movers" by the perpetra-
tors of Alt3, these victims have their minds
mutilated or lobotomised so that they could care
less what they do. Not only slaves and scientists
are hijacked: plants and animals are also in big
demand to repopulate the Martian surface.

But why go to all this trouble and expense,
huge expense? Why not be satisfied simply to
rule over planet earth? The book makes it perfectly clear why: earth is doomed...and the super powers know it. As early as 1958, the powers
knew that our ozone layer was sinking fast. Weather patterns were and are changing radically.
The greenhouse effect would make life on earth
unlivable. Hence the Alt3 plan: rescue the
crem de la crem and set up shop somewhere else..
only under stringent rules.

In Mike Cohen's article on Alt3, he tries to
show that space travel has been in the hands of the
SP's for some time. Other sources have claimed
this to be the case as well...going all the way
back to those Nazi flying saucer rumors we have
heard so much about lately.

Watkins' claim is that in 1962 the USA first
landed a controlled space probe on Mars. The
Martian landscape, once uninhabitable by us, was
made bearable and livable by the dropping of an a-
tomic bomb, which released the latent oxygen atoms
from the soil:::::now, waitaminute! you're thinking.
Isn't this getting a bit far fetched? Not in the
least. Mike sent us a copy of an article from the
Nov/Dec. 1980 issue of Science Digest that echoes
Alt3. It is called "Preparing Mars for Life".

Right off the bat, the article asks us "Will
we use microbes or H-bombs to change the eco-sys-
tems of planets, so that we may one day be able to
inhabit them?" And of course you know the answer
is going to be yes. At least, according to alleged
"terraform researcher" James Oberg...doesn't that
name sound familiar??? To continue: "Nuclear bombs
dropped from orbit into the huge, but dormant,
Martian volcanoes could prompt eruptions that
would presumably fill its rosy-colored sky with
gases such as carbon-dioxide and water vapor..."
Is this deja vu or what? Did Oberg know of
Watkins, or vice-versa?

One thing is a fact: just about everything
that is detailed in the book Alt3 is possible
within our present technology. The events that
are going to happen to earth in regard to the
threat of pollution seem imminent. If anyone
thinks   for a minute we aren't in big trouble
in the weather department (ozone/greenhouse effect)
just look through some of the clips in this ish...
its only a small sampling. It is a known fact that
the USA government has instigated its own program
of weather modification in an attempt to turn
things around. A last ditch attempt?

The most frightening aspect of the whole
scenario is the state of the art of mind control
the SP's have attained since WWII. The book is
heavy with grisley details like "hot jobs" (that's
when they scramble your brains with microwaves
like some omlete; and somnambolistic suicides for
those who would get in the way of Alt3. Again,
newsclips in this issue are only a minor sample
of what is in our files on the subject.

There are still some nagging questions to be answered, however. For instance: if Alt3 is true, then what are the super powers up to in their constant quarelling, their "arms race", their stupid statements and actions? Is it all a big con game? Are the Breznevs and Reagans simply figureheads to make us feel like business is going along as usual? If so, it will have been one of the most elaborate scams of all time, with the world population as the poor mark. What a sting!

Watkins reveals that there is a counter plot to destroy (or at least delay indefinitely) plans for Alt3. Like the IRA, PLO, SLA...ie. the Underground. If their purpose is to keep secret space projects from happening they might be getting positive results. I just heard over the radio today that the space shuttle is over 2 years behind schedule for every imaginable reason. Alot of satellites have been disappearing lately as well, and its making someone very upset. The work of the Underground... or just our imaginations?

In a zine as small as this one, it is impossible to go into that much detail on Alt3. If anything, this is just an addendum to the book. If you haven't read it, try to find a copy...write to the publisher. Then decide for yourself. We have reprinted some excerpts from the book on certain pages with news clips to help show the relationship between the clips and Alt3.

Now to other business!

We have a new contributor in this issue: a Dansk (that's Danish to you!) illustrator, writer, traveller and hopeful film maker, Max Fyfield. While on a tour of the USA, Max found a copy of Shavertron in New York, and subbed as soon as he got back to Denmark. Max has his own version of Alt3 to discuss in "It Was Top Secret"...we might call this article "The Other Side of Alt3". We also appreciate his expertise in the illustrations that appear in this issue.

We are also announcing that foreign sub prices went up starting with this issue. USA postal rates are making our "worldwide sub drive" very difficult.

Remember new subscribers: when making out your check or money order, please write it out to the publisher: Richard Toronto, not to the zine. California red tape and such make this the case.

See you next issue...in the meantime, write a letter to the editor...

MEMBER:

THE HOLLOW EARTH RESEARCH ASSOCIATION

Read THE HOLLOW HASSLE- PO Box 255, Santa Fe, New Mexico 87501 USA;;; Journal of THERA.

8-29-80   19

Lance Rails At 'Powercrats'

Calhoun, Ga.

Bert Lance says he is working on a book that will expose the workings of what he calls "powercrats" — government agents who he said use their power to ruin people's lives.

"They need to be identified," the former U.S. budget director said in an interview yesterday in the Atlanta Constitution. "They need to be pointed out. They need to be talked about. They need to be sued. They need to be fired — whatever it takes to stop them. And I'm gonna try to do that."

Lance charged that the "powercrats ... put things together...to try to bring about the results they want to see brought about — without regard to the truth, without regard for what is right, a regard only for what suits their purposes.

"They can do anything they want to, without ultimately having to face up to whether they've been right or wrong."

He said "powercrats" were instrumental in pushing the investigation that led to his resignation as President Carter's budget chief in September 1977, then to the indictment of him and three of his friends on charges of bank fraud and bank fraud conspiracy.

Lance eventually was acquitted on all counts.

"I've seen it. I've seen the way they do things, their tactics," said Lance, who now is a financial consultant with an office near his hometown of Calhoun.

"There are those in the Justice Department and in other governmental agencies who, in their misappropriation of power, will do anything to make sure that this power never leaves them," he said.

Associated Press

Teenage Girls Kidnaped

Zamboanga City, Philippines 2-13-80

Eleven teenage girls have been kidnapped recently in the southern Philippines, according to authorities.

Police said Monday they still had not received ransom demands for six of the girls, seized in an eight-day period in late January and early February.

Associated Press

3

a Mute Point

(And a Strange Tale)

The following letter was received by Tom Adams at the Project Stigma offices last year. It is a very strange letter, which is why it is printed herewith. It may have a connection with the Alt3 puzzle. We thank Tom for permission to reprint it...anyone who is interested in the subject of cattle and other animal mutilations should sub to Stigmata, the best on-going zine on the subject in this country...PO Box 1094, Paris, Texas 75460.

The Letter:

My interest in reading Stigmata was to see whether there was a rationale for explaining "slow motion mutilation of humans". What I have in mind is the existence and use of highly sophisticated equipment which can surveill a human...ie. see and overhear conversations (even when cloistered within the walls of otherwise optically opaque confines) and secondly to debilitate him clinically. Not knowing all of the gory details of mutes, I thought perhaps that such equipment was responsible as part of a training program to prepare personnel to use such hypothesized equipment. Having now read Stigmata, I can offer a scenario that embraces both issues.

Before we get into the issue, you will see that I am simplifying the explanation of the source of mutes but at the expense of embracing a far more insidious and more insoluble problem.

To start things off, let us consider first a model problem. I have in mind "The Prisoner", a tv series dealing largely with a 1984-type society. Frequently, in this Psycho-sci fi story, scenes are shown of surveillance-headquarters. Personnel are shown who man equipment used in surveillance. On occasion, such personnel are called upon to zoom in on a person, who may be sleeping at the time, and in some way bother, annoy, or do something else unethical. The question posed is-- what sort of training do such staff members undergo and what sort of ancillary exercises are necessary to maintain skills, proficiency, etc? Also, just what makes such a person tick?

And now a short step into the real world-- maybe:

(a) Refer to Peter Watson's book, "War On The Mind" (Basic Books, 1978, p.242). Chapter 12 deals with atrocity research. With regard to ex-service men who had committed atrocities in Vietnam: "All the men went to psychiatrists in order to confess their part in atrocities in the Vietnam War...The incidents reported ranged from mistreating prisoners to mutilating the bodies of dead Vietnamese-- cutting off ears, genitals and breasts." Watson continues, "These studies suggest that although the conditions of war may make anyone a potential mass murderer, some men are more prone to kill indiscriminatly than others."

(b) Two books of note have surfaced. The first is "Techno Spies" by Ford Rowan (Putnam) and SPOOKS-THE HAUNTING OF AMERICA by Jim Hougan (Morrow). The latter reference has nothing to do with ghosts. Techno Spies deals with the types of government personel who fancy themselves to be super patriots who can do no wrong and are the custodians of our system. They seek ways to protect the system from threats as they perceive them. In part, this can have translated into the Animal House mentality, typified by the quote of one George White in John Marks' book on CIA Mind Control studies (The Search For the Manchurian Candidate)-- namely, 'Where else could a red-blooded American boy lie, cheat, steal, rape and pillage with the sanction and blessing of the All-Highest?" (p.101). Hougan's book illustrates further the types of personnel who are trained in a Techno-spy background and leave the govt. service for other sectors.

(c) Suppose there exists in combination: surveillance headquarters, maybe a prototype of the one that we taxpayers funded which was lost in Iran, and a class of satellites which are similar to or are advanced forms of SALT II verifiers. Suppose further that these satellites can "see" with superfocused EMR (note: electro-magnetic radiation) of wavelength much longer than 7,000 Angstrom units, say more like the order of centimeters. Then it follows that individuals could be "seen" and also could endure all the rights and privileges of individuals who are illuminated (call them "lumes") with long wave-length EMR. To find out the consequences of illumination with long-wavelength EMR, consult Paul Brodeur's book, "The Zapping of America", (W.W. Norton, 1977). Another good reference is the "Bibliography of Reported Biological Phenomena" and "Clinical Manifestations Attributed to Microwave and Radio-Frequency Radiation" by Zorach R. Glaser re: NTIS-AD-750-271. Thus, lumes could be seen remotely and would endure in slow-motion the various types of maladies attributable to illumination of this sort... (for whatever reason).

(d) Finally, if personel staffed such hypothetical equipment, the question is-- what sort of people would they be and further, what sort of additional training would they require? Part of the answer resides in "War On The Mind". They would have to be savage types who have little regard for life and could easily perpetrate such deeds, particularly, in the name of meeting the best needs of the country. Such patriots are re-

4

cruited from the characters written about by Hougan and Rowan. And they need just a touch of the Mafia-type view of the value of life.

Now-- where does the issue of mutes fit into all of this? Put yourself in the shoes of a psychologist-consultant who must decide on ways to keep skills at a high level. He is dealing with personnel who are on mundane 8-hour shifts. These people are savages who must slowly peck away at a person in methodical fashion. Savagery must be maintained...ferocity must be intensified sporadically. Under such circumstances it seems reasonable that mutilation of animals would be ordered much as has been described in Stigmata 4. The description of the mutilation (last paragraph on p. 9) ie. the bull sans rectum and sex organs, provides a technician a brief respite while in the act of also committing this very same activity on some tax-paying lume perhaps during a five-year period while the lume and his many diagnosticians witness the transformation from some incipient condition to a full-blown case of cancer of the colon or incontinence or impotence, etc.

Those who are engaged in slowly destroying a lume's eyesight would be revitalized by frequent rapid mutilations which involves removing eyes from the sockets of a cow or bull. The act of mutilating an animal permits the perpetrator to cope with the staleness that otherwise would arise and furnishes an outlet for the technician to see in moments an accomplishment that he otherwise is charged with synthesizing over a period of a long time on an unsuspecting lume.

So why do it the way it is done ...ie. risk being caught or having one's helicopter shot down? The only answer here is, that to have any value, the act must be committed under some uncertainty.
                                        (Name Withheld)
                                        Eastern USA

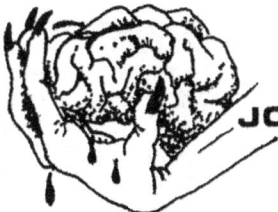

JONESTOWN LINK TO ALT 3?

Was there more to the Jonestown tragedy than most of us knew of? Your humble editor taped the following news report from television around July 31, 1980.

No follow-up stories were noticable, and readers will note that NO mention of the CIA, drugs or mind control was included in the newspaper article that appeared one day after the taped tv news spot. Wot hoppened? More slaves for Alt3? It would seem that an $8 million suit against the USA government isn't such big news after all...

" There are people who believe the entire story of what happened at Jonestown has never been told. One of those persons is San Francisco attorney, Marvin Lewis.

In filing an $8 million wrongful death suit on behalf of the Leo Ryan and Don Harris families, attorney Lewis says the US government knew there was danger in going to Jonestown, but it failed to warn the congressman.

Lewis says the CIA was using the followers of Jim Jones as guinea pigs to experiment with mind control drugs.

Lewis: "The inference is that it could have been possible, and I won't say that it was, that some deal was made between the CIA and Jones that these drugs were used on people who were taken into this colony at Jonestown, and experiments made from that time."

Lewis is still pushing for a Congressional investigation of Jonestown. In San Francisco, David Louie, Channel 7 News Scene."

The Kampiles Affair

Friendly skies full of eyes

By William Hines
Chicago Sun-Times

WASHINGTON — Although the Pentagon's space program is top secret, enough can be inferred from basic laws of nature and from the widely trumpeted accomplishments of civilian satellites to derive a pretty fair idea of the powers—and limitations of "spies in the sky."

The first thing to understand about intelligence gathering from space is that the technology that makes it possible is both rich and mature.

Development has been under way for more than 20 years, and in this period the military has spent more money on space projects than the National Aeronautics and Space Administration has spent on all its manned exploits, including the 1969-72 conquest of the moon.

The second thing to understand is — to paraphrase a golden oldie — "anything NASA can do the Pentagon can do better." NASA avowedly limits the sharpness of its satellites' vision out of respect for other nations' privacy. This is something the military doesn't have to worry about.

The third thing is that the military program is a continuing effort — slower of late than that of the Russians, to be sure, but still moving at a respectable pace. Up to now, the armed services have sent more payloads into orbit than NASA has. (Up to 1978 about 400 of the 700 satellites launched were defense-oriented.)

In 1964 NASA was sending back high-resolution stills in "real time" — that is, instantaneously — from spacecraft diving down to destruction on the moon, and by the '70s was using live TV movies as part of the command and control system of Project Apollo. High-speed film emulsions and instant-development still and motion picture systems also came out of the space effort, mainly from the military side.

Guyana Death Suits Seek $8 Million
8/1/80

The survivors of two of the five persons who were fatally shot at the Port Kaituma airstrip near the Peoples Temple compound at Jonestown, Guyana, in 1978 sued the U.S. government in federal court yesterday for a total of $8 million.

The family of Congressman Leo Ryan asked $3 million in general damages and $1481 in funeral expenses.

The survivors of television cameraman Don Harris asked for $5 million in damages.

Both suits, filed by attorney Marvin E. Lewis, said the government denied wrongful death benefits claims filed by the survivors earlier.

The suit claims that the Department of State "knew of the extreme risk and danger involved" in Jonestown but failed to advise Ryan when he said he planned to go there to investigate reports of mistreatment of U.S. citizens at the Temple settlement.

The airstrip shootings by Temple members preceded a mass murder and suicide of 911 followers of the cult.

Retrospeck:

BY RALPH HOLLAND

The following article is reprinted from the now de-
funct zine called WONDER (Summer, 1951). It has
been supplied to us by a long-standing (maybe some
day he'll sit down) friend and fan of the late Rich
Shaver...Lucius Farish. It will be presented in installments for the benefit of those readers who are
not totally familiar with the famous Shaver Mystery.
Thanks, Lou!

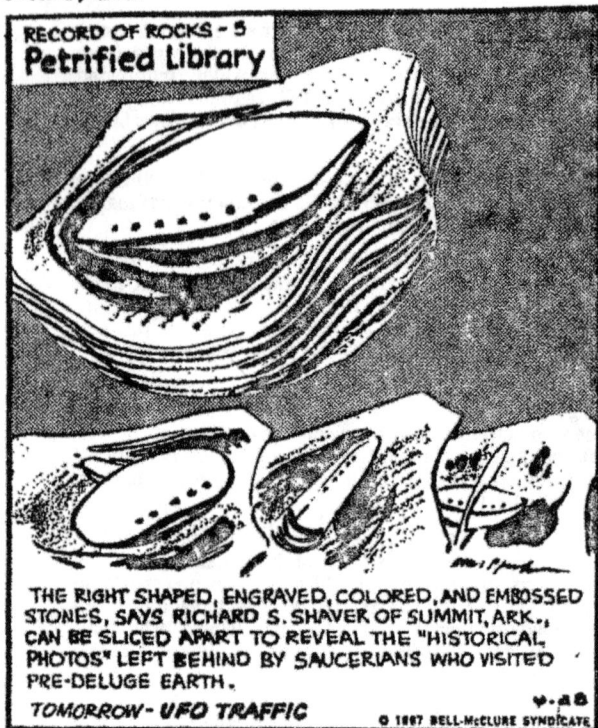

RECORD OF ROCKS - 5
Petrified Library

THE RIGHT SHAPED, ENGRAVED, COLORED, AND EMBOSSED
STONES, SAYS RICHARD S. SHAVER OF SUMMIT, ARK.,
CAN BE SLICED APART TO REVEAL THE "HISTORICAL
PHOTOS" LEFT BEHIND BY SAUCERIANS WHO VISITED
PRE-DELUGE EARTH.
TOMORROW- UFO TRAFFIC
© 1967 BELL-McCLURE SYNDICATE

Foreword:

Late in 1944, Richard S. Shaver wrote what later
became known as the "Shaver Alphabet", a list of the
meanings of sounds used in speaking. This, he said,
was "Mantong", the language of the ancient "Elder
Race" who inhabited this planet long before the present human race appeared, and the basis of all spoken languages in the world today. By its use the
correct meaning of many words could be found. It applied to any language but the more ancient the tongue
the better it would respond to analysis by Mantong.

Raymond A. Palmer, who was then editor of AMAZING
STORIES became enthused about the "Alphabet" and published it. The reader response was quick and volumi-
nous. Some challenged his claim that he had secured
the information from the telepathic "thought Record"
tapes of this ancient people. Others verified the
fact that Mantong did correctly interpret almost any
word in any language, and demanded more details of
the Elder Race. The result was a series of stories
which both Shaver and Palmer claimed were either
based on some actual fact or were typical descriptions which were written up in fictionalized style.
The subject was too unbelievable to be presented in
any other manner they said.

The readers became sharply divided into two war-
ring camps. On one side were the supporters of Shaver
and Palmer. On the other were the psuedo-scientists

and the members of many cults, "ists" and "isms" to
all of whom Shaver's claims were   the rankest heresy. The owners finally gave way to the latter groups.
The Shaver Mystery was banned from all of the Ziff-
Davis chain of magazines and a short time later, editor Palmer left to manage his own chain. (Editor's
note- The details of the Ziff chain's banning of
RSS' stories is detailed in issue 4 of Shavertron).

Plans were made by both Shaver and Palmer to
handle the Shaver Mystery on a factual basis for the
benefit of those who were trying seriously to evaluate it. Shaver announced his intention of publishing a series of non-fiction books.

Palmer made plans to handle it on a non-fiction
basis in FATE magazine. The plans of both were
brought to naught by a series of misfortunes so
strange that many of Shaver's followers are convinced that some sinister unseen influence does not intend to let the facts be made public.

Shaver himself is, of course, the logical person
to sift the fact from the fiction in his stories.
However, he is clearly unable to do so at the present
time. Therefore, I am attempting to do the job temporarily in order to answer numerous inquiries from my
friends. The material has been taken from Shaver's
stories, and from other articles and material to which
he has given at least tacit approval by publishing it
in the Shaver Mystery Magazine. In so far as I was
able, I attempted to omit any expression of personal
opinion or belief in all details. R.M.H.
(To Be Continued) ...

IT WAS TOP SECRET!

by MAX FYFIELD

According to calculations and common sense it is too late to save all mankind! A few members of the SUPER POWERS have also discovered this, and therefore are now working on a plan to preserve a tiny nucleus of HUMAN SURVIVORS. It is TOP SECRET-- it is ALTERNATIVE 3-- but someone "talked", so now we can say it was top secret!

There is no reason to doubt the authenticity of the book. It all checks with facts, the same facts I have studied for over 10 years. The major world-problems are all discussed in a serious manner. However, the names of the various government officials may have been changed, but is that so strange? The book was banned for 2 years in the USA-- why ban fiction?

The way the book presents the world problems coincides exactly with the results of research done during the last 15 years by serious groups like the Club of Rome. Some years ago it was suggested that clean air would save mankind! (No mention of religion). Nuclear bombs should punch holes in the envelope of carbon dioxide surrounding Earth, all cars should be made illegal, etc.-- that was ALTERNATIVE 1 -- but it was rejected, too risky to blast a hole in the ozone layer.

Then someone came up with ALTERNATIVE 2 which was to go UNDERGROUND. (Not a bad idea, really, if only they had known that the earth is hollow). This was also rejected, though both TUNNELS and CITIES were mentioned, it was crazy and unrealistic, they said, who would want to live like a human mole? (Editor note: Max hasn't yet heard of the half-dozen or so cities under govt. and CIA rule that are at least 5 to 6 miles under such large USA cities as Philadelphia...yes, real live cities with traffic lights even! Your humble editor has received this info from two separate sources...one whose father was actually in the CIA and living in an underground city!)

At last the few top men of the Super Powers (who work well together behind the scene) came up with Alternative3, which could be called Operation Noah's Ark. They know now that the only way to survive (at the very last) is to get off the ground. Perhaps 1994 will be that last year? (If we are allowed to mention dates in this zine?) Who, then, decides which people shall be evacuated in the "arks"? These anonymous men have assumed the right to decide who shall live and who shall die. First the top men themselves will go (of course), then for the rest of the small nucleus, computors will decide who goes with them to Mars. Yes, Mars has been chosen, just take off at the right time, and you can't miss it. By the way, I wonder if the Martians know about this?

There is one thing the Earth Super Powers have overlooked: The existence and reality of the Space People...(yet they ought to know). There is a positive group of Space People who have planned their ownversion of Alternative 3. They come from Jupiter, Venus and Mars (so perhaps they do know), they will contact Earth People from every walk of life, everyone will get their chance-- yet, not all will accept. But those who do (144,000?) will be "the cream of

Strange 'Roads' in New Mars Pictures

Pasadena 6-25-76 SF. Chronicle

Mars appears to be crisscrossed by a number of streak-like roads, space scientists announced yesterday after studying pictures from the Viking I spacecraft.

"This is a most strange feature," said Harold Masursky, Jet Propulsion Laboratory scientist in charge of Viking's July 4 landing in search of life on the Mars surface.

"We often see things in these pictures and we say that looks like so-and-so that we have seen on earth ... and this looks like so-and-so that we see in aerial photographs but they all turn out to be roads."

The puzzled Masursky told a press conference: "We don't have the vaguest notion what this picture is because roads seem to be a little extreme."

He added: "We tried to determine whether these were single or double lane freeways but the resolution isn't good enough."

Masursky said the road-like streets on Mars were interrupted in places by lava flow from volcanic craters.

Pointing out one example of where lava had slowed over one of the streets, he said to laughter from the press corps: "So it's not only a road but a very old road."

Reuters

the crop" to start the next era...the Era of Aquarius. This will be Operation Lift (Operation Rapture), how many of us will be part of the "cream"? Perhaps we have decided by the way we live our everyday lives.

Then comes the Tribulation (1987-1994)?, Armageddon and the Return of Christ in a Space Ship (what else did you expect me to say?) It will be interesting to see how these Earthly Operations will coincide with the Space People's...will the Earth's Super Powers get to Mars before the Space People? Silly question? Of course, especially to us who know that there is life on other worlds.

In the meantime, I am working on scripts for the trilogy: "Free of the Past", "The Latter Days" and "The Mighty Millennium". These films will show how a man (Max Fyfield) and a woman (Gina Lollo) live through itall, from 1951 to 2000, and then some. The idea is to show all future happen-7gs as realistic as possible, especially how and why some people will be "lifted" by flying saucers and later returned to "The New Earth" to begin a new life in The Mighty Millennium!!!

I am only a writer yet, but the producers of Star Wars have asked to read more of my work (after I had sent them my script "The Underground--Top Secret") they think I have an "extraordinary and inventive imagination"-- so perhaps the trilogy will be a more serious follow up to the Star War series! Perhaps the word "war" will be eliminated -- perhaps Richard Toronto will go into film work again and work with me on these films? How about it, Rich?

LETTERS

Dear Rich,

I found Shavertron extremely interesting and dealing with matters one should know. Interesting of the mentioning of the Ashtar lot...(Ashcan). I know well of him. He really got the fertilizer moving, apparently too much and his own people of Venus threw him out as he was advocating mind control and getting their world into a war. The Ashtar group I have met up here (Ontario) years ago. Once they find out who you are and what you're into, lo and behold they introduce you to Deros. I had a live one waiting for me when I got home from their meeting. Within a few days I was almost killed by them. That is how I knew what Shaver was talking about.

Deros were originally prisoners sent to the caverns for going against the lord of light or positive people who ruled. Teutonic myths tell of this and the head Dero in Gorm's expeditions. Then in the lost Books of the Bible of the Abandonderos who Christ freed against Satan's will. Strange indeed as to why? To test mankind apparently.

Deros are in fact very big cowards when confronted, but one must not allow the fact of their overblown mech mind controls get to them, for fear of them is the device they use to gain control. Once you understand them, then you can battle them.

But what is the source of the Deros power besides mech devices? Apparently it goes beyond this planet and right through Alternative 3, to Saturn and then to Algol where Galactic versions reign... but not too much longer. It is through them that the earth is ruled now, and has caused previous civilizations here and elsewhere to fall. But there is now a large Alt3 underground to battle this, and soon it will show its hand to give man a chance to think free and revolt against these alien invaders.

Of the book on the Alt3 scenario...there is much in it, but also much left out. The earth has had space flight for ages, this is known, even NASA has had saucers for the last 37 years. Remember they confiscated Tesla's saucer which was test-flown to the moon and back, also Marconi's scientists in Brazil who have saucers, but are part of the freedom movement against Alt3.

Not all scientists and people who disappeared in that book went to Alt3, but to the underground too. I myself and others know of these people as does Dr. Raymond Bernard, who fled to the underground. This, too, is where the Nazi ufos come in, as part of the underground against Alt3.

Mars is named in the book as the Alt3 base, but that's BULL...Mars itself is against Alt3. The base is on Saturn. I have had dealing with them and they are lethal. Having been to many of these places in the past, I found out a great deal and have been approached by Alt3 agents to shut up. But they were warded off by theunderground.

P.S.: Recently, last week 70 top Russian officials including the Admiral of the fleet were killed. They were agents of Alt3. Each day in the papers and tv news many new things are brought to light, such as the plane accident in which many executives were killed which all fit into the little war that is going on between inner earth and the underground against Alt3 set-up by the Galactic deros, as one could call them.

Man has often during the ages revolted against the Deros who live on the surface too, but they cry discrimination and pass laws to protect them. Take the Second World War...it was a war with the Deros and Vulcan himself returned to take them on. And now wars on them under the earth as they clear them out of this realm, and to form a free world working with the other positive Teros.

Ivan Boyes

Dear Rich,

I always look forward to reading the letters section of S, it helps promote the interest when readers state their views and experiences.

Henry Steele seems quite a character, but I don't laugh at his claims (for I have had some strange things happen to me also on this line. I admire his guts in telling the world. Or should I say trying to?

An interesting book came into my possession recently called "The Illuminoids" (a 1978 paperback by Neal Wilgus...New English Library). There is even a mention of Palmer and Shaver in there. Its on the Secret Society the Illuminati and possible connections with beings originating from Sirius, etc. mentioning in chronological form, ufos, political assasinations etc. I am also proud to own now "The Secret World" by Palmer and Shaver.

I now think that the red race Indians were the ones who went underground. Indians: In Dions? (Editor note: see Ray's Mantong article, last ish). Didy they come from Mars? George Hunt Williamson in his book "Road In The Sky" hints that some links of cultures to Mars on pottery etc. seem to indicate this is so.

With your permission, in a future article I hope to show that projection mech are still at work below us. The ghosts persons are observing now are really peculiar, many accidents have been caused, or nearly so, by phantom furniture vans and lorrys (trucks) around England. A hum has been driving people to suicide, it all makes sense when looked at from the sub-mech angle.

Not only this, some of these weird things fall along straight lines, possibly leys, and after the Forest of Dean episode, I'm wondering if the leys are being utilised by unknown forces.

All the Best,
Ray Archer
England

R-- Ray is doing a great job of keeping us informed of British goings-on, and we hope to be pubbing more of his intriguing articles in the months to come. We are doubly grateful to Ray for sending the original Alt3 ITV television broadcast on tape. Almost as good as seeing it first hand. To those who never did see it, it follows the book almost to a "T".

8

Dear Richard,

I am sorry that it's been so long since I last wrote, but I have been having problems. In the pst 5-6 weeks my angina problem took a turn for the worse and got to the point I couldn't do much of anything without chest pain. Two weeks ago it became real bad and I had to enter the hospital, where I am now. I need a bypass operation so that will lay me up a couple more weeks here.

I have not been able to keep up with anything along the hollow earth line, even my mail. I would appreciate it if you would let some of the fans know that I just have not been able to keep up with all their letters. It will take time, but I will get around to ansering them.

The booklet out from Bruce Walton is about the best thing I have seen in the past few years... (B. Walton, 2880 N. 840 E., Provo, Utah 84601). That David Lewis book, "The Incredible Cities of Inner Earth" just strikes me as a wild yarn like most of Lewis' stuff. He offers no proof whatsoever.

Been trying to locate Robert Charroux's book, "Agharta and Shamballa", but without luck. This may have been published in England.

Best Wishes,
Frank Brownley
29 McCall Rd.
Rochester, NY
14615

R-- The strongest of wishes for your speedy recovery are sent to you from Shavertron, Frank. And we are sure that each SM fan reading S feels the same! Get well soon! We miss your letters.

Dear Mr Toronto,

I must comment on something I read in issue number 6 of your zine. You published a news clip about the town of Xucurus, which you say it is near Buenos Aires...please be advised that no such town exists in Argentina, because the name is Portugese. This town, if it exists, must be at the neighboring country of Brazil. Also, the name of the man who dreamed he would find a treasure if he went to a determined spot, Mr. Cordeiro, is typically Brazilian.

Another important comment: there was an American, Dr. Walter Russell, who had a divine revelation but concerning science instead of religion. This man wrote about his revelations on a series of books-- available from the University of Science and Philosophy, Swannanoa Palace, Waynesboro, VA.-- and several of his statements are closely aligned with those of Richard Shaver in "I Remember Lemuria". It would be interesting to those studying the scientific side of the Shaver Mystery if they purchase and study Walter Russell's books, since he died in 1963, his wife has been carrying on his work.

Sincerely Yours,
Jorge Resines
Buenos Aires

R-- Thanks, Jorge, for the correction of that newsclip we ran in issue 6...and if you ever find any other discrepancies in our info that comes from South America, please feel free to let us know...we could use a correspondent from the Southern hemisphere.

Dear Rich,

Our special Shaver issue is shaping up quite well. We have a good article by Jim Pobst, and two separate articles on Hidden Worlds and one on the Shaver Mystery Magazine. The official obit from Lucius, and some evaluations and perhaps a checklist of his stories. I don't think it would be possible to do an index of his articles or Shaver/related articles.

Since you are the only one doing a Shaver zine at this time, I wonder if you would care to submit something? Jim Pobst is mainly covering his fiction, so perhaps something detailing the history of the Mystery, or how you came to be involved with it or the creation of Shavertron would be of interest.

I have had many inquiries about the project since we started. The interest seems quite widespread. I am a little unsure how many copies to run off. I should run off a few more than I regularly do. I don't want to run off too few and have some super rare item overnight. I want the edition to be large enough that they will be easily available to interested parties, yet I dont want to end up holding copies for 20 years either. Odd position. The interest in Dick Shaver is more than I had anticipated.

Well, all the best in 1981, for the continued success of Shavertron!

David Bates
P.O.Box 161
Putnam, Conn.
06260

R--Haven't heard from David since I sent him the ms. he requested...although it is one that he was not exactly expecting: "Issac Newton Vail and the Shaver Mystery." Maybe he got it too late! I procrastinated...

Shavertron is pubbed quarterly @ $6 per year. Address all mail to 309 Coghlan St., Vallejo, CA. 94590, USA. All unsolicited mss. will be handled with utmost care, but we cannot be responsible if something goes awry...Deromania. Foreign subs cost $12 in American funds.

Greenhouse Effect Can Be Checked

Napa Register
12/5/80

MOUNTAIN VIEW (UPI) — Space agency scientists have used data from the Pioneer Venus orbiter to develop a method of measuring the deadly greenhouse effect threatening Earth.

By humans' burning of coal, wood and other fossil fuels, carbon dioxide collects in the earth's atmosphere to produce a greenhouse effect causing the atmosphere to retain ever-increasing amounts of heat.

If, with growing population, carbon dioxide in the atmosphere doubled in the next 50 years, as estimated by some, earth's temperatures would be boosted 3 to 7 degrees. That could be enough to turn vast areas such as the northern United States, into drought areas and to melt enough polar ice to flood coastal areas worldwide.

Dr. James Pollack of the National Aeronautics and Space Administration said Thursday that Earth's greenhouse problem may now be compared to a very strong greenhouse effect on Venus, a searing planet of about the same size.

Because of Venus' thick atmosphere, which is 96 percent carbon dioxide, the temperature in the upper atmosphere of minus-300 degrees rockets at the surface to 900 degrees, hot enough to melt zinc.

The reason, Pollack said, is that sunlight penetrates the atmosphere faster than heat, with longer wave lengths, can escape. As a result, heat simply builds up.

The Venusian situation is extreme compared with earth's, whose atmosphere now contains only .03 percent carbon dioxide, but Pollack said Venus now provides a model showing how greenhouse effects work on a gigantic scale.

With lessons from Venus, he said, scientists will be able with reasonable accuracy to calculate the future effects of specific amounts of carbon dioxide in earth's atmosphere on surface temperatures. Until now, such calculations have been vague, as have estimates of the actual amount of the gas retained.

Pollack's announcement was made at a meeting of top space scientists sponsored by NASA at its Ames Research Center, a meeting also confronted with Venusian data seeming to contradict some previous ideas about how the solar system was formed.

It had been thought, for example, that since terrestrial planets were formed by the same materials, their relative amounts of rare gasses would be roughly the same. Unexpectedly, 700 times as much argon as krypton was found on Venus, while the ratio on earth is only 30.

Dr. Tom Donahue of the University of Michigan said this means basic notions about planet formation have "something wrong with them."

The Pioneer Venus orbiter reached Venus Dec. 4, 1978, dropped four probes into the atmosphere and began a circling of the planet that will continue until 1992. So far, it has returned 40 billion data bits.

With the data, earth scientists now have an explanation for the atmosphere's remarkable circulation. Clouds move in zones from east to west so fast that they circle the planet at the equator in four days while the planet itself takes 243 days to rotate. Such a situation on earth would mean the stratosphere would circle earth in a half hour.

Summer's Heat and Drought Killed 1,265 And Cost Nation $20 Billion, Study Says

10/16/80

By a WALL STREET JOURNAL Staff Reporter

WASHINGTON — Last summer's blistering heat wave and drought claimed at least 1,265 lives and cost the nation nearly $20 billion, according to a government estimate given to Congress.

The heat-related death toll, mostly poor or elderly people living in homes without air conditioning, was seven times greater than normal.

The tally of fatalities and economic cost attributed to the scorching summer comes from statisticians at the National Oceanic and Atmospheric Administration. Officials said it was the first attempt of its kind to assess the impact of bad weather over a whole season.

The $20 billion cost estimate is an adding-machine total of the economic impact of several factors reported by federal agencies, private organizations and officials of 26 states hit by the heat wave and drought from June into September.

One major expense was an extra $1.3 billion spent for electricity, mainly to run air conditioners longer. Electricity use was 5.5% above the summer norm.

The estimate also includes damage to corn, soybean and spring wheat crops, plus weakened livestock and the loss of millions of chickens. The statisticians said prices for raw agricultural products rose 19% during July and August.

The heat wave buckled hundreds of miles of highways in the Midwest and softened asphalt roads in Texas and Arkansas. In Illinois alone, road damage totaled $100 million.

The heat caused an unusual surge in auto-repair costs, the report said.

The heat wave began in mid-June when temperatures topped 100 degrees Fahrenheit in Texas. By mid-July it had spread into the Ohio Valley and, by early September, much of the East. On July 13, three cities broke their maximum temperature records, with 107 degrees in Augusta, Ga.; 105 degrees in Atlanta and 108 degrees in Memphis. Temperatures in Dallas ran above 100 degrees each day from June 23 through Aug. 3.

Britain's Drought Threat — Worst in 200 Years

5/3/76

London

Britain is undergoing its worst drought in more than 200 years, attributed to a persistent change in Atlantic weather patterns.

Harvests are threatened after a year of phenomenally poor rainfall, and huge forested areas have become fire risks.

though the rest of Europe has been affected to some extent by a change in weather patterns, Britain is the worst hit.

The edge of the polar ice cap has receded after a number of mild winters, they say, and this has tended to shift the North Atlantic weather pattern northwards.

Volcanic Threat To Ozone Reported

Washington   7/19/80

A government geologist killed in the Mount St. Helens eruption said in a report he wrote early this year that explosive volcanoes may spew 20 to 40 times more ozone-destroying chlorine into the stratosphere than previously believed. His report was published yesterday in Science Magazine's July 25 issue.

The First Sahara Snowfall in Memory   2/19/79

Algiers

Snow fell in the Sahara desert yesterday for the first time in living memory.

Snow fell on Hassi R'Mel, Berriane and Laghuat and Ghardaia, in Southern Algeria.

A half-hour snowstorm in Ghardaia was so heavy that it stopped traffic. The snow melted a few hours later.

Agence France-Presse

10 Human Rights

1. It is your right to do anything as long as it does not hurt someone else.
2. It is your right to maintain your self-respect by answering honestly even if it does hurt someone else (as long as you are being assertive opposed to aggressive).
3. It is your right to be what you are without changing your ideas or behavior to satisfy someone else.
4. It is your right to strive for self-actualization.
5. It is your right to use your own judgment as to the need priorities of yourself and others, if you decide to accept any responsibility for another's problem.
6. It is your right not to be subjected to negativity.
7. It is your right to offer no excuses or justifications for your decisions or behavior.
8. It is your right not to care.
9. It is your right to be illogical.
10. It is your right to change your mind.

SHORT RIBS

WE HAVE PROVED CONCLUSIVELY...

THERE ARE NO INTELLIGENT FORMS OF LIFE ON THE PLANET EARTH.

HOW CAN YOU BE SO SURE WITHOUT A DEEP PROBE?

WE'VE BEEN MONITORING THEIR TELEVISION SHOWS.

from HIGH TIMES - DEC.75/JAN.76

Microwave Tapping Now in Use

Amidst speculation that the United States is developing psychic snooping potentials, CBS News recently reported on new electronic eavesdropping equipment capable of monitoring radio microwaves and rendering anti-wiretap laws obsolete.

The equipment is capable of picking conversations out of the air, and has been used to monitor all calls between an unnamed Latin American country and the United States as part of a narcotics investigation.

—P. J. Sampson

Extinct Mammals

Mexico City 7-28-76

Of the 100 species of mammals that have become extinct on earth during the last 2,000 years, 75 have disappeared within the last 200 years.

Associated Press

To get your copy of Alternative 3, send $3 (this includes postage in USA) to Avon Books, Mail Order Dept. 224 West 57th St., 2nd floor, New York, NY 10019.

PURE BLISS

W.G. Bliss

Anybody in the fixit trade gets scads of negative thinking. The late model is a lot of people under 23 years of age bring fixit jobs in and in a few minutes are talking about not fixing it, and fixing it would be too much trouble-- they actually say that-- for me. Somebody has gotten to their brainbox. Bibliography-- "Operation Mind Control" by Jerry Bohart. It is vital to keep up that good old fashioned crackpot image these days. A few simple excentricities usually foster that impression well.

I leave the shop look junky, and outback sunflowers have replaced most of the grass. Sandburrs had replaced a lot of the grass anyhoo. I drive a car with rust holes. I bore the heck out of customers with scads of technical details-- tell 'em everyone needs to know more these days. They dont want to know-- so they label my elucidations crackpot stuff and intellectual overkill-- fanaticism.

* * *

Just for the heckofit, I been telling ye clientele that I am the only rogphoto expert--but why bother nobody is interested because it has never been on the boob tube. Been telling a chosen few that I sure wish somebody else would take up an active interest in rogphoto-- I'm the only one left. And it likely would fade into obscurity eventually otherwise. Free course available here. It actually is the most potentially valuable research there ever was. Tremendous source of useful info. And naturally, ye establishment would glom onto it eventually.

* * *

Or why Shaver and I were gunshy about yakking about how technically valuable rock pix are and so the SECRET WORLD is almost totally barren of technical detail. We thought there should be a good market for just the art images. If Palmer hadn't messed up TSW, chances are good it would have swung on the art book market.

(Editor note: We've given over most of one entire issue to Bill to whomp up a special, technical edition of Shavertron. The only problem we'll face here is sufficient photo reproduction).

Mercury Pollution Perils Jakarta Bay

Jakarta 6-6-80

High mercury and heavy metal pollution threatens to turn the Bay of Jakarta into a new "Minamata case," the mercury poisoning incident in Japan's Kyushu Island 24 years ago that killed 800 persons, Indonesian

ecologists warned yesterday.

A non-governmental group led by scientist Meizar Syafei said recent surveys have "established without possible doubt" that the Bay of Jakarta has been polluted by mercury particles

beyond the acceptable level."

The situation is considered especially serious because 85 percent of seafood sold in Jakarta comes from the polluted bay.

United Press

CIA's Memo On ESP Spying

Mon., Mar. 12, 1979

★ San Francisco Chronicle

Washington

The CIA once looked into the possibility of using a team of ESP spies to scan the world for such intelligence targets as underground submarine pens, it was disclosed yesterday.

ESP or extrasensory perception is the ability of the mind to perceive things beyond the five senses.

CIA documents made public under the Freedom of Information Act indicated the agency also expressed interest in Nazi studies on ESP and even considered using dogs as ESP spies.

But the information, distributed by American Citizens for Honesty in Government, an affiliate of the Church of Scientology, failed to reveal whether the CIA ever got around to setting up an ESP espionage team.

A heavily censored April 8, 1952, memorandum said the CIA gave "some serious consideration" to subsidizing research into applying ESP "to matters of pure intelligence.

"If a number of individuals could be found in the U.S. who have a very high ESP capacity, these talented individuals could be assigned to intelligence problems," the note said.

The memo said the ESP spies could work on such problems as whether a nation "had a submarine pen at a given port or area."

A Jan. 31, 1952, memo described a CIA conference on the possible use of ESP. An "outstanding authority on ESP," whose name was censored, briefed officials at

the session.

The expert was quoted as saying researchers were "approaching a solution to the problem of how to control and direct this ESP capacity.

"He insisted that the knowledge on ESP at this point was far in advance of the basic knowledge that was held on atomic energy and atomic weapons before the first atom bomb was developed," the memo said.

A Feb. 7, 1952, memo said an undercover CIA agent contacted a scientist about the possibility of using dogs for an ESP espionage team.

But the scientist "disqualified himself and his department from any work on ESP perception in dogs, pointing out that they had not a great deal of specific experience with dogs as subjects."

The scientist, whose name was censored, advised the CIA official to look for "a research psychologist, strong in comparative animal psychology," and provided a list of potential candidates.

A Jan. 7, 1952, memo calls for a discussion about Soviet ESP experiments and "what the Nazis undertook to do," but gives no other detail about the other work.

The unidentified writer, who was apparently being considered as head of the CIA's ESP program, said he didn't want to become involved without a firm, long-term commitment.

The Church of Scientology, a controversial religious group that began in 1950, has been engaged in a running battle with the government.

Associated Press

Scientists draft plans to make Mars livable

But they warn it could take 10,000 years

Top U.S. scientists have come up with fantastic plans to make it possible for man to live on Mars. But there's one drawback — they say it will take at least 10,000 years.

According to a report drawn up by NASA scientists, there is no "limitation of the ability of Mars to support" earth life.

Scientists say the key to making Mars a second earth is creating a "greenhouse effect." This means melting the Red Planet's polar ice caps to get water vapor and oxygen into the planet's atmosphere. That will make the atmosphere reflect heat back onto the planet's surface to warm it up — now it reaches temperatures of 200 degrees below zero.

Paul Deal, a biochemist at NASA's Ames Research Lab in Mountain View, Calif., says that monster atomic bombs could be exploded to melt Martian ice caps.

Dr. Joseph Burns, a professor of astronomy at Cornell University in Ithaca, N.Y., suggests another method.

He wants to spread carbon black on the surface of the ice to absorb sunlight and heat which will melt the ice.

In addition, Burns suggests directing laser beams at the ice and putting huge mirrors into orbit to reflect sunlight onto the ice.

Dr. Robert MacElroy, a biochemist at Ames Lab, heads a group of scientists who favor covering the planet's surface with plants like algae or lichens. These will give off oxygen which will not only thicken the planet's atmosphere so it can reflect back heat, but also provide an atmosphere where man will be better able to breathe.

"Introducing lower forms of life, such as lichens, would be the most immediately do-able and most practical way as a first step toward making Mars habitable for man," said McElroy.

The NASA study concluded that it would take from 10,000 to 100,000 years for the plants to produce enough oxygen to warm the planet and put enough oxygen in its atmosphere.

However, the NASA report says that a possible combination of methods to melt the polar ice caps and cover the planet with plants would "significantly decrease the time required to create an acceptable human habitat on Mars."

But Dr. Ronald Bracewell, director of Stanford University's Radioastronomy Institute, says that man could begin to live on Mars within 10 years in domed mini-trenches. These would be created by digging trenches and covering them with a mylar top which would let in sunlight but reflect back the heat.

"These would create mini-greenhouses which would provide an atmosphere within the trenches within which man could function and begin agricultural tracts," he said.

After setting up these tiny greenhouses, man could begin changing the planet's outer atmosphere.

A Girl, 15, Forgets Her Mother
C.1973

TORONTO — (AP) — Rose Ann Hebert had to be told that the woman who had just walked into her hospital room was her mother.

Then she broke into tears.

Rose Ann, a 45-year-old Saint Jean, New Brunswick, girl, has no memory of her life beyond a little more than a week ago, her doctors say.

Her mother, Elizabeth Hebert, who hasn't seen her daughter for 15 days, spent about 35 minutes in the room Friday night.

"She seemed very bright and normal, but she couldn't remember." Mrs. Hebert said. "I mentioned several of her girl friends back home but the names didn't mean anything."

Doctors say Rose Ann, who hitchhiked to Toronto after "waking up" outside a pool hall in Fredericton, is suffering from amnesia, probably brought on something she saw or heard that "terrorized" her.

She was identified after a picture of her on television was seen by her brother Leon, 17, who lives in Orillia.

Weekly World News 1-13-81

U.S. Drought

HERB CAEN

FRIDAY NIGHT. A fatal accident on the world's greatest bridge — with mysterious overtones straight out of an espionage novel. A Honda Civic driven by a Russian engineer swerved across the dividing line into oncoming traffic — everyone's Golden Gate nightmare — and smashed head-on into a car occupied by three FBI agents. Purely coincidental, but many an espionage novel has begun with a less dramatic scene. The Russian died, the agents survived, and once again we look askance at "safety" precautions on, to repeat, the world's greatest bridge. Millions for ferries, not a cent for dividers that would keep cars from ploughing head-on into each other. After all these years, still only those plastic pegs that transform the bridge into — the world's greatest cribbage board. Combine that with Doyle Drive, which has yet to be "improved," the narrow tacky toll lanes, the lack of traffic control and the deteriorating roadway and you may have the world's greatest dangerous bridge. Millions for buses and not a cent for suicide barriers. Why spoil the fun?

★ ★ ★

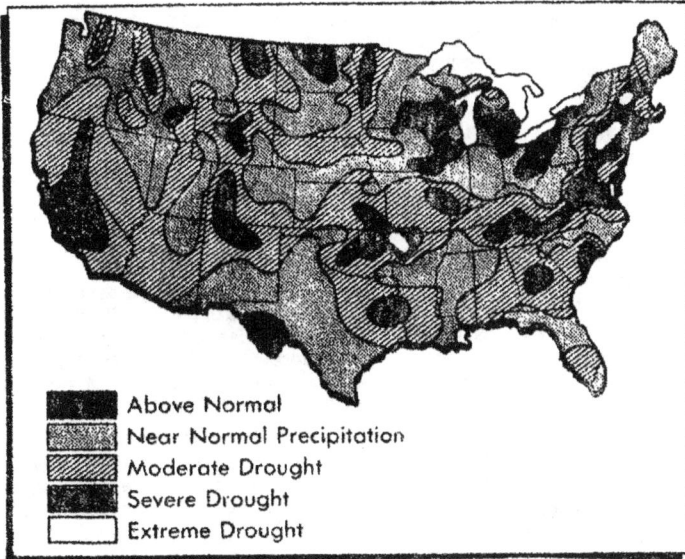

Above Normal
Near Normal Precipitation
Moderate Drought
Severe Drought
Extreme Drought

Memphis 2-81

For the past four months, a single weather pattern has gripped most of the United States, causing a coast-to-coast drought unique in the annals of weather recording.

Water emergencies have been declared all along the East Coast; farmers from Colorado to Pennsylvania are seeing damage to winter crops and are fearful about their spring ones; ski resorts, despite some snow in the past few days, have reported disastrously low levels, even bare ground in several areas that usually have 60 or 70 inches.

The drought's most visible effects are in the Midwest. The Mississippi River, which draws water from 40 percent of the United States — from the Rockies to the Appalachians and from Canada to the Gulf — dropped off the water gauge at Memphis in early January.

The low water has struck fear into the hearts of the river pilots. Scores of towboats and barges have run aground in the mud and sand between Illinois and Louisiana, closing the river to traffic at least six times since Christmas and for up to five days at a time.

According to several meteorologists, there are two reasons for the current weather pattern, both extremely unusual:

First, there are two very large and very persistent high-pressure systems that have planted themselves over the West Coast and Rocky Mountains and remained there for four months. In America, such long-lived weather centers were almost unheard of until 1977, when a similar one blocked the West Coast for months. Last summer, another pressed down on the Midwest and part of the East, causing record high temperatures and continuing the water deficit that began the previous winter.

Ozone worse off than thought

11-9-79

WASHINGTON (AP) — The Earth's protective ozone layer is being depleted by chemicals twice as fast as previously predicted, raising concerns about possible climate changes and increases in skin cancer, the National Academy of Sciences reported yesterday.

The academy's National Research Council said new calculations indicate atmospheric ozone could be reduced 16.5 percent because of worldwide use of fluorocarbon chemicals. Half of this depletion will occur in the next 30 years, it added.

In 1976, the council predicted an eventual 7.5 percent ozone reduction. But new atmospheric measurements and improved mathematical models revised the estimate, it said in a study done for the Environmental Protection Agency.

Scientists have estimated that for every 1 percent of ozone reduction, there is an estimated 2 percent increase in the amount of ultraviolet radiation reaching the Earth. Earlier studies have indicated that there would be a similar increase in easily-treated and curable skin cancer. More ultraviolet rays could also trigger climate changes and affect animal and plant life.

The report expressed concern about increasing use of two hydrogen-bearing halocarbons not used in aerosols.

Use of a chemical called F-22, largely in refrigeration, has increased 25 percent in two years. Production of methyl chloroform, an industrial solvent, is doubling every five years.

The council said it did not attempt to evaluate possible ozone depletion due to these chlorine-containing compounds because of limited knowledge of how they react in the atmosphere.

But the report said these chemicals "require careful attention" in the future.

Even if all release of the ozone-destroying gases were stopped today, the committee said ozone would still be depleted during the next 15 years. Then, the report said, the ozone level would gradually recover.

Dark Arts
2/5/81

Jack Anderson

LAST MONTH, I revealed a Pentagon secret that raised eyebrows from coast to coast. To the thousands of skeptics who wrote in, the brass hats are, indeed, dabbling in the dark arts.

They are seriously trying to develop weapons based on extrasensory perception. If the research is successful, the next war could be won presumably by casting an evil eye on Moscow.

The true believers are convinced that our national security can be preserved only by spending millions of dollars on such comic-strip concepts as the "hyperspatial howitzer," which supposedly could transmit a nuclear explosion in the Nevada desert to the gates of the Kremlin with the speed of thought.

Representative Charles Rose, D-N.C., for example, is a respected five-term congressman and a member of the House Select Committee on Intelligence. He has advocated psychotronic weapons.

* * *

BY PENTAGON standards, not much money has been invested on psychic warfare — a trifling $6 million. Rose thinks the United States should be spending a lot more money on these ethereal weapons. "They could make every other weapon obsolete," he said.

The congressman is quite correct: the Buck Rogers weapons would certainly make plain old nuclear bombs obsolete — if they should ever work.

One such weapon, it turns out, has been blessed with an Air Force contract. It's an anti-missile system that would throw a time warp over the North Pole. Incoming Soviet missiles would fly into the time warp and explode harmlessly in the past — perhaps blowing up Commander Robert Peary or, if the time warp mechanism was tuned to really high frequency, killing a few dinosaurs.

The National Security Agency, to cite another example, has tried to use ESP to crack Soviet codes. When the agency's computers have failed to break the codes produced by the Kremlin's computers, the NSA technicians have enlisted the help of local astrologers and palm readers. So far, according to my sources, the swamis have been no more successful than our computers.

* * *

REPORTING ON the bizarre research is not without its hazards. Several self-styled psychics have accused me of being an unwitting victim of Soviet success in the field. I am, they say, acting under long-range Kremlin hypnosis intended to persuade the American populace that Pentagon attempts to close the "psychotronic weapons gap" with the Soviet Union are a ridiculous waste of money.

But there are more skeptics than advocates. One critic of ESP warfare, physicist Martin Gardner, characterizes the budget for psychotronic weaponry as a monetary "black hole," into which bad research sucks good money forever. Others suggest the ESP efforts should be classified as "Top Stupid."

CR: Mike Cohen By MICHAEL KNIGHT
Special to The New York Times

NANTUCKET, Mass., March 7 — On a bitterly cold, blustery night last January, Dr. Margaret M. Kilcoyne disappeared from her vacation home on the deserted moors here, creating a mystery that seems to deepen almost daily.

It is not clear to Paul Hunter, the Nantucket Chief of Police, why the 50-year-old Columbia University medical researcher and perhaps one or more associates came to this island 30 miles off Cape Cod, only to disappear a few days later amid a trail of puzzling clues. But he now characterizes her disappearance as probably an elaborate hoax.

Dr. Kilcoyne vanished after boasting of a breakthrough in research on the causes of hypertension. She left behind a tape recording saying that she was "sitting on top of a Nobel Prize."

"It's a very real possibility that she engineered the whole thing for purposes of her own," said Chief Hunter. He took up his duties as head of the island's 18-member police force only hours after Dr. Kilcoyne was reported missing on Jan. 26 by her brother Leo, a vice president of I.B.M. Canada Ltd.

"We have definitely eliminated murder, kidnapping, any sort of foul play, and the evidence points very clearly away from suicide," the Chief continued. "In fact, it now points to a deliberate attempt to make believe there was a suicide."

There are those who disagree, like Nantucket Brownie, a grizzled and gray-bearded man who looks so much like the kind of old salt the summer tourists expect that his picture is on many of the postcards they buy. "Surf got her and that's that," he said, adding that his real name is Wilson Brown. "She fell in the sea and got drowned."

Just in case he is right, the police patrol the beaches here every day at dawn looking for her body.

Mary Peterson, a cab driver who helped her load $850 worth of groceries into a taxi the morning before her disappearance, said she seemed "excited and in good spirits, but normal, like anybody else."

"But everything she bought for the press conference was in threes, and multiples of threes — six gallons of peanuts, 12 toothbrushes, six tubes of shampoo, and so on, which was kind of strange," she added. The groceries, along with $250 worth of liquor, were later returned to the store by Dr. Kilcoyne's brother.

Richard and Grace Coffin, members of the island's leading family since it was settled in the 1600's, had dinner with Dr. Kilcoyne and her brother that night and said she appeared happy and not at all distraught.

But her brother told the police that his sister sounded overwrought and "burned out" from work when he talked to her from his home near Toronto a few days before her disappearance.

Brother Arrives Concerned

He told investigators that he flew here on Saturday, intending to persuade her to seek psychiatric help, but found when he awoke early the next morning that she had disappeared from her six-room $100,000 summer house near Tom Nevers Pond. No suicide note was found, and a search of her apartment at 330 East 33d Street in New York City turned up no additional clues.

India Engineer Vanishes in S.F.
5/18/78

A young engineer from southern India was reported by members of his family yesterday to have been missing in San Francisco since May 6.

Police said Varadarajan Ponnuswamy, 25, arrived here aboard a United Air Lines flight from Memphis, Tenn. His baggage was picked up at the airport, but he has not been seen since.

The young engineer, a graduate of Notre Dame University, was supposed to have gone to the Japanese consulate to obtain a visa to visit Japan but he never showed up there, police said.

Police learned of Ponnuswamy's disappearance from a brother, who is a medical doctor in Dearborn, Mich.

The missing man, who was said to be carrying $2500 in cash and traveler's checks, had suffered a nervous breakdown last month and had been under the care of a psychiatrist, police said.

Ponnuswamy, a tall, thin man with a long nose and black hair, is one of seven brothers. The family, according to the Indian consulate, owns a steel mill in Madras.

Another brother, Venkatesan Ponnuswamy, has arrived here from India and is staying at the Hyatt Regency to assist in the search.

VARADARAJAN PONNUSW
He was last seen May

Ex-Congressman Jack Anderson Dies

2/10/81

DID THEY GET THE WRONG Jack Anderson?

Hollister, San Benito County

Former Republican Congressman Jack Z. Anderson, who served in the House of Representatives for 14 years, committed suicide in his home yesterday with a single pistol shot to the head.

During World War II Anderson served on the Naval Affairs Committee. He was one of a small group of congressmen selected to witness a test of the atomic bomb at Bikini atoll in 1946.

Satellite in Space

6-15

Vandenberg AFB 6-15-78

A satellite was shot into space aboard a Titan 3 Space booster by the Air Force Space and Missile test center yesterday.

United Press

A secret launch

6/11/78

CAPE CANAVERAL, Fla. (UPI) — The Air Force launched a classified satellite from its Eastern Test Range yesterday, the second classified launch at the site in a little more than two months.

The Instigator did not contact The German when he returned to Earth. He fled into hiding. And then, with a small group of trusted collaborators, he founded his action group, Anti-Alternative. This group, unlike organisations such as the IRA or the PLO, could make no public statements for such statements could lead to them being rooted out and destroyed. They dedicated themselves to disrupting, by guerrilla tactics, all work connected with the exploration and exploitation of space. Their actions, they felt, might force an eventual re-think on Alternative 3.

On October 1, 1977, the *Daily Telegraph* carried a story, written by Ian Ball in New York, which was headlined: SATELLITE ROCKET No. 2 BLOWS UP.

"For any action as dramatic as self-destruction there would almost certainly have to be a synchronization of many factors," said Dr. Danningham. "For example, it would be easier if the intended victim were at precisely the right period of his biorhythmic psi sensitivity cycle and . . ."

"But surely the instinct for self-preservation would countermand any instructions calculated to result in suicide . . . unless the sleeper wanted to kill himself anyway . . ."

"Not if the telepathic instructions were cleverly presented," said Danningham. "Let me give you an illustration:

"Imagine you want to kill a man who, let's say, lives high up in a skyscraper block. Now you're not going to tell that man to kill himself by jumping out of his bedroom window because—as you so rightly say—his instinct for survival would very likely intervene and reject the order.

"So what you do is feed him false information. You tell him telepathically that there is some wild beast rampaging around his room or that the building has caught fire. You tell him there is a safety net spread under the window and that, to save himself, he must jump. So, in a desperate bid to stay alive, he jumps—and breaks his neck.

"It is possible, of course, to play all sorts of permutations on this tack. You might persuade your sleeping victim, for instance, into believing there is some venomous spider attached to this chest, that he must stab it and kill it before it kills him. And so, in his sleep, he stabs himself.

"The variations, my dear Mr. Benson, are almost limitless. If the telepathic messages convinced your sleeper that he had accidentally drunk some corrosive poison and that the only antidote was in a bottle marked cyanide . . . well, I'm sure you see what I mean."

Big Rocket Knocked Askew on Pad

1/23/81

Cape Canaveral, Fla.

A launch tower door hit a Delta rocket being prepared for launch yesterday, knocking the rocket from its upright position, officials said. No one was hurt.

National Aeronautics and Space Administration spokesmen said the damage was "considerable," but had not been assessed. Delta rockets cost $17 million in 1977.

The rocket, owned by McDonnell Douglas Corp., was being prepared for a March 12 launching of a weather satellite. The accident had no connection with the space shuttle, the first reusable U.S. spacecraft, which is scheduled for its maiden launch March 17 from another pad here.

"Officials don't know how much damage has been done, and nobody knows whether the launch will have to be delayed," said NASA spokesman Hugh Harris.

The rocket's first stage and inter-stage had been set up on the launch pad earlier this week, and the first of nine solid fuel boosters used for the launch were placed in a sling inside the mobile launch pad tower, officials said.

As the tower moved into position to install the booster, a large door struck the Delta, officials said.

The moving tower pushed the Delta several feet from its upright position and pulled free two of the three bolts that hold the rocket to the launch pad, they said. The Delta tilted back into the tower and was left leaning into it, they explained.

Associated Press

These two clips appeared on the same day! A photo went with this one. Terrorists?

Top Security

NASA guard Tom O'Connor patrolled Kennedy Space Center in Florida in combat gear and carried an M-16 rifle in a stepped-up security program that was instituted this week to protect the space shuttle against terrorist attacks. The space vehicle has been rolled out onto its launching pad, and extra security measures included boat patrols along the coast three miles away and vehicle searches at nearby beaches.

1-23-81

AF Silent on Satellite

6-12-78

Cape Canaveral, Fla.

The Air Force maintained strict secrecy yesterday about the status of a satellite launched Saturday aboard a powerful Titan 3C rocket.

United Press

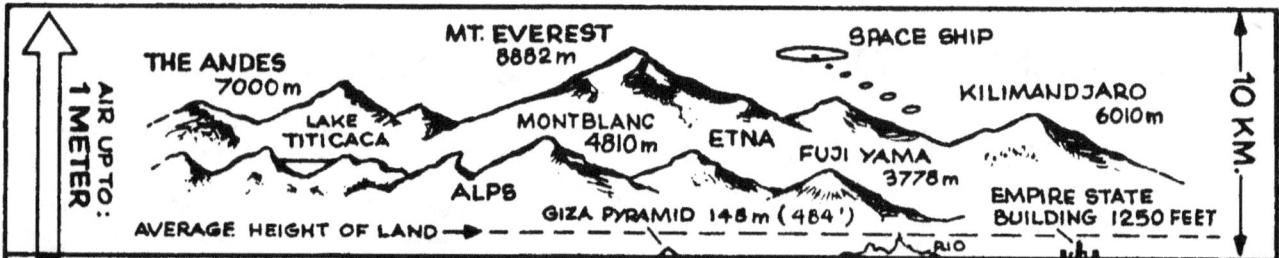

THE HOLLOW EARTH

FACT OR FICTION?

THE ANDES 7000m

MT. EVEREST 8882m

SPACE SHIP

KILIMANDJARO 6010m

LAKE TITICACA

MONTBLANC 4810m

ALPS

ETNA

FUJI YAMA 3778m

EMPIRE STATE BUILDING 1250 FEET

GIZA PYRAMID 148m (484')

RIO

AVERAGE HEIGHT OF LAND →

AIR UP TO: 1 METER

IN THE SAME SCALE: 16 METERS TO CENTER OF EARTH

10 KM.

DEEPEST OCEAN

ADMIRAL BYRD'S FLIGHT 1947

SAUCER TO VENUS

MELTING ICE

"TEST" ATOM BLAST: COLD AIR RUSHES BACK TO EARTH THROUGH CENTER OF SHAFT

HEIGHT OF ATMOSPHERE 200 MILES

KENTUCKY MAMMOTH CAVE

-50°

MT. EPOMEO ITALY

PYRAMID OF GIZA

LAKE

CLOUDS

AGHARTA
LAND OF
ADVANCED RACES

CITY OF SHAMBALLAH

CITY

CLOUDS

MAN-MADE TUNNELS

CITY

CENTRAL SUN

FOREST

KING SOLOMON'S MINES

MANAUS

VOLCANO

MATO GROSSO

CAVE CITY OF SEMI-ADVANCED RACE

MOLTEN BASALT

BRAZIL

OCEAN

IGUASSU FALLS

SPACE SHIP BASE TO & FROM OTHER GALAXIES

MOUNTAINS HIGHER THAN ON OUTSIDE

DERO CAVES WITH STOLEN SAUCERS

SEDIMENTS

GRANITE

BASALT

PLASTIC BASALT

RAINBOW CITY

OCEAN

TUNNEL ENTRANCES TO INNER EARTH

ICE

CENTER OF GRAVITY 400 MILES DOWN

SMALL ENTRANCE

0   500 1000   2000   3000   4000   5000   6000   7000   8000

SCALE IN MILES

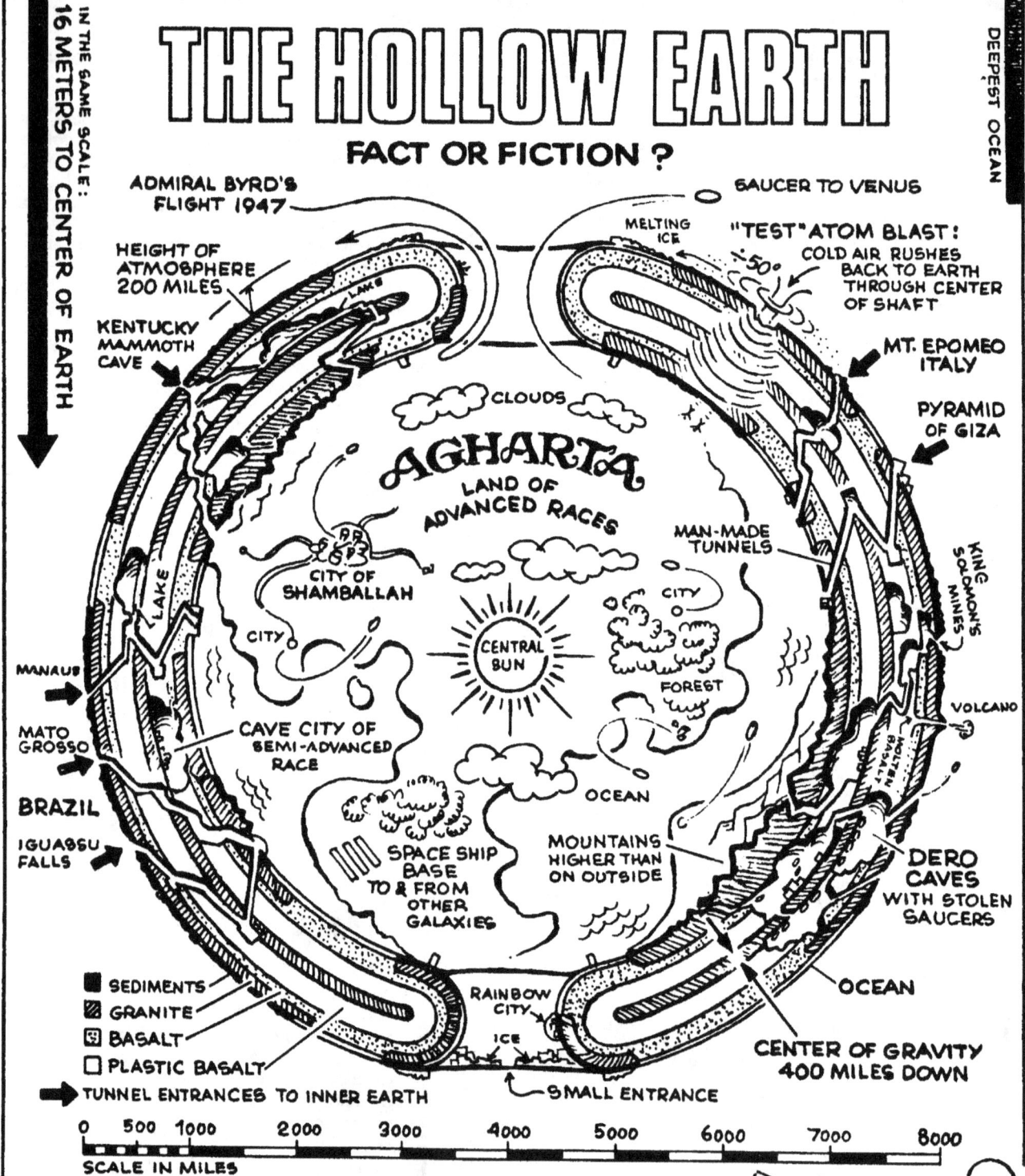

INNER EARTH TO BE RE-DRAWN BY SOMEONE WHO HAS BEEN THERE! THANK YOU...

TAHITI DENMARK FLORIDA CALIF. ITALY

1 METER: 40" APPROX.

MAX FYFIELD

SHAVERTRON

"The Only Source of Post-Deluge Shaverania"

FALL 1981 ——————————————————— ISSUE 9

INTERVIEW: CHARLES MARCOUX

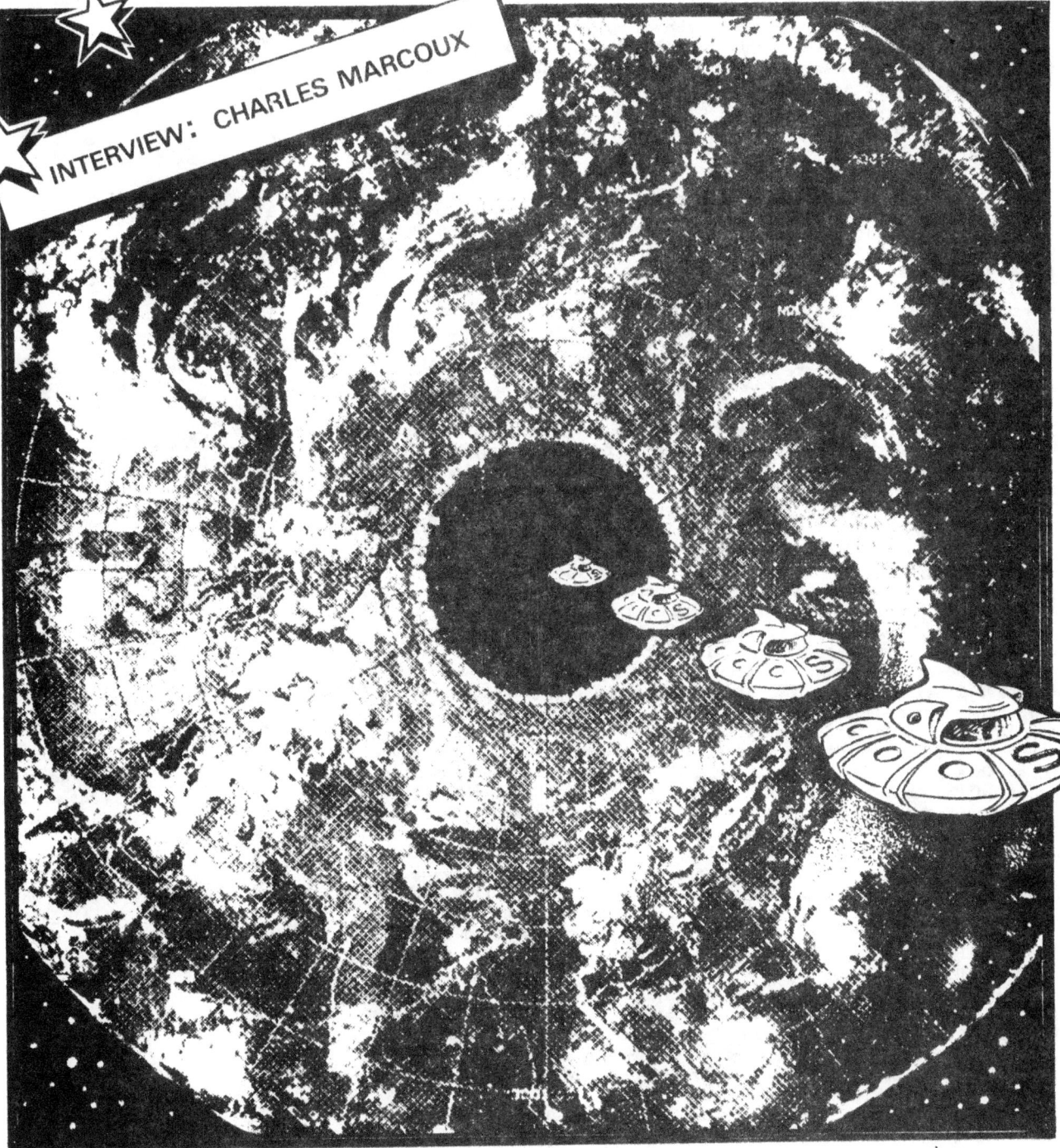

SATELLITE PHOTO OF NORTH POLAR OPENING $2

notes from the underground

Naturally, as editor of this infinitesimally small bit of copy hurtling toward who-knows-where in this crazy universe, I get alot of unusual and oft as not weird mail that never gets shared with you readers. Shavertron copy space is at a premium and that has alot to do with it. But some of our mail has gotten so nasty that we thought we'd share some of it with you as a change of pace.

In the 2 and a half years we've been pubbing S, we've received only 3 reviews of the zine. Two of them were bad. The most downright obscene one we've gotten so far has oozed out of SCIENCE FICTION REVIEW (Summer, 1981, pubbed by Richard Geis), who denounces both your humble editor and our readers in one fell swoop:

"Toronto and his readers believe Richard Shaver was onto something with what is known as the Shaver Mystery-- remnants of a master race living in caverns far below, able to affect human minds on the earth's surface by means of ancient evil machines...etc. One could say if you're an anal-retentive paranoiac this is right down your hole." Mr Geis' language may hint at where he is coming from, and just to show that we can take it, we'll continue: "The zine...is a disorganized paste-up of bits & pieces...news stories, clips, editorials, letters, ads..."

Enough of that. In a preceding review, this time from THE GMS INFOR-MANT (editor-Don Miller, Nov. 1980), Shavertron was lambasted by Dave & Su Bates. Unhappily (for them) this was the INFORMANT's last issue. Said Bates: "I find this hard to review. Though it is indeed printed and illu-strated, the layouts are nearly impossible to follow...everything is scattered seemingly at random. This is the only active fanzine dedicated to the late author, Richard S. Shaver, and it is worth struggling through if you are a fan of his. With better organization, more serious graphics, and an attempt at serious layout, it would probably be better received... but what can we do when this is the only game in town?"

To be quite honest, your humble editor confesses that he modeled S's layout on the crumbling foundations of John Keel's ANOMALY. A was free until the day it folded. The big finale Keel had planned was to be a big, two ounce issue (readers had to send in 2 stamps on their SASE instead of just one), and yours truly sent his in right away. This story has a sad ending,however, because the issue never came...maybe it was never published, I never heard. Then Keel moved on to bigger and better things.

Your editor presumptuously assumed that S readers were following what was going on in each issue, but it would seem that only Shaver Mystery fen, persons in-the-know about the SM and SM topics could readily grasp the gist of this zine. We noted that in both reviews no mention was made of content (although Geis tossed a very ripe tomato at the SM itself)... only "layout" and "organization" were grated over the coals.

Sooooo, in an attempt to go commercial, your humble editor donned his Hollywood sunglasses, his shirt and tie,and sat down at his desk in a deliberate attempt to improve this issue in both layout and organization. We hope it will not only make it easier for everyone to follow, but also bring us some reticent subscribers who would have scratched their heads in confusion on their first look at Shavertron. Oh, the Good Review? That's in the file under Top Secret, just for now...you might call it our Ace in the Hole.

Regardless, however of our detractors, Shavertron is pleased to note that other media sources have taken our lead in regard to the Jonestown/ CIA link (S no. 8). A recent VideoWest tv broadcast pointed out that the American embassy in Guyana was staffed and run by the CIA, and had ties with Jonestown. Cases of CIA-style drugs, frequently used in CIA mind-control experiments were found in Jonestown.

Congressman Ryan's close friend and associate, Joe Holsinger, claims that Jonestown was code named MK-Ultra. He believes its purpose was to see if a large group of people could be made to commit suicide. According

2 cont pg 8

SHAVER TRON

Editor/Publisher
Richard Toronto

Associates:

Rogphoto Tech
Bill Bliss

Art Director
Max Fyfield

Literary Research
Jim Pobst

SM Adventurer
Charles Marcoux

Hollow Earth Research
Bruce Walton

Moral Support
Mary LeVesque

Cartoonist
Henry Steele

Our Man In:

Britain: Ray Archer
Rome: Francesco Savorgnan
Washington, DC: "X"
Private Idaho: R. Finley

Shavertron is quarterly at $8 per year domestic, $9 overseas via surface, $13 via airmail. Make out all checks or money orders to the publisher, not to the zine. Address all mail, including mss. to 309 Coghlan Street, Vallejo, California,USA 94590.

Advertising Rates:

$20--full page
$10--half page
$ 5--quarter
$ 2.50--eighth
Cover by Max Fyfield

Letters

Dear Rich,

I have a few comments on the subject of outerspace survival.

In the highest levels and ranks of what I could call the new "Gods" and rules of this planet there are plans to extend the domination and denial systems into other areas of this universe. But a number of us give these plans very little hope for success. In the first place, there are certain Human Componets related to mind action that simply will not function beyond the Van Allen Belt. The first astronauts for instance, were carefully programmed in their proceedures once in space.

Yet beyond earth they often reverted to a simple mental process that played hell with the procedures and rules. After bad mouthing their superiors motives and things which they felt unethical, it was finally decided necessary to stop the open communication channels and keep the conversation censored. Without a great deal of automation, high level mind function simply is to weak in space to run the sophisticated technology.

What most persons fail to realize is the fact that the Creator has this universe under complete

and perfect control. One atom out of law and it would be a junkpile. Under free choice law the highly motivated domination leaders are free to enslave the minds of weak men on this "containment" planet. But beyond this planet there are safeguards that are far too effective. It is continually tried. I grant you I am aware of such attempts dating back 10K years.

The body and the technology can be sent into the universe, but the higher level components of the Human are still sencered if they are of what we term, "reflection" origin--a long subject.

Underground flight and safety is also a joke as it is being applied. The great mormon underground installation for example, will be at a frigid area far too cold for survival when the final accounting time arrives...another very long tale.

Al Fry

Dear Rich,

In his book, Watkins says that if the Apollo astronauts on the moon had anything unusual to report, they would be told to switch to a "private" channel. SAGA mag seems to have some supporting evidence of this.

Way back in 1974, they published (in 2 parts) an article on the astronauts' transmissions from the moon...(the non-public transmissions)..about finding strange "tracks", Ufo's, dome, etc. This was in Saga March & April 1974.

I am looking for a book by Phil Hruskocy that deals with the Alt3 subject, but as yet have not found it. Search mag had a short article on it in their Fall issue. (Article is in this issue...Ed.). If any S readers know of where I can find a copy, please let the editor know. Thanks.

Anon.

Dear Richard,

About Reagan's assasination attempt, I think it was definitely a conspiracy on the part of the rightwing. The attempt took place one week after Reagan stripped Haig's power--giving it to Bush. The General represents the right wing (although the right wing literature claims he works for the Rockefellers) and I believe they decided that Reagan betrayed them when he attacked the General. They were getting fed up with because he did not deliver on his campaign promises (ie. cut welfare and starve the niggers, etc.) There is little doubt that it was a conspiracy-- the different guns involved--- .22 and .38 calibre, explosive bullets and NBC-TV claimed right after the attempt that the man caught was in his 40's! When the Gov't. claimed he was in his 20's NBC said that "their reporters were not crazy and they could tell the difference between a man in his 40's and one in his 20's".

Of course, the real assasin (who could not be identified because the police put a coat over his head) was released and the son of that right wing millionaire was made the goat. I feel his father wanted to get rid of him because he was a bum, drug addict etc. and these rich families don't stand for that kind of behavior.

As for the Richardson affair, I understand that right after the attempt on Reagan, there was a tremendous number of threats against politicians in this country &

in other areas of the world. The Govt. in my opinion, had to make up the Richardson case in order to threaten potential assasins or tricksters that they will go after you if you either say or do anything against the politicians. Jody Foster was just part of the fiction--all made up just to make the plot look real. I dont even think that Richardson exists...he could be a completely fictional character made for the media.

MC

Dear Richard,

I have just heard that Capt. Tawani Shoush, head of the Missouri centered Hollow Earth Society, just returned from the South Pole where he led an expedition to search out the alleged polar opening, however I haven't heard any details yet of any possible findings--hope to soon.

Bruce Walton

R-- This is one expedition we've been waiting for. We wonder if he got ahold of the dirigible that he wanted to float down into the polar opening? Did he find his Rainbow City Aryans, we wonder?

Richard,

Prisons are full of ignorant/crazy people, not all, but most. These jails, prisons and mental-institutions breed hate and violence...crime. The Dero and Zionist Bankers love it, it will soon, however, backfire on them ALL.

Ya know, there's really nothing "secret" because with astral travel and mental telepathy, etc. no gov't. is over another. What a joke-- man made World Gov't. It'll be based on materialism not spirit. THAT'S why it will fail. The Anti-Messiah and his ignorant 7-year middle-east plan will fail and Armageddon will be the end-result. Of course Russia will be wiped out, and its allies before this 7-year tribulation hardly gets off the ground. Alot of people will be murdered cause they'll refuse to worship this false-messiah, & take his invisible-laser-beamed symbol on either the forehead or back of right hand.

Ronnie Crawford
Missouri State
Penitentiary

3

GIANTS IN THE EARTH - *revised*

By Jim Wentworth

Revisions for possible Second Printing.
The following to be inserted on page 44- 2nd col-
umn- after first line, of GIANTS IN THE EARTH by
Jim Wentworth....(Palmer Publications, Amherst, Wisc.
USA.)

If the dero have the means of doing such "simple"
things as opening railroad switches and manhole covers
(to use only the two examples just given) they could
with equal ease do other things like...Well, as a
possible example of their evilness, let us give thought to an underwater event that occurred on May 2, 1975,
as told by Charles Berlitz in his book of 1977, WITH-
OUT A TRACE.

The person involved was Ben Huggard of Freeport,
New York. This rugged policeman and champion long-
distance swimmer had planned to swim from Sombrero
Point, Marathon Cay, Florida, to Freeport, Nassau,
162 miles away. He would swim, non-stop inside a cage
towed approximately 150 feet behind a launch equipped
with a two-way speaking unit to enable communication.

Why the cage? Because he would be swimming in
shark-infested waters. And indeed sharks showed up,
predictably, within ten minutes of his takeoff. It
should be mentioned that the carefully checked and
tested trap door-- the sole entrance to the cage--
was controlled by two double locks.

Huggard had some trouble with the strong eddies
and currents of the Gulf Stream which, taking him
off course, lasted for several hours. Then came
night, and with it normality. Floodlights of the
lead boat clearly revealed the still-present sharks
outside the cage as Huggard swam robustly inside.

Then...But let Ben Huggard tell his bizarre story
in his own words:

"I always breathe on the left side. But suddenly
I had a strange feeling to look on the right, towards
the trap door. As I looked, the door opened by itself and fell down, despite the double lock. I swam
over and reached up and locked both locks, and tested the door. I then resumed swimming. A short time
later I had an urge to look again. While I looked
to the right, the trap door opened once more. I
called for the crew to bring tools to fix the door.
They came and tried the locks and said nothing was
wrong--nothing could open them. After they went
back I kept getting the feeling the door would open
again. This went on and on throughout the night with
me swimming up and closing the door every 15 minutes
or half an hour. I called the crew every time and
they must have thought I was crazy because whenever
they tried to, they could not open it. They shook
and pulled it but it never opened. The locks held
perfectly. But every time I looked over at it, the
locks slowly unsnapped and it opened by itself. I
am never frightened in the ocean, but I had this horrible fear that caused me to jump out of a window
from a high building. I knew what would happen, with
the sharks outside, but the urge was almost irresistible. Finally, when I felt almost forced to swim
out, I swam over and grabbed the trap door, I was
shaking, but I held onto it. I kept saying to myself
'I'm not going to let it take me out of the cage,
whatever it is...' and then I slammed it shut."

And from then on it remained shut, back to normal.

Now we come to a number of unsettling questions.
Why was all this done? What caused the trap door to

RECORD OF ROCKS - 6
UFO Traffic

© 1967 BELL-McCLURE SYNDICATE

RICHARD S. SHAVER OF SUMMIT, ARK., BELIEVES HIS "STONE
PICTURE BOOKS" PROVE THAT AN ANCIENT EARTH
CIVILIZATION CARRIED ON **SPACE COMMERCE**
WITH STARMEN, WHO TODAY ARE BACK, HOPING
TO SET UP **SPACE TRADE** WITH US.

This is the final installment of our "Record Of
Rocks" series that began in issue 3. These were
created by Otto Binder, who syndicated them in
the late 1960's.

open by itself? Why this opening only in the presence
of Huggard and no one else? And what gave the swimmer the feeling, the "almost irresistible" urge, that
he should leave the safety of the cage? Was this not
irrational thinking?

The answer to all these questions, if the Shaver
Mystery enters the picture, is simple enough. It was
done by the dero. Why? As a joke. For the depraved
and gleeful pleasure it would give them to watch the
mounting terror of a hated surface inhabitant.

In this case, the unfortunate was a single individual. But how about multitudes of unfortunates
that could be the persecuted victims of the dero?
Again, from THE MOTHMAN PROPHESIES by John Keel:

"The madness that grips crowds and produces
violent riots, some of which have changed history,
seems lettle different from the madness that produced the widespread dancing mania of the Middle
Ages when thousands of people danced in the streets
until they dropped dead from exhaustion. Survivors
claimed they believed they were knee-deep in blood
and were prancing to get out of it. This was a
collective or mass hallucination. Even today there
are annual incidents in which whole towns are seized
by hallucinations, usually in obscure parts of S.
America and Asia. Such events are traditionally
explained as being caused by tinted bread despite
the fact that people who have not eaten the local
bread are also affected."

4

THE BUSY PYRAMID

by MAX FYFIELD (alias RA-MAK)

This story takes place in the years 820-22 A.D. However, the film begins with a few scenes showing Cairo and the pyramids as they look TODAY! A couple of tourists, (Max and Gina) are seen together in the King's Chamber, they both believe in the fact of Reincarnation and also that they have been in Egypt in former lifetimes-- TOGETHER!

The titles are shown and we are back in 820 A.D. Al Mamoun, Caliph of Bagdad, is admiring his favorite belly-dancer (Gina from lead-in scenes), he is hopelessly in love. They travel to Egypt where Al plans to find the entrance to the Great Pyramid, or break into it if necessary. He wants the legendary treasure hidden inside, and brings 1000 workers who begin to dig a tunnel. Many months later they are still digging, only encouraged by Al's promises of great riches for all! Al and Gin begin to argue, she is getting bored and threatening to leave him, he begs her to wait, and press the workers to hurry up.

Two years later, still digging, still arguing. During the night, she walks over to the Sphinx where she meets a procession of High Priests. The youngest is RA-MAK (Max from lead-in scenes). They take her along through the secret entrance between the paws of the Sphinx, down below and through a tunnel to the Great Pyramid. RA and GIN have to find their way (alone) to the center of the pyramid, as part of an Initiation ceremony into the Ancient Mysteries...

At the same time the workers are still digging, but about to give up when a minor earthquake shakes a big stone from the ceiling ahead. With new courage they continue to point where they meet RA and GIN who just manage to escape upwards. But the workers have to dig through another barrier.

Meanwhile, RA and GIN find their way into the King's Chamber. The High Priests tell them to crawl into the Coffer, they are left alone in the dark, they realize they have known each other before, in many lifetimes (as they will meet again in the future). Phase two of the Initiation now takes place! Their Souls leave their bodies in an ASTRAL TRIP into Higher Spheres, they see and talk with their inhabitants! Three days later, the priests come in to the 2 who have returned to their bodies and are ready to begin a NEW LIFE!

Just then the workers break through while the Initiates disappear through a secret door. Al is furious when he finds no treasure! Meanwhile RA and GIN are lead to a secret hall far below where they are shown the real treasures: Scientific equipment from ATLANTIS! At last they enter tunnel vehicles which will take them to their final destination--the land inside this HOLLOW EARTH!

(an 18 page Motion Picture story-
outline is written)

Sequel will be: "EMPRESS OF AGHARTA"

to appear in an upcoming issue (No. 10 or 11).

(SHAVER) (TRON)

5

Charles Marcoux

Shavertron: Did you ever get to meet Richard Shaver?

MARCOUX: No, I never met him in person, only by mail. I met Ray Palmer, though, in 1966.

S: What were the circumstances of that encounter?

M: I met him sometime in the early summer or late spring, during my vacation, when I lived at Rice Lake, Wisconsin. I found out where he lived and was told how to get to his home. I discovered him walking in his front yard, recognised him, and I introduced myself. I knew that he was "sizing me up" to see if I was another one of those trouble makers, or what? Anyway, we walked up by the lake on his land and talked for over an hour or more.

When I asked him if Shaver was around, and if I could meet him, then, RAP said he didn't know where Shaver was. I became "aware" that he was "covering up" so, I just dropped the subject concerning Shaver. But I know that he was "on guard", so to speak, and he didn't know that I was psychic enough to pick up his physical and mental thoughts. He was "tense", and that meant "on guard". Also, his words were guarded, which I could detect in his voice and in his eyes. Being a healer, I pick up these three things that a person gives away of themselves, their conditions and fears. Outside of that, RAP and I got along fine, and he sold me a bunch of books, which I still have. I told him that I would try to visit with him again, when I came by his way, but I never made it.

S: Well just how did you come to be involved in the famous Shaver Mystery in the first place?

MARCOUX: During WWII, I was working at Continental Motors on East Jefferson, and I had an apartment near Temple St. in Detroit, Michigan. There was, at that time, a used book store in which I often browzed, searching for books that contained unusual material in which I had hoped to find some link that would explain some of the personal experiences I had had since I was born.

It was in March of 1945 that I was impressed to go into this used book store, which also carried new books and magazines. As I was browzing about the shelves, my eyes were drawn to the book shelf that contained magazines pertaining to the "Science Fiction section". I was so drawn to those magazines that I walked over to them, and there appeared a stell-blue light around them. So, I began to look at the mags., and the cover of a certain mag seemed to burn into my eyes and mental mind. There, stood a mag with a cover in very bright colors, titled AMAZING STORIES, and "I Remember Lemuria" by Richard S Shaver.

Well, since I had to get to work, I took the mag with me, but all during the night, while I was working, I just couldn't forget that magazine. It continued to burn into my mind, and after work (I was working 12 hours a day at that time), I went home and read the whole story of "I Remember Lemuria". I didn't put it down until every last word was read. As you can guess, I was extremely excited and didn't get any sleep that

MARÇOUX & HIS WIFE— NOV 1980

day. For a long time after that, I couldn't wait til the next issue of AMAZING STORIES appeared on the book shelf.

S: Then you were convinced from the very first Shaver story that the "Mystery" was on the mark?

M: I just simply knew that Shaver was right!! Since I was born, I had been in contact with unknown beings who showed me the cavern world, but I never had any kind of confirmation until Shaver came into my life. Many times I was taken into the "Underworld" by a large, tall "being". He told me about the existence of their world, and he took me to a large, dome-like building that had a long set of steps.

There were other "beings" going in and coming out of this building carrying large books. The "being" would take me into this building, which was like a library, and show me books that were of gold. I never seemed to remember any more than that, nor what was in those books. I do not know how many times I was taken into the Underworld and to the Library. Now, as I look back, I am aware that I was taken there astrally.

S: From that time onward, then, the SM played an important role in your life.

MARCOUX: Yes, I was personally involved with the SM since   1945. I joined the SMC right from the start, as well as the first Saucer Club in Chicago. I still have all 9 issues (of the SM Mystery Mag), as well as over 80 copies of AMAZING and FANTASTIC ADVENTURES magazines. I wrote to over 85 different people in these clubs, but I didn't have my own zine until 1966. I did publish this zine from '66 to May '67, but I don't have any copies left.

When Palmer created FATE Magazine, he advised many of his followers to start their own clubs. This began a new movement, and the first "saucer" club was organized in Chicago, by a group of college students. This started a long series of chain letters to a group of more than 80 people. Each would add their experiences to this letter, and it would be sent to the saucer club in Chicago. After awhile, that died out, for the chain letter seemed to take too long to get the information to the center of operation. When the college students left the University, the saucer club died with them. Others joined together to keep it alive by having their own zines or bulletins.

I organized several saucer clubs in Mich., Ohio, Indiana, and then organized a saucer club in Phoenix in 1959. Shaver was a taboo subject, even though I did lecture about Shaver in Phoenix, as well as in Palmdale, California. I couldn't get any real support-- too many parasites. I went to Giant Rock two years, but he wouldn't let me lecture about Shaver, Palmer or on my UFO pictures (he, meaning George Van Tassel). But Van Tassel is dead now and so is his organization.

A GROUP OF UFOs IN PETRIFIED FOREST, AZ—1959
Photo by Marcoux

S: Where have you looked for the legendary Underworld entrances, and what have you found during your expeditions?

M: I have personally explored, investigated and searched for the Elder Worlds throughout Arizona and New Mexico since 1958 and have photographed proof that the so-called "entrances" (to be EN-TRANCED?), portals, pillars, etc. do exist, and they are as physical as you are.
There are, also, interdimensional beings that can transmute from levels of other dimensional worlds, and they are intermixed with our own physical world. That is to say, they communicate with each other, and most often, do not interfere with their passage through the different worlds--they pass right through solid to non-solid, visable and invisable. So, Shaver and Palmer are right, and so is Oahspe, regardless of the difference of opinion which existed between RSS and RAP. These interdimensional beings can, and do, take physical form and mingle with people of our own world, without

Marcoux's psychic photo of a "Haunted Church."

them even knowing that they exist. I have seen them and have telepathically communicated with them personally. Yes, there are Teros, Deros and Durjas.
S: When did you begin your successful career in "psychic photography"?
M: My psychic photography began in 1943, but my best experiences have been since 1958. I have hundreds of pictures, and I had personal communication that made it possible for me to take my pictures of the paranormal world.

My psychic eye is attuned, in some way, to my cameras, which makes paranormal photography possible. The fact that I am a psychic healer augments the ability to photograph paranormal phenomena--they are all tuned together. Another thing which is very important is that I get in a light "trance" state, and that is why I can see the "hidden world".

Others that are around me often do not see a thing. They don't believe me when I tell them that there is an object, or something around, but then the pictures are developed, and there they are. People are amazed, especially when they were right beside me and didn't see what I saw.

S: I don't like to dwell on the negative, but there was a negative side to the SM. Can we attribute this to dero tamper?

M: As I watched the Shaver-Palmer movement, it became apparent that there was a sinister movement against them, as well as all the followers that were involved. Who were the ones that put pressure on Ziff-Davis? Was it the Dero alone? MIB? The government and its "yes-men"? Or, just people, themselves with their paranoid personalities or ego and mental problems, seeking to secure their own unstable society? I assure you that all of the above mentioned were, and most likely, still are involved with the ancient system of inquisition and heresy. They were are are, religious, and they religiously pursue the ancient secret.

As the Science Fiction group, as well as many "Spiritualist" organizations, put the pressure on Ziff-Davis Publishing company, it put an end to the Shaver Mystery as published by AMAZING and FANTASTIC magazines. Palmer quit and started his own publications. To me, Palmer has done more good for the world than anybody else in the paranormal field. Shaver was the key that opened the door, but without Palmer's insight, there wouldn't have been any Shaver Mystery movement. Palmer's real contribution to the world was by getting Mankind to think and to open the Portals so that Mankind could get a glimpse of the hidden world.

It is not difficult to understand the "why" of this type of persecution. It happens because these people live in fear and ignorance. They hold back the progress of Mankind, refuse to remove old taboos, superstitions, and ancient religious customs. They want to keep the knowledge of the ancients for themselves. The "yes-men" and the "know-it-all" scholars are the worst, as well as the most dangerous. Many are Communists or "leaners" who know not what they do. They cover up, but don't really know...they only know what is in books or what professors tell them to think-- to be a copy of their professor's image. The leaders know and have access to the ancient's secrets, and they give thirty pieces of silver to keep the "yes-men" and the scholars happy with their child-like toys such as TV, sports, liquor, social security and a pension. People are dead and have no real purpose, for Mankind is no more advanced than 10,000 years ago. No wonder the Underworld is kept so secret. It's no wonder that Shaver and Palmer were constantly being harassed.

S: It sounds as though you are speaking from experience.

M: Yes, it is the same with my own experiences, information and evidence that I have accumulated by my personal exploration into these matters. Try as you will, you cannot sell, or even give away your knowledge. It is like that man who stands on a street corner and offers five dollar bills in exchange for a one dollar bill. People think that you're a "nut" and it won't take long before the paddy wagon comes along. It wasn't too long ago (on a TV program) where a man was trying to give away money, and people shied

away from him like he had the plague. That is the way people are, and that is what happened to Shaver, Palmer me, and anyone else that had any knowledge.

S: I hear that you are writing a revised version of your recent book, I SEARCH FOR THE PORTALS. How is that coming along...any problems?

M: I finally got my manuscript to the printer today (April 21, 1981). Now, I just have to get the front cover finished and off to the printer.
Yes, there was "Tamper", ever since last January, in my attempt to rewrite my book. It is still entitled I SEARCH FOR THE PORTALS, but it is not just like the last book. I have changed the pictures and had them screen printed, instead of using the old system. It is completely redone, with some exceptions, from the last book.
Most of the tamper was from people, business managers, and the price-con-schemes, raising the price so much that it would make it impossible to sell it. With advertising and mailing yet to come, I can only say that I will have to sell it for $8, plus $1.40 for postage. So let's say $9.40 postpaid. Please advise your readers to make out any payment to me, only. And I would appreciate BANK MONEY ORDER or POSTAL MONEY ORDER.

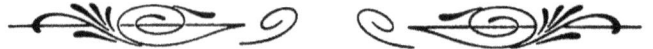

In future articles, Mr Marcoux will present material pertaining to artifacts. His letters sent to RAP and RSS, showed that the followers and readers did very little to explore, investigate and search in the deserts, forests, mountains and caves.
Why do the Forest Rangers cover up so much? Why do they "police" the forestry? Do the shepherds still guard the entrances? Of all Shaver Mystery Club members and followers of Shaver and Palmer, Mr Marcoux is one of the very few who personally explored and found the Elder remains and the entrances to the Hidden world.

-See ad page 14-

---

to Holsinger, the CIA simply moved its mind-control experimnts away from prisons, hospitals and schools at some time during the 1960's. And from another source (THE GLOBE, May 12, 1981) we get basically the same info, except that we find the mind-boggling claim that Jones is still alive and hiding in Brazil, a claim that Shavertron will not endorse at this time.
Hollow earth scholars will be interested to know that a new book on this topic has recently appeared on the scene. HOLLOW EARTH MYSTERIES AND THE POLAR SHIFT by Floria Benton (Future Press, Elkton, MD. USA, and available thru Arcturus Book Service, 263 N. Ballston Ave, Scotia, NY. 12302 USA...$5.65 postpaid). In her book, Benton claims that the hollow earth subject is not well-known worldwide because of a cover-up by inner earth societies who wish to keep their presence a secret. The reason? Soon, our civilization will be wiped out by a pole shift due to the radioactivity building up within the shell of our hollow planet. Evidently, the hollow earthers could care less about us, as they look forward to our demise...they confuse us into thinking nothing is going on. Benton also takes the offensive against such authorities as Carl Sagan, whom she says is playing devil's advocate for the inner earthers by publicly disclaiming such ideas as ancient astronauts, ufos, ancient advanced civilizations, etc. She wouldn't be surprised, she says, if Sagen gets to hop onto a rescue ship at Endtime, as part of his reward from the inner earthers. Another interesting comment she makes is in regard to Alternative 3... Benton says the droughts and gradual heating up of the Earth is caused from within the planet, not without...due to radioactivity, not due to manmade pollutants and erosion of the ozone layer. The real secret is

cont p.15

SUNDAY STAR, DECEMBER 7, 1980

Would the course of 20th century history have been changed if **Harry Tandy** hadn't been a compassionate man?
When Harry was fighting for the British in France in World War I he came upon a German soldier and was about to kill him when he saw the man was wounded. He held his fire and the soldier escaped in the confusion soon afterwards.
On now to 1937, to a meeting between Britain's **Neville Chamberlain** and **Adolf Hitler**. Hitler told his visitor how a British infantryman was about to kill him on the French battlefields of World War I but stopped when he saw Hitler was wounded. Historians say Harry was that private.
The story came out when Harry's Victoria Cross, earned for valor in the Great War, was sold a couple of weeks ago for $70,000. Harry died in 1977 at the age of 86.

From Jim Wentworth

The Mysterious Roman Mine

by Ray Archer

This particular Iron Mine is situated in the Forest of Dean area of Gloucestershire, in the West of England. The mine's entrance is more or less circular in shape. Because of rain seepage, all of the passages are quite wet within.

The layout of the mine consists of a long passage -- a tunnel at least 150 feet in length, which bends slightly to the right halfway in. Another smaller passage branches off to the left from this a little way down from the entrance and leads into the final passage that ends like the long one in a dead-end. The main passage is rather dry after the bend, although it is littered in places by fallen pieces of stone. It is here that our vigils have been held, ever since the first odd incident I will now relate:

The first unusual incident to do with this old mine occurred during a very hot spell of weather and a welcome break from my normal routine, spent down at the Forest of Dean.

On Saturday, 26 June, 1976, a friend told me of a previous visit he had made to the mine, and as it was quite close to where we were caravanning at the time, we both agreed to pay it another visit. Eventually, we came upon the mine (looking to me more like a cave) and entered switching on our torches, and proceeded down the long passage. The roof or ceiling of the tunnel is about 7 feet high from the floor, so we could walk perfectly upright inside, but you do have to stoop a little on entry.

On reaching the end, we decided to stop a few minutes before exploring the other passages...besides it was cooler than the sweltering heat outside... and struck up a conversation. Suddenly, John, my friend, drew my attention to a strange roaring noise (such as a lorry or truck makes) gradually getting louder, and coming from somewhere deep below the floor of the passage, moving towards the mine's entrance. The noise lasted at least 3 or 4 seconds and faded into the distance-- an estimation, as we did not have our watches-- and all was again silent as before.

Since that experience, periodic visits have been made (and still are) in the hope of photographing or taping something unusual there. I now give a brief summary of other strange occurrances also associated with our vigils in this old working...late at night and quite recently. How much of this can be explained by natural phenomenon I leave each individual SHAVERTRON reader to draw their own conclusions.

On May 27, 1980 a vigil was kept during which a musty smell was noticed on entry, a tape in the cassette recorder decided to come out blank,etc. We agreed to leave the cassette on its own for about half an hour and then about 15 minutes was spent inside, during which I among other things, felt an energy (like electricity tingling) pass into me from the floor, setting me buzzing (shaking). John felt nothing at all, but I found after this, I was much calmer than before, having been on edge a little on entering the mine that night.

During the same week, another visit was made at night on 30, 5, 1980. This time the atmosphere in the place was entirely different from the last occasion, but even so, for some reason, many of the flash cubes on the camera would not fire, ruining several pictures. In spite of this, two black and white prints did turn out, one of which (shown in this article) is of the entrance. The starting point of both passages can just be made out, the one on the right being the longest one of the two. The "ray" lower centre, had me wondering at first, but it is obviously a reflection off a can or bottle from the flash cube when the picture was taken.

Our vigil began at 10:20 pm. and lasted to 10:50 pm this time. The cassette recorder never let us down, and came out quite good. On this occasion, too, the recorder was left inside. After about 15 minutes outside, we were thinking of going back in again, when unusual BOOMING noises sounded from the interior. All told, we counted seven, almost one after the other. After getting back to the recorder, the last boom no. 8 sounded..this I think can just be heard above the noise of the recorder although one can't be certain. Some time after, the tape finished and we left.

During the most recent watch, Don, another friend joined us, and even though nothing of real significance happened that evening, some good colour pictures were taken of the interior. On this night, 8-23-80, we stayed inside the main passage, more or less in close proximity with the recorder. This time, the vigil had started later, due to unforseen circumstances. From 11:40 pm. to 11:55 was devoted to the flash photography, already gone into before. At about midnight, we all became aware of a significant change in the atmosphere of the place and also a strong smell of sulphur.

On moving a little up the passage towards the entrance, a vapour was seen (blue smoke) issuing from part of the ceiling, reminding me of films depicting "genies" escaping from their lamps. At this point, one of us panicked, which had us all hurring in the direction of the entrance again. After realising we had been rather silly, there being no real reason for running,

9

we turned round and walked back to the recorder.
The smell and the smoke were no longer present
by this time and nothing further happened, up to
the time the tape ran out at 12:40pm. and our
vigil ended.

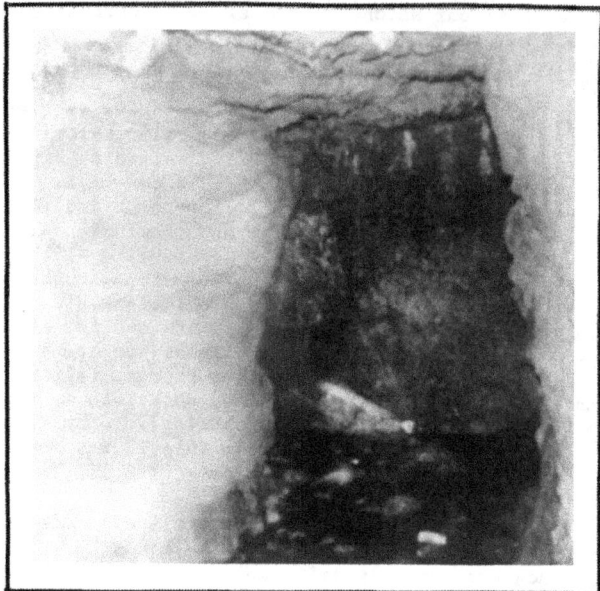

"Entrance to Roman Mine taken by Ray Archer"

TWO UNUSUAL ENCOUNTERS

A very significant phenomenon of the Forest
of Dean area is the number of "ley lines" passing through it.

Not surprising either is the discovery while
plotting these lines, I found at least one passes through the region of the Roman Mine. When
we spent a week taking in the area and parts of
Wales, in May of 1980, there were two reasons
we went: the mine and the leys. You could also
say the ufo flap, a few months before, also
prompted us, but this appears to have been centred
around the town of Gloucester itself.

On Thursday, May 29, my friend and I were returning to the Dean, from Wales, in a motor caravan. At
about 1:00am. we were driving down a quiet road in the
country that had very high walls on both sides. Suddenly, what we took for a house cat seemed to rush
out from these walls in front of us, and under our
wheels-- we felt a jolt in the caravanette. But when
we got out to see, there was nothing on the road. There
was a weird flapping noise and squeaking sounds, seeming to come from the tree-tops, but nothing was found
even with our torches.

The second incident happened on the Stourton Road
about half an hour later. While driving along, a
long trailer lorry, its lights coming on all at once,
suddenly came out of a lay-by right in front of our
vehicle...turning onto the same road as us. It seems
from that start, this other vehicle did not appear
"right". There was no engine noise that we could detect. It seemed capable of rapid acceleration, and
suddenly shot round a bend in the road. John, who
was driving, put on the speed, but even though it
was a straight road after the bend, it had vanished
into thin air!

Before its somewhat enigmatic departure, the
lorry had been about 15 to 20 feet in front of our
motor caravan for at least two miles, so we got a
good look at it.

Its colour seemed to be grey or black, but I
cannot be sure, and neither can John, as colours
look different at night. The lorry was carrying
what appeared to be metal bars on its trailor, and
the back of the cab had two black strips, so I could
not see the driver. John thought he saw the shoulder
of a person from his angle. We travelled quite a
way before seeing a turnoff on the right, and cannot
see how a heavy vehicle could have reached this point
without us seeing it slowing down to turn, when we
ourselves were not too far behind. Was all this just
a misinterpretation of normal occurrances? Or was
something having a laugh at our expense?
30

ARE gnomes (in bubble cars) in the City park

Oct. 1, 1979

By GILL SWAIN

GNOMES, those legendary little
chaps with bearded faces, are
alive and well and living in the
technological age.

At least that's what children in
Nottingham, who claim they were
chased out of a park by little chaps
in bubble cars, believe.

Angela Elliott, Patrick Olive and
Andrew Pearce, all ten, and Andrew's
eight-year-old sister Rosie, who
live in Kennington Road, Radford,
were walking home at dusk after
playing in Wollaton Park, a mile
from their homes, when they had
their close encounter.

Angela said : 'We heard this tinkly
bell. We started running and these
little men in cars came out of the
bushes. There were about 60 of
them in 30 cars like bubble cars.
'They were half my size and looked
old. They had greenish faces with
crinkles in them and long white
bears with a bit of red on the end.
They were laughing in a funny way.

We were frightened and ran to
the gate. I don't think they liked
the lights outside because they
didn't follow us into the street.'

Andrew said he saw one of the
men standing up. 'He had a red
top on and green legs,' he said.

The youngsters told their story at
Southwold primary school the following morning and were questioned
by headmaster Mr Robin Aldridge.

He got them to draw pictures and
tape-recorded interviews with each
of the children.

Mr Aldridge said yesterday: 'I
know it sounds far fetched but they
really believe in what they saw.
These children are not the kind
who would make up something like
this.

The children claim they have
never seen gnomes before but
rumours in Nottingham playgrounds
are that Wollaton Park is full of
them.

Andrew said : 'We heard that if
you don't tell them where you live
they take you to their houses and
keep you.'

The very day after the youngsters'
fright, Patrick's 12-year-old sister
Mandy caught a glimpse of the
weird gnomobiles.

She said : 'There were about six
of them coming round the back of
Wollaton Castle. They were just like
those Patrick saw.'

Former secretary of the Fairy Investigation Society in Nottingham,
Miss Marjorie Johnson, is convinced the park is a favourite haunt
of the little people. She said : 'I
think the children's stories are
genuine. I have had other reports
of sightings near the park lake.'

Unidentified flying objects experts
are getting in on the act, too. Mr
Larry Dale, head of the British UFO
Research Association, said yesterday : 'I shall be contacting our local
investigator.'

Patrick's mother Mrs Joan Olive
took a more down-to-earth view.
She said : 'I think it's a load of
nonsense.'

Thanks to Ray Archer for these clips!

It's no fairy tale, sir

THE little people are
making themselves
really at gnome in a
quiet park.

Four children at South-
wood Primary School,
Radford, Nottingham-
shire, told their head-
master t h e y were
followed home by about
60 gnome-like crinkle
faced, laughing little
men, in tiny cars.

Mr Robin Altridge said
he had questioned the
c h i l d r e n separately,
tape recorded their
answers and after
studying them said :
"All their stories
tallied."

DAILY STAR 10/1/79

'Dream' Inspired Threat to Reagan

New York 4-9-81

Edward Richardson, arrested Tuesday for threatening the president's life in an imitation of accused would-be-assassin John Hinckley Jr., wrote that he was inspired by a "prophetic dream" in which Hinckley urged him to commit the deed, officials said yesterday.

Richardson was held on $500,000 bail in the Metropolitan Correctional Center in Manhattan after allegedly threatening to kill Reagan, Secretary of State Alexander Haig and Senator Jesse Helms, R-N.C.

In an apparent attempt to follow Hinckley's footsteps, Richardson spent last weekend at New Haven, Conn., where actress Jodie Foster is a freshman at Yale.

Hinckley is charged with attempting to kill Reagan last week — perhaps in an effort to impress the 18-year-old actress.

Richardson wrote to the actress that he had attended a Yale student production in which she was performing last weekend, intending to shoot her. But, he wrote, he decided she was "too beautiful to kill."

A friend of Richardson's said yesterday that the 22-year-old unemployed laborer was the sort of person who was fascinated by spectacular crimes.

"I remember when Gerald Ford was shot, he got real, real interested in Squeaky Fromme," said the friend, Peter H. Griffin. "He knew everything about it." Fromme was one of two women who unsuccessfully tried to shoot

Ford in 1975.

Richardson had recently lived with his sister in a small Colorado town near the Hinckley family home, and stayed in the same hotel Hinckley had used in one of his visits to New Haven.

The letters Richardson allegedly wrote during his four days in New Haven make repeated references to Hinckley. One, sent to Foster, promised to "finish what Hinckley started."

"RR must die," the letter said.

"Teenager Accused of Reagan Threat"
5/15/81--New Haven, Conn: A teenager who was apparently drunk has been charged with threatening to kill the President..."The threat was real, but she probably didn't have the means to carry out the crime"...

UPI Telephoto

EDWARD RICHARDSON
The arrested man

"He (JWH) told me so in a prophetic dream. Sadly though, your death is also required. You, too, will suffer the same fate as Reagan and others in the fascist regime. You cannot escape. We are a wave of assassins throughout the world."

Richardson is remembered as a youth who fantasized.

In his high school yearbook, he listed biology club, rifle club and the baseball team as his activities, but school officials said Richardson was not on the baseball team nor a member of the biology club, and that the rifle club was disbanded during his first year there.

"I would have to conclude that he just wanted to belong — that he fantasized," said assistant principal Mel Brodsky.

English teacher Jean Smith said she noticed a change when she saw Richardson last year. "His conversation was rambling and full of fantasizing about what he wanted to do and places he wanted to go," she said.

U.P. & A.P.

ELF unit suspected in storm

MADISON (AP) — A Navy radio transmitter in northern Wisconsin may have triggered a massive summer storm in 1977 that killed two persons and caused $50 million in property damage, Stop Project ELF has claimed.

The group, admitting that its theory has not been scientifically proven, called for an investigation into the possible effects that the ELF transmitter at Clam Lake could have on weather.

The group said transmissions from the facility during a routine thunderstorm converted the storm into a massive downburst. The ELF system transmits extremely low frequency electromagnetic radiation.

"An inspection of the facility's operating logs shows a direct correlation between the time the transmission went on at full power and the intensity of the storm," John Stauber, a Stop Project ELF board member, told a news conference.

"The Navy's ELF system may have inadvertently triggered a weather bomb," Stauber said.

2/15/81 Minn. paper CR. Mary LeVesque

Pennsylvania Man Arrested For Threats to Reagan 4-13-81

Hatboro, Pa.

A Philadelphia area man who was arrested for allegedly threatening to kill President Reagan was jailed yesterday on $50,000 bail, awaiting arraignment on federal charges.

Secret Service agents Saturday arrested James T. McCaughey, 42, for the alleged threats.

McCaughey was being held in Montgomery County prison on charges of assaulting two Hatboro police officers who accompanied a Secret Service agent to McCaughey's apartment, police said.

A Secret Service spokesman said yesterday that McCaughey would be charged in U.S. District Court in Philadelphia this morning with threatening to kill the president and with assaulting the Secret Service agent.

Hatboro police said McCaughey resisted them, punching and kicking them, once they were inside the police station. He was arraigned before a district magistrate on three counts of assault on police officers.

Kevin Tucker, Secret Service agent-in-charge for Philadelphia, said McCaughey made his threats against Reagan by telephone directly to a Secret Service agent Saturday morning. McCaughey was arrested soon after.

United Press

11

INSTANT DERO
MEAN MACHINE

By AL WISEMAN

A few short years ago, Ray Palmer published a special book-length article (name not recalled at the moment- was it "Hidden Kingdom"?) in FORUM. The surprise mini- edition cited existence of a newly- crashed saucer (reported originally in the mass- media via auspices of TRUE MAGAZINE). The non- confirmed (to date, that is) incident occured some while back, probably circa 1947 or thereabouts. The fantastic disc contained several dead human- like occupants. The bodies were found to be dwarf- sized bipeds garbed in curious, ana- chronistic costumes of a bygone era (Spanish variety). Of course such as this could not fail to stagger the post- atomic, workaday individual.

The Scientific Community was even then being challenged by the recent event of "impossible" high performance ufos which had current- ly blistered the air over California's towering Cascade Mts. Now, according to Einstein's marvelous Specail Theory Theory of Relativ- ity, the way the "composite" cosmic Universe is built causes a num- ber of unusual phenomena to occur in space travel which approaches the astronomical speed of light (apprx. 186,000 miles per second, for ye ready reference "number" freaks). These phenomena include: 1..CLOCKS slow down. 2..AGEING processes, ditto. 3..The SIZE of tangible objects decreases considerably. 4..A notable INCREASE in weight of objects is affected.

Time dilation and the Lorentz- Einstein contraction of mass, ergo, is an experimental fact (recent experiments suggest that ageing is linked to "motion"!) Regarding the downed saucer above, the writer suggests that a disc- shaped ufo, in a time long past, set out from Earth on a journey into deep space. The amazing spacecraft was based UNDERGROUND in secret, hidden caverns which honeycomb deep beneath medieval Spain (with its then still tenable ancient cities!) Now, historic fact is that once, in a century set in the Medieval Age, in the same country, two different contingents of well-armed Spanish Army troops vanished without any trace while traversing rugged mountain terrain known to be rife with cavern openings.

It might be labeled a sci-fi dreamy dream or Moon Smoke by some, nonetheless, the writer contends that near-light speed travel under conditions prevelant in outer space subjects voyagers to freakish unknown biological processes. PERMANENT molecular changes in both human and humanoid physiognomy and PSYCHOLOGICAL make-up can occur bodily. Abnormal, mutative-like changes-- a strange atrophy, a pronounced shrinkage in bodily structure. Thus, the resultant typ- ical "Dero" characteristics as per related above in "disc-overy" of the crash-landed ufo! Probably a fatal mishap and violent descent to earth was how the saucer finally came to be captured on the floor of the great American desert.

The clothing of the "time travel" saucer crew would, of course, have had to be the highly stylized sort contemporaneous with the historic period in which they embarked originally on the trip thu through outer space. As per already outlined in the foregoing, traversing space at near-light speed may well subtly affect the e- motion-effusive, sensuate human nervous system; the body chemistry, and the intellect or mind-- perhaps beyond all repair. It might well be productive of zombie-like humanoid "robots"-- ghastly dero with glassy-eyed murderous fixations! In which case someday (may- be sooner than later) we may say hello to the first modernday ver- sion of the new "Instant Dero..Mean Machine".

Tunnels & Caverns Under NYC

by R.L. Blain-Somers

Under NYC exists a tunnel which connects a Masonic Engin- eering school called "Cooper U- nion" at 8th street and 3rd Ave with the "Flatiron Building", a triangular-shaped building loca- ted at 23rd street and 5th Ave where Broadway and 5th Ave "X" each other.

The third point in this tri- angle is interestingly enough, a homosexual bar known for its, a- hem, hot heavy action in the ba- sement tunnels which apparently go for 100's of feet. This is located in the heart of the meat packing area, (the cattle muti- lation connection) at 14th St. and 10th Ave., called the ANVIL. (Again, the Masonic connection, for the CYCLOPS or eye in the PEER-AMID were Smith's as well as Masons). There appears to be a number of "5's" connected with this triad along with an X-ing or crossing of force lines as is apparent.

In the ANVIL there are "SA- TANIC" insignia as well as own- ers of the same breed. (From an ENOCHIAN CABALIST who used to work there). There are also stories of rape by inhuman, stinking, wretched things (pro- bably Dero). The owners were taken aback at any of the Wiccan charms our friend wore or aero- gramic Pentacles drawn astrally in their presence. The aversion probably having to do with the fecund-male origin of that par- ticular art.

Retrospeck:

BY RALPH HOLLAND

"Our continuing saga of the history of the SM."

Many ages ago when our solar system was young -- long before any of the present human races had appeared-- its planets were colonized by the space travelling "Elder Race". There seems to have been at least three different groups of these people, but all allied to some degree. Their sciences were far above ours of even today. By means of medical rays they had conquered disease and were able to extend their lives to unbelievable spans-- thousands of years. Since it is an inescapable law of nature that nothing can remain stationary, but must either grow or decay, their great age was also accompanied by great size which continued to increase as long as they lived.

Synthetic foods, clothing, and all other desired articles were made by fully automatic machinery (mech). This robot mech was so well made that it required very little, if any, attention and was practically indestructable. A sort of super- television could pick up three dimensional images and sound from any place, in natural color, and despite many miles of intervening rock. A reversed variety of this mech, the "telesolidograph" could project sound and images to any point.

For defense purposes, these ancients had several weapons. "Stun Rays" would temporarily paralyse persons without doing any harm to them. Other rays could act upon the brain and circulatory system to cause the death of persons at great distances by inducing a "stroke" or "heart attack". Blast rays would cause explosions at distant points, while "dis guns" and dis cannon would destroy persons or objects by disintegrating them into pure energy.

In addition to their many medical and healing rays, they also used "stim rays" which could play upon the emotions, plus accomplishing by direct means what we seek to do with music, literature and plays (and sex too..Ed.). Perhaps the most important of their rays was "telaug", which picked up, amplified and transmitted telepathic thought radiations.

This was originally used as a means of communication between persons and could be recorded on tapes for later "scanning". It is from these tapes that Shaver claims to have secured most of his information about these people. Telaug could read the thoughts of a person at a distant point, or implant the thoughts of the sender into anothers brain without his knowledge, although the ancients apparently considered this unethical, and had strict rules against it. In the latter days of the Elders, however, after they had become degenerated, corrupt rulers used a variety of telaug as "control ray" to control the thinking of the people and thus keep themselves in power.

Attention all Ufozine editors/publishers!
Ufologist, Tom Lind is compliling as complete a listing of Ufo-oriented zines as possible for future publication. If you pub, or know someone who pubs a Ufozine, please give all pertinent details to: Tom Lind, 124 Ivy Drive, no.8, Charlottesville, Virginia 22901. Any help is greatly appreciated.

GREAT MOMENTS IN UFOLOGY

Here we find the Italian contactee, Zanfretta, wearing alien medical gear. Behind him stands "the egg-headed man", who often tormented Zanfretta in his many close encounters of the 4th kind. The "ship" that Zanfretta has experienced, is similar to the classic Adamski saucer, according to Luciano Boccone, the investigator of this case. Dec. 2, 1979.

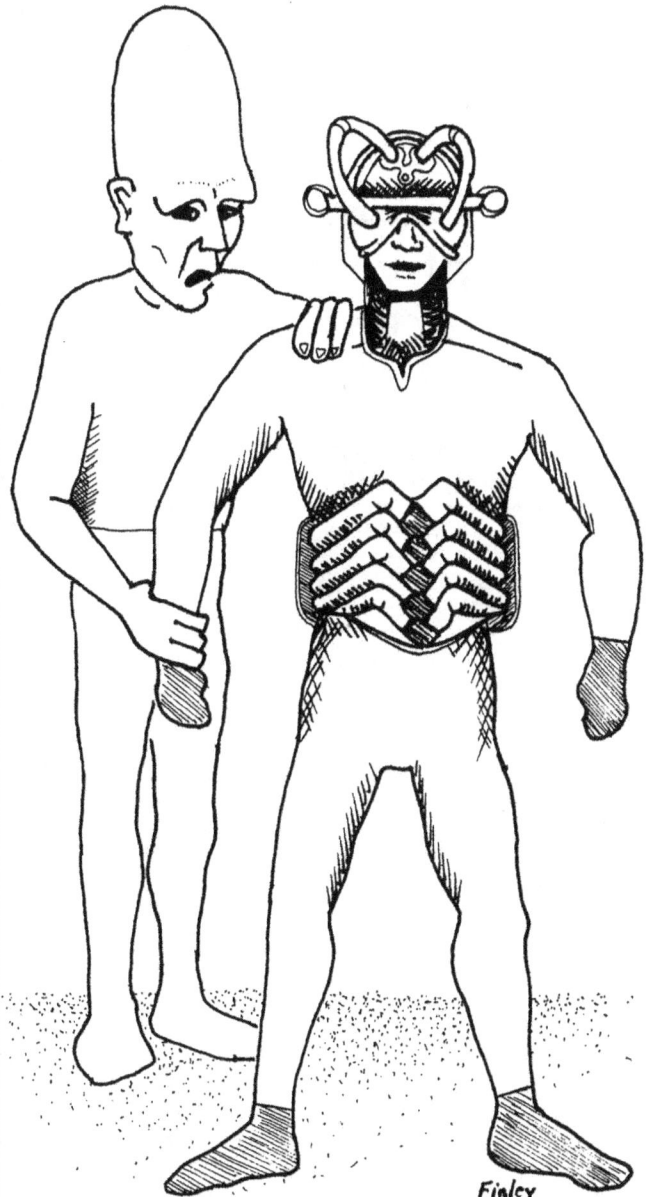

Finley

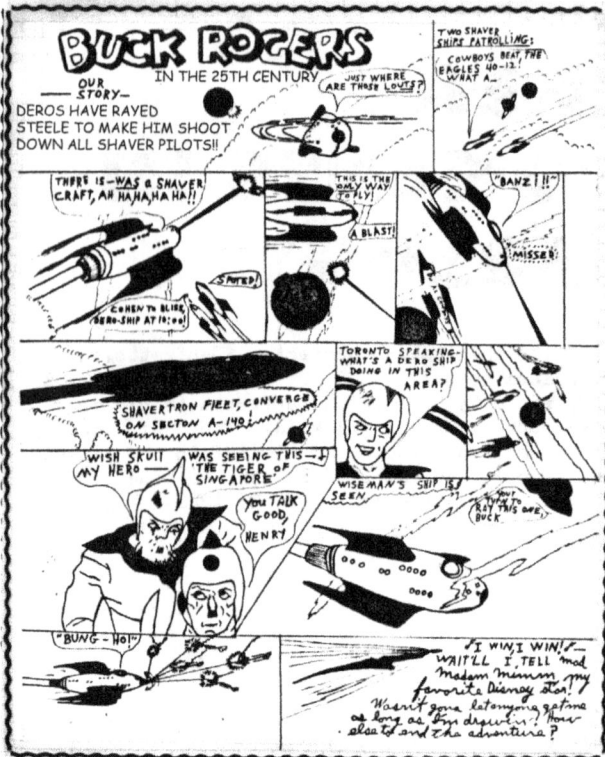

Alternative 3: Survival of Man

A Computerized Nightmare?

PHIL HRUSKOCY

In regard to the controversy on Alternative Three, the alleged international manned Mars space effort to assure the survival of the human species, let us try and look at the timetables for such a move.

1. May 5, 2000: The Earth will tilt on its axis. According to many geophysicists as there will be a planetary alignment far more acute than the one so ofter discussed for September, 1982.

2. Our world economic system, if it is controllable, would only collapse AFTER THE CONSPIRATORS ASSURRED a Mars civilization to become viable. This would mean they would "pull the plug", usher in their one world mark-of-the-beast computer system, when, if it backfired, they could flee this planet and its atomic inferno.

3. Our world economic system is OUT OF CONTROL, would imply the hurrying up of the batch consignments, and technical personnel needed to make up for lost time due to the previous setbacks.

4. The collapse of the economy would make the computer systems a reality, only for recruitment for the project under the guise of simplifying our already complex world.

5. All space research must be viewed in the light of making life on this planet continue elsewhere.

The cover-up of the book, its ramifications, and serious debate on the theory(?) leaves one thing clear—we are in a vacuum as to what our secret rulers have been working on since the end of WWII; we know little of just how far technology has gone; and we care little of how much time we have in the cosmic clock for this planet. We are in a race against many things, population, pollution, ignorance, and psychological warfare. Only how many are still thinking outside their little smug world.

6. Dr. Beter's assessments of the world condition can be seen to make sense now that we have an independent authority (from Great Britain) saying the space race wasn't just an olympic event, nor even a military one, but rather a life and death assault on another place to start life anew.

I challenge every reader to the ultimate thought:

One world government when all minds are linked via one wavelength. Hence, NO INDIVIDUALISM THEN!!

No rebellion, only a computerized nightmare.

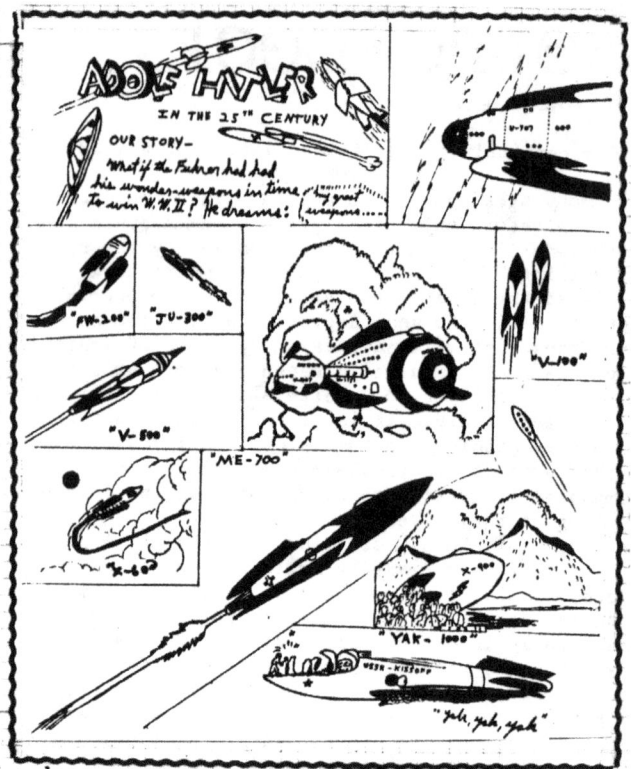

PURE BLISS

This ish will be devoted to reviewing a box of sci-fi books Shavertron's editor sent to the Fixit shop in Chillicothe.

All four of these paperbacks are the Timescape series pubbed by Pocket Books, Simon & Shuster, NY:

THE CAPTIVE by Robt. Stallman

Herein, the werewolf legend is inverted with a creature from space which can change into human form. Later in the book it is referred to as a big pussycat. The tale takes place in the 1930's. The fascination factor is high, and Stallman succeeds in getting the reader to look out through the critter's eyes.

FIREFLOOD AND OTHER STORIES by Vonda N. McIntyre

A collection of short stories featuring Le 'Femme with far out problems. All guaranteed to generate a tremendous empathy in readers who have at a time in the course of their lives felt trapped. Recourse Inc. has a humour element, unless of course, the reader had difficulties with computors and dubious firms. All very readable, though often inclined toward the morbid.

GOLEM 100 by Alfred Bester

Bester has been well known since the pulp era. Another Gully Foyle? Nope. A perfume chemist in a world that is overpopulated and has a bad case of B.O. He becomes involved in the plot whena Hindu detective consults him. Meanwhile, a ladies' club dabbles in the occult, and unintentionally foments a monster. Profusely illustrated by Jack Gaughan.

A FOND FAREWELL TO DYING by Syd Logsdon

Another post atomic war tale. This time the planet needs the big terraforming kit. Among other things, there is a high water problem. Meanwhile humanity behaves as usual. Almost at atomic war again. Cloning is a major factor in the story and explores the question: If your entire mental stock is transcribed to a clone of you, is the clone you even though you are still you? The prose is a bit old-fashioned, but readable.

*   *   *

Received a letter from Jessica St.George today. She has commenced tuning in on rock images--direct eye-balling and psychic methods:
"I think I have found about 5 more rock books," writes Jessica. "I, finally in desperation, meditated on where to find them. I saw this dark creek with skinny trees and the next day found the location. My meditation said that in creeks with sandy bottoms and lots of rocks is a good possibility. And the other place, which is not around here, is on the sides of mountains. What do you think about that? Well, you see I'd only one rock book which was polished and that made it difficult for me to determine how the others should look. Well, I started finding others which I think are rock books. I would not dare to polish them. I think that there are many kinds and that some wear better than others. Well, think of all the types of books printed...types of papers, etc."

By Bill Bliss

Con't. from page 8

Is there truly a "wave of assasins" as described by copykat assasin Richardson in our featured newsclip this ish? Since our last issue appeared, there has been so much news we don't have space for it all. The attempt on Reagan's life in late March was part of a vast scenario that played and then replayed itself over and over...please note our newsclip on Hinkley's copykat, Edward Richardson.   A rash of threats against political figures flared up during late March. Dero scatter ray? Hinkley followed the same scenario even down to the Jody Foster connection. There is also a Right Wing Extremist theory concerning this assasination attempt, and it is expressed by one reader in our lettercol. Along this line is the SPOTLIGHT's article hinting at trouble in Reagan's own ranks (4-27-81). The power struggles between such gov't. heavies as Haig and CIA types make Reagan's presidency all the more dangerous to him.

Six weeks later, we find the Pope ducking bullets in Rome. A worldwide conspiracy? No, never, of course not. Has the USSR begun its version of our newest war? WWIII? A war of the mind, rather than body? Or is it the USA? At this point, its hard to tell who's working for whom.

Something of interest along this line is an article called THE HELGE FILE--MIB IN SWEDEN? that appears in the Oct/Dec. 1980 issue of the Swedish ufo paper, Nyhetsblad AFU Newsletter...(PO Box 11027, S-60011, Norrkoping II, Sweden). It is a tale in the same genre as Al Bender's "Flying Saucers and the 3 Men". We quote: "whoever these people are they are working on a global basis. They look almost exactly alike as reports from all over the world confirm. The Ufo-mafia connection has been mentioned by other Ufologists and contactees. Woodrow Derenberger, the American contactee, who was visited by the MIB referred to them as the mafia...I also would like to mention Richard Shaver, who claimed that the largest group of cave dwellers were the "gangster" groups who are "in active and frequent contact with both criminals and corrupt politicians on the surface." Even though some of this fine zine is printed in Swedish, (wadya mean ya can't read Swede?) at least half is printed in English.

Another Ufo zine from this side of the world is Gil Ziemba's "The New National Ufo Newsletter"...
($10 a year, monthly, RR2--Box 335, Crab Orchard Estates, Carbondale, Ill. 62901 USA). Gil has made an impressive start with an expose' by Kal K.Korff on the Meier contactee case. The Meier contact has been described in a very expensive and heavily advertised book called "Contact With the Plieades". It is being billed by The NNUNewsletter as the "most infamous hoax in Ufology", and if you suckered into the book, you will no doubt want to find out more. Even some of ufology's finest have become mired in this deal ...Wendele Stevens being one of them.

In this newest issue of S we bring back our British correspondent, Ray Archer, with an account of his vigil in an ancient Roman mine. An interview with valedictorian Shaver Mystery explorer and writer, Charles Marcoux is also featured. Al Wiseman relates his formula for becoming dero "instantly". Henry Steele tries his hand at cartooning Shaver style. A short article by Rande on tunnels under NYC, and our usual features including Jim Wentworth's "Giants"...Shaver Mystery fans couldn't ask for more (but we know they will...and we intend to give it to you). Next issue will mark our 10th... and to celebrate this milestone we intend to pub Richard Shaver's last known unpublished interview, with photos...sooo!

From our Rome Correspondent we've received some

New Facts On Space Meanies

Ms. Germana Grosso, from Italy, apparently after having
been sick, started getting very strong telepathy messages
from several space dwellers. She said it just started
one day, and through the years, she learned how to send
a message back, by means of telepathy. Anyway, one of
her closest space friends is a guy that goes by the name
of Ithacar, from planet Masar...that isn't Mars, though,
not the one we know. They moved out of Mars long ago,
and now they only keep robots and machines, and have a
crew there to service them periodically. Ithacar and
his people had to find another Mars (Masar). Among the
many messages that Germana Grosso got from Ithacar was
a particular one telling her about some "negative" planets, and their inhabitants. One of them is Saturn,
where the people look very much like us, generally
brown haired, good looking, very mellow, but under the
surface they turn out to be very very mean. These negatives, who represent absolute evil, are in constant
fight with the people from Masar, and other planets
also, who try to stop their intentions to permanently
invade the Earth. Apparently, these "negatives" have
no fixed bases on Earth. The people from Etenya, where
the Egyptian race came from, and the people from Masar,
Lioaki, Algol, won't let them. Over the next issue, I
will tell you more about some other "meanies" who often
visit this planet...and I will try to contact Ms. Grosso
asking her some questions about inner earth...although
I am not so sure she will answer.

Francesco Savorgnan
Via Barnaba Oriani 91
Roma, Italia

PS- Ms. Grosso wrote a book about her space contacts,
with V. Sontorio, an Italian journalist.

Lou Farish tells us that he has hundreds of Ufo/weird
phenomena books for sale. Some are one-of-a-kind, and
all are first come, first served. He is also offering
a book-finding service for hard-to-get titles...at a
reasonable fee. For a copy of his list, send an SASE
to Lou Farish, Rt.1--Box 220, Plumerville, Ark.72127.

SHAVERTRON

First Class

SHAVERTRON

"The Only Source of Post-Deluge Shaverania"

WINTER 1981 — ©Richard Toronto

NEVER BEFORE PUBLISHED: LAST SHAVER INTERVIEW !!!

10th MILESTONE ISSUE

INNER EARTH

AGHARTA

R. TORONTO

MAX PYFIELD -81

RICHARD S. SHAVER

HIS WORLD(S)

$2

notes from the underground

SHAVER TRON

Editor/Publisher
Richard Toronto

Associates:

Art Director
Max Fyfield

SM Adventurer
Charles Marcoux

Rogphoto Tech
Bill Bliss

SM Consultant
Jim Wentworth

Literary Research
Jim Pobst

Moral Support
Mary LeVesque

Inner Earth Research
Bruce Walton

Our Man In:

Britain: Ray Archer
Rome: Francesco Savorgnan
Washington, DC:
"The Librarian"
Private Idaho: R.Finley

The Shaver Mystery lives on as you will soon see in this issue. This is something of a milestone for S, being our 10th issue and going on our third year of publication. Wish we could say that all was going well with other small zines around the country. As many of you know, The Pyramid Guide folded with its 55th issue, after nine years of publishing. Bill Cox, the editor, says that mailing and printing expenses were getting to be too much, as well as the time it took to pub the zine. Another "old timer" on the zine publishing scene, Riley Crabb, is also feeling the bite.

Reagan isn't helping us out much with the postal rates, he points out, as they have just raised the rate on 3rd class mail by 70%! "Whereas it used to cost 40 cents to mail a Journal" he says, "it now costs 69 cents! That's the First Class rate! Postal people tell us the goal of the Postmaster is to eliminate all postal classes and have only one, First Class Rate." Your humble editor went to talk with postal minions today, and yes, it is true. They said that S cannot get a cheaper rate than First Class, unless we hit the 4-ounce mark, or get enough subscribers to get Bulk Mail rate (we're no where near it). Unhappily, we've gotten complaints from readers whose issues look as though they were used as paper filters in a Mr Coffee machine, and they plead with us to use envelopes and a cheaper postal rate. Well, here's the envelope-- wish we could get a cheaper mail rate. If anyone can give us a super-cheap rate on 5 by 7 inch manila envelopes, please let us know.

Make a special note to yourself to fill in the Shavertron Survey on page 9. The more of you who fill it out, the better S can serve your needs and desires. Note, too, that we have instituted a new column at the urging of Ray Archer, among others, called Contact. You are all invited to use this service and it's Free...an almost unheard of word these days.

We got a note from Dorris Van Tassel the other day. Seems she wants to buy a printing press to pub some of Van's out-of-print works on flying saucers. Says there are "negatives" working against them down there: "Would believe anything could happen to those who are Spirititually trying these days...Two fellows lost good jobs because they talked of Van Tassel. Van told me of the opposition in the Press, but I never dreamed it was as stacked as this!" says Dorris. If you have an extra one lying around, she could use a Chief 15, or AB Dick 360 or a 1250 Multigraph...PO Box 3867, Landers, CA. 92284.

Want to mention MAPIT, the British ufo organization/journal. They are doing some excellent research on ufos Over There, and are fighting like cats, dogs and ufologists constantly do. They are going to create an honest-to-goodness ufo research library open to everyone, with a computor, no less! All we need is a ticket to England, and we're set. More on MAPIT later...their address: 92 Hillcrest Rd., Offerton, Stockport, Cheshire, England SK2 5SE.

We wanted to use this column for our review on Vallee's newest opus, "Messengers of Deception", but we see our space is shrinking fast:

Shavertron's Review of Mesengers of Deception

It's that contactee crimefighter, Jacques Vallee, here to save the world from the threat of irrationalism! Jacques thunders: "We are being manipulated by persons unknown somewhere on this planet!"

Jacques believes at this point in his ufo-crimefighting career (you remember how well he handled Richard Dreyfus in the box office smash, Close Encounters of the Third Kind?) that we are entering a new Dark Age, which will extinguish the brilliant light of rationalism fired by his fellow countrymen in France. To listen to Jacques, one would think that France is one of the last bastions of logic in the world-- and that California is trying to shove the remnants of that logic over the Abyss.

Basically, Vallee states his fear that an age based on irrational thinking is looming ahead of us, while we blithely let ourselves be

Shavertron is quarterly at $8 per year domestic, $9 overseas via surface, $13 via airmail. Make out all checks or money orders to the publisher, not to the zine.

Advertising Rates:

$20--full page
$10--half page
$ 5--quarter
$ 2.50--eighth
Cover by Max Fyfield

2   cont pg 16

Dear Richard,

I have one complaint and a suggestion. Many readers consider "Shavertron" and other HE newsletters as collectors' items. It really gets me "hot" to see the way the mail gets beat up and since "Shavertron" is a quarterly, a couple days longer in delivery would make little difference. I would suggest that you mail Shavertron in an envelope or at least a sturdy wrapper and send it at a reduced rate.

I've been helping Tillman L. Martin and Bruce Walton compile a HE bibliography. Martinhhas a list out now, though not complete, it would be an enormous help to new fans of the HE subject. Though my files are a total mess, I could probably list around 200 items on the subject. At least another 200 science fiction and fantasy items could be added to this list. Tillman Martin's address is 298 Cahal St., Hattiesburg, MI 39401. He is revising his list as I recently sent him a long list of items that I copied from my files.

I enjoy Shavertron and hope it will continue on and on. Am sending along my renewal.

Frank Brownley
Rochester, NY

Dear Rich,

Got number 9 a few days ago. Have to honestly say that it was not one of your better issues. In my opinion, you're using far too much stuff which is total nonsense. Reprinting the entire Holland article would have been better, as it is excellent background info for those just becoming interested in the SM. I have no real complain t about the new format, but I certainly hope number 10 (and all subsequent issues) will be better than this one.

Lou Farish
Rt.1-220
Plumerville,
Ark. 72127

R-- It's guys like Lou that keep us awake at night thinking of ways to make next issue more wonderful than the last! Believe it or not, Lou will be featured in our famous Shavertron Interview in issue 11. Lou has been in the ufo field for as long as we can remember, and its rare that we see him interviewing (he's shy). Readers won't want to to miss this interview!

Letters

Richard,

Have been getting constant mail from Henry Steele. He claims he's going to put out Shaver Mag--that RSS is still living--in caverns-- that there are all sorts of conspiracies against him...etc. He sent me correspondence that he has apparently sent to you--xeroxed copy to me. Well? What do you think? In spite of my interest in his drawings, and in the SM, he seems to be a bit off, to me.... mentally unstable. I say that not because of his way-out claims... Shaver's were rather way-out! But because too much of what he says just does not stack up with other sources of info. Of course, dero tamper ray could have affected his brain, as apparently with RSS. Thus the paranoia/persecution complex. But everything that happens he attributes to the cavern world-- makes one awful suspicious. Well?

Harvey Larsen
PO Box 4080
Torrance, CA.
90510

R--It probably wont soothe you to know that you are but one of many being bugged by this ersatz newsletter publisher! Due to so many readers asking us what the heck is going on...we reveal the whole sordid tale in this issue. Hope that no one has lost much in this enterprize!

Dear Rich,

I am very intrigued by the descriptions of some of the cavern creatures given by RSS in his writings. In some ghost cases, these creatures, or ones similar to them, keep cropping up. Either RSS had really seen these things or the phenomenon is patterning itself on various articles or books just to confuse us or mislead us. The latter, of course, indicates something watching the human race. It's certainly baffling, and it seems there is no complete solution, all one can do is speculate.

The zine is getting better each issue. Number 9 was very good. Max is doing a great job on the covers. His art reminds me of the late RSS to a certain extent. I liked the layout and the pics looked great. You certainly have been receiving some criticsim lately as shown by your interesting editorial, but this might help in the long run, and shows your zine is becoming known to other publishers.

Ray Archer
6 St.Margaret Rd
Stoke, Coventry
West Midlands
England CV1 2B2

Dear Mr Toronto,

We are an information-gathering group in touch with many peopleall over the USA who are doing research on the nature of earth's structure and the hollow earth theory. Most of these people have graciously agreed to compile their information into articles and contribute them to our quarterly newsletter. We hope to pub our first issue in July.

Membership in our organization is $15 per year to join and $10 per year and includes the newsletter and certificate of membership.

For further info please feel free to write me.

Dennis Feeback
791 Ridgeview Dr.
Frankfort, KY40601

Dear RT,

Ish number 9 of S arrived today...yipeee. a breath of fresh air at last!

Religion and the SM: did you know the Worldwide Church of of God (HW Armstrong) believes the world will be rayed, made to belive the second coming will be phoney and instead a non-spirit entity "invasion" via Outer Space Beings? True AND-- did you folks know a local L.A. relig ous group (not WCOG) believes they live forever in their physical body? "We will be alive to usher in the Millenium" they claim...something to do with the water from the Jordan River. Their pastor is "Ray" (name deleted) So you guys and dolls thot the "Aquarius Church" was far out huh? All for now. My "T" force be with ye.

Al Wiseman
636 N Plymouth
L.A., CA90004

3

SHAVERTRON

The Man Who Gave Us The Shaver Mystery

Richard Shaver

INTERVIEW

The following interview was taped from July, 1972 to October, 1972. Parts of it are therefore dated, while other sections could have been taken just last month. So, from the Rock House Studio in Summit, Ark. we bring you Richard S. Shaver:

Toronto: What do you think was the main reason for the huge interest in the Shaver Mystery? Were readers interested in the story lines, or was it the fact that you declared your material to be in fact, the truth?

Shaver: The huge interest in the SM was there all the time in people, it just lacked a channel, a way of saying anything...and we opened that channel by publishing letters from people about voices and mysterious occurances. It seems that every single person has had singular experiences that he can't explain. The whole occult world lives on that same fact: that everyone has these experiences and doesn't understand them.

I explained these things as being due to the ancient mechanisms underground being used by people who didn't care about us and who liked to fool us. That's the fact of the matter. This opened up the door. Every person found a way of relating to it, because he had the same experiences to some extent. They've heard or seen things they can't understand or explain ... occult things: voices in their heads or visions and so on and THAT'S what it's all about.

You see, the Shaver Mystery, the whole hullabaloo, was due to a new explanation for the old mystery of occultism and spiritualism. All of which are real and alot of people openly pretend to doubt. But inside, they have similar experiences and know there is something to 'em. To friends they doubt them, because they can't explain them and they're afraid of 'em. That they should explain this as being due to spirits of the dead and so on is too ridiculous to think about to a rational person who knows better.

And that's the mystery. The whole occult world and, in fact, every person who understood what we were talking about at all became vastly interested because he had the same puzzlings and questions in his mind about what in Hell it was all about.

You see, not many people up here on the surface realize that we're ruled from underground, we're really guided mentally and ruled and don't know it. And when somebody says (tape went blank here for about 4 seconds--RT)...up on their hind legs and holler because it's supposed to be secret and they're afraid not to have it kept secret. But actually, the whole secrecy angle about it is rather ridiculous because millions of people know better: they know all about it...except publicly it isn't published or written about...which I did. They had a great time about it and that was the Shaver Mystery.

Toronto: Do you think that your publishers believed in your stories? Were they personally involved?

Shaver: I knew that as long as my writings produced profits at the news stands, I was on the payroll. Nothing personal about it. I got up among the top 3 sci-fi writers before tv took the wind out of all their sales...sales, that is, as in news stand sales. I worked for several publishers which means I mailed manuscripts to them like you put a letter in a box. They sent back checks...nothing personal about it. Hard to imagine doing things   that way isn't it? The only way you get a check in the mail nowadays is to be 65 and get soc-sec checks: social security. It's hard for you modern people to visualise a world without tv isn't it? In those days people READ instead of looking at the idiot box to see what to think next. In those days publishers were the big thing, not TV producers. Publishers estimated profits at the news stands in dollars and cents rather than ratings and sponsor reactions. I never met one in the flesh, I just worked for them.

Toronto: What about Ray Palmer?

Shaver: Palmer was my editor, not my publisher. I went out to Chicago and met him, and bought a house out there. We got to know each other pretty well. Palmer and I met outside the office. I was only in that office (Ziff-Davis, no doubt--RT) once, or at most twice. Thats how it was.

Toronto: I've read alot about the fanmail that the Shaver Mystery used to get, what was it really like?

writing you talk of yourself in the third person. Is there a difference between Shaver the man and "Shaver" of the Mystery? Is one a public image?

Shaver: You talk of public images in a modern sense. I dont think we had 'em in those days. A writer wrote, but the people didn't really know him or hear him. They had to judge him just on what he wrote. A public image was an entirely different thing from the sort of thing you've got now. Today, looking back, I don't know how the Shaver Mystery looks to you people, but it wasn't on radio, and I was just writing it in the magazines... the only channel there was for it.

Toronto: It would seem, then, that television, with all its vast potential for story-telling slipped right by you...and in the process it pulled the rug right out from under you.

Shaver: I didn't really grasp the rest of that picture, I was too busy writing back and forth to Shaver fans. It was just about at the peak of that thing (the SMMag)

"I used to show off my muscles."

Shaver: Well, uh, Palmer has told me about tons and tons of mail...from the millions of readers we had then. Nobody ever really read all that mail, I don't think that 1% was read. It just came and piled up and was thrown away, eventually...stored in the basement in bags. I probably got more mail than anybody that ever wrote for tv, because they just didnt know what to do with it all. That's really why I started the Shaver Mystery Magazine, so I'd get to read some of my own mail... The SMMag was really three or four of us who put it out mainly as a business gamble sort of. And I did get to answer some letters and get into contact with some of the readers, but it was a very small percentage of the total that reached us...2 or 3 thousand out of perhaps a million. I eclipsed what was then the science fiction fan world. The SMMag had something like 3 thousand paid subscribers. And the whole sci-fi fan club membership was only around 1,200 paid memberships and fan clubs. So Shaver was really about twice what the whole total of all the others were, if you estimate it by paying fans.

Toronto: Just a moment ago, you refered to yourself as "Shaver", and I've noticed that in alot of your

when tv started to take over, and within just a few months subscriptions and news stand sales' total volume dropped over 60%; and that drop went on to 90%, and the number of science fiction magazines on the market dropped from 36 to 6, then the 6 dropped to 2. Now I understand that it's up to 4 or 5 again, but I'm out of touch with it now. That picture is not understandable in today's terms of tv producers and the limelight was an entirely different sort of thing then than it is now. Then was a matter of print and photographs, now its personal appearances. When the tv took over, all the money dropped out of publishing. Publishers went out of business all over the place. I could still sell, but I couldn't make enough out of it to really call it a living, so I quit altogether. Most of the rest of them did too, even the best, the very best quit and took up something else, they had to to make a living. So they went into other sidelines. So did I. I never tried to sell after that, I'm probably the only writer who has no unsold mss. I never wrote anything unless it was already sold.

5

Toronto: Throughout your writings, you constantly attack the educational system. As far as I know, you never really got an "official" education yourself. So how did you become "educated"? Are you bitter?

Shaver: You bet I dislike the educational system in the world today. YES I'm bitter about my own education. And then again, I'm mighty glad that I got my education the way I did. You know how I got educated? I went to the library and I stayed there day after day. You know what started me? Chess problems. I was always playing chess and I went to get chess books at the library and I met the fellows who worked in the stacks in that big public library, and they got to know me and they used to bring me art books and chess books and what have you in a whole cart, so I'd spend the day there. That went on for years. That's how I got my education: following a reading course in the public library. It's faster and better than any college can give you. That's the truth about education, education is available to anyone who wants to go to the library and dig it out. I didn't have any money, then. When I was going to the library, there was a Depression. You couldn't get a job in '32, '33. You know how I used to pick up pocket money? Modelling in the art schools. I used to show off my muscles. If you ever try standing on one foot for 35 cents a half hour, you'll find out that's earning money the hard way! (laughing) But I liked it. I was really a kind of hippy around Detroit, hanging around the studios. The hippies today think they got everything. We had much the same kind of thing in those days.

Two kids from this lost flower generation just left here. They're on their parents' ranch, running from a city job. I always wish there was some way to set 'em on their feet, when they come along like that. But when the best painter, that's me, and the best writer, that's me, can't make out, what can you tell a kid about how to make out. All I tell 'em is "don't worry". Ambition is empty. After you work all your life for some corporation they fire you just before you qualify for the company pension. So why worry when welfare is better to begin with?

Toronto: Getting back to your education...then you actually feel better about charting the course of your own education, than if you had attended an acredited college?

Shaver: They teach the young people an enormous amount of misconcept...mistaken ideas about life and thought and so called logic. The young aren't able or equipped to convert this nonsense into sense. It forms a mish-mash of utter idiocy. Unrelated parts form into what I call false syllogisms, because they are false, based on assumptions and old ideas that should have been disgarded centuries ago. I learned to think for myself from little known philosophers and little known volumes, skimming through the stacks I remember one author I recall only as Schmidt, a German whose logic struck me as PERFECT logic, which is rare.

To think for yourself, you have to throw out every thought that you don't absolutely know is correct. And to accept for thinking purposes, nothing you don't know from observation and deduction that you do yourself. Few people ever do this, and it is necessary to unpollute your mind in order to fill it with clean and correct information. Our educational system fails to educate, especially today. I correspond with college graduates, quite alot of them... (RSS often had his letters appear in the MENZA newsletter--RT) and some of them are really ignorant creatures who can hardly write and who print everything, yet they went through school. Our education system

suffers from a vicious sabotage unseen and unknown to most. It is this sabotage my writing and my stories and life work was all about...was fighting against. How to boil this sabotage down into a few words so you can understand it isn't easy.

Toronto: When did you make the changeover from writing your scifi stories to writing about the rock books?

Shaver: Well, this occured over a period of 5 or 10 years when on the ranch, and there wasn't any way to sell anything. There was very little publishing going on, and I had no contact with 'em. I was depending on Palmer to publish, and Palmer wasn't in a position to pay anything, so there wasn't much point in writing anything. So I raised cows. I picked up the rocks in the field and got interested in them. Now, the books aren't mentioned in my writings earlier than that time: '50, '52, something like that.

Toronto: How do you use your time, then, today?

Shaver: Today I put in my time on rock books, the pre-deluge artifacts of a vanished civilization, a great civilization of the past we call the Golden Age. There are plenty of these artifacts, and they are tremendously faginating, and the only reason they aren't known is ignorance, pure ignorance in our so-called educated society of today. They don't even bother to know what their own rocks are, what's on 'em and in 'em. I look. That's what I do as a hobby, I look into stone. And if you try it you'll learn something about the past...it's the only way you'll ever learn something truthful about the past, because most of what's published and written about it is false. Theorising and assumptions based on things like the Piltdown skull, which was a forgery.

Toronto: Alot of people have a hard time reading these rocks, though.

Shaver: In rock books you don't really learn to see until you reverse your black and white. Alot of rock books are very plain and easy to see, but they are negative, which means you have to reverse 'em. About the first thing you learn is that better optical methods of a radically better kind are needed to properly study them. We need a zoom that instantly responds to varying sizes which run from 6 inches to a half inch in the same print. Better lenses, a more flexible kind of lens, better light with a more penetrative quality. All I can do with present day photographic methods is to try and demonstrate that in picture rock is a full gammut of movies in 3-dimensions, in negative and postive both. We only need the right methods to show our own ancestors a million years ago in action. Right here in front of me are life-sized cuts of the features of early man, amphibious man. What is needed to appreciate such things is not the rock or the picture or the photographs but the mind, the mental obstacles between understanding that the photographs of our own ancestors and the things that happened in the past are perfectly available, if we look for them. This darkness of mind of today's people is the only obstacle, and I think this darkness of mind has been produced by our so-called educational system, which has not educated people, but closed their minds to the realities of life around them.

The works of giant early men are everywhere to be seen, if anyone looks but they haven't been taught to look and to see when they do look.

Toronto: I guess that the most often asked question you get is this one: "how do I get into the caverns, and when was the last time you personally went there? Shaver: What you don't seem to get about that is that it's like the Iron Curtain in Russia. You can cross it and you can go back and forth, but that curtain is

6

Shaver posing with rock books in his studio. Note the rock book painting on right.

there, and there isn't much point in going because you can hear about it and see it without going. If you're in contact, and you are if they want you to be, if they dont want you to be, there's no point in going, 'cause you wouldn't get anywhere. It is a tremendous organization all over the world, sort of like the UN, trying to do something sensible about things. We are defeated many times by the deros actions, like the murder of the head of the UN, Dag Hammershold. You're always in contact telepathically with such an organization, whether you know it or not...lots of people don't even know it, but its there. The harder you try, the more you improve and the better results you'll get. Yes, going into the underworld is very much like going to Russia: you pick up a secret agent and they hang onto you and you don't see anything or hear anything.
Toronto: What do you think about   semi-religious books such as Ohaspe?
Shaver: I think much the same thing about churches and religious teachings (as I do about the schools),

which are not teachings, but misteachings. It is utterly ridiculous and insane to accept life after death as a rational concept. It is just about as ridiculous to accept the evolutionary theories because it is so obvious we are in fact DEVO-luting, and have been in the process of devolution for a long long time. When Newbrough started writing Ohaspe, They took over.

The deros took over and fed him alot of bullshit instead of the original ancient book that he was supposed to re-write by telepathy. As a result, everything that we have of that kind is based on a lie, a purposeful lie not an accidental lie. They lie to us on purpose about the past, to hide their utilization of the ancient mechanisms.
Toronto: How old are you, Mr Shaver?
Shaver: How old am I? Just between you and I, I'll be 65 in October next.

Continuing our listing of the works of Richard S. Shaver, we present the following. As far as we can ascertain, we're picking up this list from issue number 3, and that's a long ways back...

OTHER WORLDS
Fall of Lemuria .... Nov. 1949
((Where No Foot Walks, by G.H. Irwin))...Nov. 1949
((Sons of the Serpent, by Wes Amherst))..Jan. 1950
Lady .....Mar. 1950
((The Gamin, by Peter Dexter))... Mar. 1950
((Marai's Wife, by Edwin Benson)).....Mar. 1950

((Palace of Darkness, by Peter Dexter))...Sept. 1950
((Glass Woman of Venus, by G.H. Irwin))...Jan. 1951

Journey To Nowhere.....Oct. 1951
Lightning Over Saturn...Oct.1951--with Chet Geier
Yelisen....Dec. 1951
The Sun-Smiths....July, August, Sept. 1952
((The Scarpein of Delta Sira by G.H. Irwin))..Nov 52
Beyond the Barrier....Nov, Dec. '52..Jan, Feb. 53
Quest of Brail...July 1957
((Pillars of Delight, by Stan Raycraft))...Sept. 57

List compiled by Jim Pobst.

7

ancient occult/technology located in the SUB-CITIES they have RE-ESTABLISHED...)"

The twelfth century monk, Gervase of Tilbury, who set down the facts concerning the famous appearance of the "Green Children of Wolfpittes" from a cave in England, also recorded another bizarre account of an emergence of a strange being from the underworld.

The incident occured in the Brunia Monastery in the fabled Trier region of ancient Prussia in the year 1138 A.D. (the story also appears in Eric Normans book The Under People).

There had been several nocturnal visitations to the monastery's wine cellar and the stuard, suspecting that the monks had been sampling the casks, voiced his suspicions to the abbot, who went to the cellar to inspect the damage. The night before the culprit had forgotten to close the bunghole, resulting in a whole keg of wine being drained onto the cellar floor. After annointing the cellar with holy water, securely locking the door and placing a saint's relic above the entrance, the abbot declared, "None of our monks would dare to transgress against the power of the Cross".

The following morning, upon entering the cellar, the abbot found the floor again covered with the rich, red wine. Suddenly, he spotted a movement in a dark corner of the cellar, and ordered the monks who had

THE SURFACE CONNECTION
By BRUCE WALTON

Do the cavern dwellers have representatives and followers here on the surface? Humans who are working in secret with those "below" for some unknown purpose, be it good or evil?

Such an idea may seem a bit far-fetched to some, but in light of recent information which has come to my attention, this idea may not in fact be that impossible to believe.

Several individuals have suggested that many of our large cities have their subterranean counterparts built deep beneath them, inhabited by subterranean races. Tokyo, New York, Moscow, Buenos Aires, Sao Paulo, London, Cairo and Cuzco are just a few that have been mentioned. Your editor sent me an interesting letter concerning an alleged system of tunnels beneath Washington, DC, which I quote here:

"...The tunnels under Washington DC is a new one on me too. I paid good $$ to a researcher for info on Shaver, and I wound up with this. The guy's name is L. Frank Hudson. He says he talked with an engineer in Washington about it. The engineer claimed the tunnels are encased in a kind of hard glass-like substance, and have been carbon dated to 100,000 years old. He claims that the founding fathers knew all about these tunnels when they built Washington DC...laid it out according to these tunnels... said that Washington (the President) often went with Ben Franklin to a cave for meetings..." ((We intend to pub this entire ms. by Hudson in a future issue of S-- RT)).

Tal Levesque sent me some related data which supports the above idea of a system of tunnels existing beneath the Washington DC area:

"...And then there are reports of an ancient network of tunnels; caverns and even the land of NOD (Atlantean) under Washington, DC. NOD, for those who may be unfamiliar, is an underground cult of power-tripping members who are plugged in on the highest levels of National Authority, (NSA) and in contact with Sirius "Star People". They have access to the

entered with him to apprechend the transgressor. Two large monks rushed forward and grabbed the shadowy figure and brought him into the light. All stared in amazement at a dark-skinned dwarf.

One of the monks then discovered a displaced stone that covered a small tunnel leading down into the earth, leading, the monks suspected, to a lair of demons. The captured dwarf was acepted into the society of holy men. But in spite of the kindness shown him

8

by the monks, the dwarf refused to utter a single word. He sat quietly on a bed in a cross-legged position, staring directly ahead and refusing to eat or drink. Eventually, the dwarf escaped from the monks and fled to the cellar and its underworld tribe.

In his book, Adventures in Arabia, Wm. Seabrook tells of his visit to the mystery temple-shrine of Sheik-Adi, on Mt. Lalesh in eastern Arabia. While being shown by a priest the various attractions in the Temple, a friend of his, Mechmed Hamdi, began telling him a story in French. The priest understood none of this. The tale revolved around supposed caverns hidden in the bowels of the mountain. Mechmed had on various occasions asked for permission to see the caverns but was flatly refused. This timehhowever, the leader of the order, Mir Said Beg, reluctantly allowed them to go a short way into the caverns, which were entered through a secret passage in the bottom of the Temple. They descended a very old flight of damp stone steps and found themselves in a vaulted cavern, partly natural, it seemed, and partly hewn from the rock, and around a corner they heard the sound of running water. They could not guess how far it extended into the depths of the mountain, and could not see the whole of the cavern they were in. "Its floor at the foot of the steps was covered with water, which I guessed from the slope to be not more than ankle deep. But the priest made it an excuse to detour us from going further, declaring that there was no use getting our feet wet, since there was no more to see". Despite their protests, the priest would let them go no further into the caverns. The author then states the following:

"...our partial penetration of it was interesting chiefly as establishing the fact that the whole temple edifice was constructed over subterranean caverns and streams and springs, some of the water of which was led into the pools we had seen in the temple and courtyard above. I learned later that the Yezidees (the people who inhabit that region) believed these waters flowed underneath the desert, from the miraculous spring of Zem-Zem in Mecca..."

"I would have given a month of my life to explore those caverns completely, and shall always wonder what I might have found around the angles of the rocks-- what other chambers, what alters, what relics of ancient or modern sacrifice. I have since had nightmare dreams of wading ankle deep through the water at the foot of the stairs, of turning the corner and, beneath a great vault like a cathedral, coming upon a dreadful red, fiery alter-- but actually there wide awake, the only thing which made me believe that there might be an alter of some sort in the cavern was the fact that there was no sign of one, or even an emplacement for an altar, in the templeaabove..."

In a remote region of northern Tibet, Theodore Illion, playwright and world-traveler, found a mysterious shaft and an underground city devoted to evil. He tells the story in his book, Darkness Over Tibet, which contains a detailed account of his observations and almost miraculous escape.

After receiving a letter of introduction and directions from a native Tibetan occultist, Illion found the city near the Sangpo Valley, 20 miles from the nearest village. It is known as the "City of Initiates", and consists of 7 underground buildings that drop at least 14 stories below the surface, the tops of these subsurface constructs being level with the ground.

They are built around a shaft, the top of which is surrounded by a wall four feet high and 10 feet in diameter. Several hundred inhabitants are under the rule of a Prince Mani Rimpotche, a tall aged Tibetan with a white beard who speaks six languages, including English,and is remarkably well-informed about world affairs.

Illion learned that only one other Westerner had ever visited the city, and he had lived and died there under a Tibetan name. Life in the city resembles that of an anthill under the absolute control of its ruler. No one is permitted to leave the city without permission, and every action of its dwellers is rigedly regulated.

The shaft itself appeared incredibly aged and very deep. Stones weighing up to 20 pounds were thown in but no sound reached Illion's ears. His inquiries revealed that only a few of the highest initiates knew what was at the bottom, and any other person who found out would die-- "there are such secrets"-- with death automatically following the discovery.

I first heard about this story from an article by Vincent Gaddis which appeared in the June, 1947 issue of AMAZING STORIES. In this article, he puts forward the idea, due to various information that had reached him, that the "City of Initiates" was apparently the headquarters of a widespread secret organization with agents scattered throughout the Orient-- perhaps even the West.

((Continued))

SHAVERTRON SURVEY

This questionaire is meant to aid us in serving you better, and to aid the staff in understanding the readership. There is no need to sign it, but please fill it out and send it to us. Thank you...

1. What would you like to see more of in Shavertron?_____

2. What would you rather see less of?_____

3. How would you respond to a new zine of similar format, size, price etc. to S, but with much less emphasis on RSS, the Shaver Mystery and HE topics-- but with more on Fortean events, occult/psychic phenomena, futurism, mind manipulation and ufos? Would you want this at the expense of losing S? YES, Favorable___, NO, Never___, Don't Ever Get Rid of RSS___

4. Is the SM and Shaverian topics the main reason you sub to S? YES___ NO___ OTHER_____

5. What other zines do you sub to?_____

6. Do you have friends who are interested in these topics? YES___ NO___

7. Do you think there should be more or less editorial comment each issue? YES___ NO___ JUST RIGHT___

8. Is your age: between 18-30___ 30-45___ 45-60___ retired___?

9. Do you think you might some day have something to contribute to S? Clips___ Mss.___ RSS info___

9

Retrospeck:

BY RALPH HOLLAND

"Our continuing saga of the history of the SM."

The various mech was powered in different ways. Some of it cut the magnetic lines of force of the earth to secure power. Other variaties tapped into the cosmic flows of energy which permeate all space. Some types of wheeled vehicles were gravity powered. "Gravity", according to Shaver, is not a mass-attraction, as we have been taught, but the flow of energy which the ancients called "exd". This flow could penetrate and pass through any object, but the denser the object, the greater the resistance to its flow, and the greater the "weight". This flow could be directed so that one side of a wheel would have zero "gravity", thus causing rotary motion.

The Elders apparently spent very little, if any time on the surface. It may have been that the surface was unsuitable for habitation at that time. There is also mention of certain radioactive rays in the solar radiations, to which they seem to have been particularly sensitive, and which could be successfully filtered out only by considerable thickness of earth. Others have deduced that persons of such gigantic size may have had trouble existing under surface gravity, and wished to go down to a point where its influence would be decreased. Whatever the reason, they began to burrow into the ground, disintegrating the rock with rays, and then packing the energy into the walls and roof where it rematerialized, making a substance harder and denser than any-

thing which we know today. Huge caverns were carved out many miles below the surface of the earth, far below the unstable surface rock strata. In these they built their cities, connecting them with tunnels which ran under the seas as well as under the land. Eventually, the surface area of this "underworld" was much larger than the surface world, and it included a great many different levels. After the first ancestors of the present human races had appeared, each of the huge underground cities had its surface "colony city" which was reached by elevators. Apparently, no mech was permitted on the surface, all necessary services being taken care of by the under-city mech.

According to some thought record tapes, the present human races were bred in the biological research labs of the Elders, They were constantly seeking to develop a better physical body...one which would be more resistant to the detrimental effects of the radioactivity in the solar radiations, and better adapted to the other characteristics of this planet. With the discovery characteristics of this planet, With the discovery of rays which would cause dissimilar genes to unite, innumerable cross-breeds were developed experimentally, The many monsters of fable...the centaurs, the fauns, and others...are said to have actually existed. Like most hybrids, these were sterile, and thus incapable of reproducing themselves. And so they died out. The only two successful crosses were the "Adams" and the "Pythons". The Adams, ancestors of all the present races of man on this planet, were a cross between some man-like beast and the Elders. The Pythons were a cross with some reptile life form, probably a two-footed erectile animal rather than a snake, as we use the term today. This was considered a particularly desirable cross because reptiles are almost totally immune to radioactivity, and have very long lifespans.

Little is known about the Pythons, except that there seems to have been bitter strife between them and the Adams from earliest times. This is indicated by the many legends which consider the serpent to be the source of all evil.

Actually, their morals and ethics were as high as those of the Adams, according to the tapes, but their thinking processes and customs were alien even to the Elders who sired them. It is said that "serpent peoples" still exist on other planets, but they disappeared from Terra at an early date, either as a result of mass migration or a bitter campaign of extermination.   ...((Continued))

MEMBER:

THE HOLLOW HASSLE

The HH is the newsletter of THERA pubbed by Mary LeVesque. Subs are $8 USA... $10 for foreign overseas. Write to HH, box 255, Santa Fe, New Mexico 87501 USA.

Serpent Writing? - Copied From Desert Stones by Author

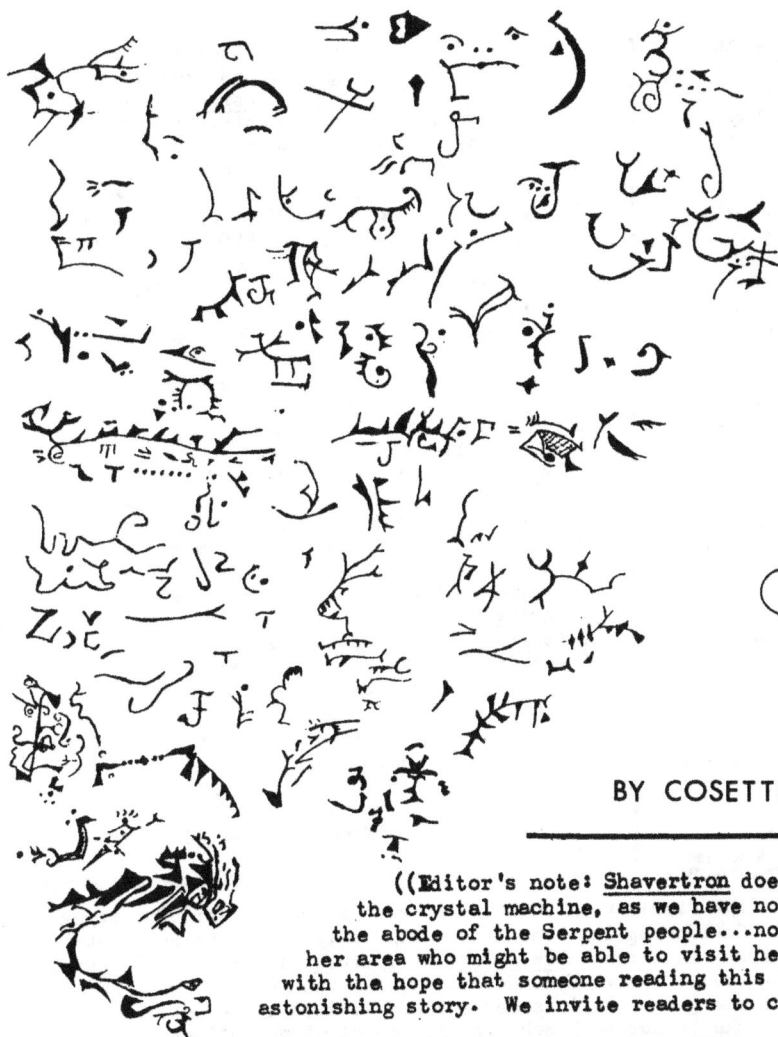

THE CRYSTAL MACHINE OF THE SERPENT PEOPLE

BY COSETTE WILLOUGHBY

((Editor's note: Shavertron does not endorse Ms. Willoughby's claims of
the crystal machine, as we have not been able to view the rock itself, or the
the abode of the Serpent people...nor have we been able to contact anyone in
her area who might be able to visit her. Regardless, we present her article
with the hope that someone reading this issue may be able to investigate her
astonishing story. We invite readers to comment on the following...))

I have been contact with these strange people for about 3 years. I have seen them
many times but only in glimpses. They are masters at camoflauge and their main purpose
is to not attract attention. I have tried to make friends with them and they have just begun to do little things that let me know they want to be friendly.

I know where the entrances to their caves are. I never tried to disturb or enter them. I have given
them candy (which they seem to like very much), a few pieces of clothing and once I gave them a mirror.
After several months I saw them flash it at me.

Recently, they began leaving things in places only I would go. Twice they gave me little plastic toys,
once they gave me money (a quarter, a nickle and two pennies). Once a babulously carved piece of golden
glass, and my fabulous crystal machine. I want to tell you a little more about them before I tell of the
crystal machine.

In the times I have seen them I have noticed that some of them are monkey-like, yet they all move in
a flowing motion like a serpent. Some of them leave a three toed track, and some leave a huge track like
what is known as Bigfoot. I saw one of them that was like a small dwarf. He didn't wear any clothes
that I could see and he had all his hair piled on top of his head in a big glob.

They speak a language which sounds ecoish, like they are throwing their voices like a ventriloquist.
They can also mimic. One of them can sound like a whole yard full of children yelling and laughing.

Many times I have been up on some cliffs which house their caves and I have heard heavy footfalls
coming from underground. They display a primitive nature yet it would take a far advanced artist to make
the beautiful stone amulets they make and strew all over the desert. I believe they do this to ward off the
rattlesnakes. I know I hardly ever see any rattlers when I hunt for these beautiful carvings and when I
do they warn me beforehand.

Now, to tell you about the fabulous crystal machine. I found it on one of the little low hills where
I go frequently to hunt for these stone carvings. When I found it I noticed right off that it was no
ordinary stone for it had a carving, a sort of little carved window on the side of it. After examining
it with a magnifying glass, I discovered it had an endless series of pictures appearing in it. The pictures
were small but so clear and real looking you have a feeling you're seeing a much bigger scope than it really
is. I saw beautiful cities with great marble buildings. I saw the insides of great palaces with much gold
and fabulous jewels. The people look so real you catch yourself speaking to them. The clothes they wear
are very rich with much gold and jewels. Women crowned with huge rubies and pearls and every stone you

you can think of. I began to ask it specific things.

I asked to see the wizzards of olde. I saw six of them dressed in elaborate gowns, and wearing pointed turbans. They all looked at me as if they really saw me. They bowed and greeted me. It made me feel that they really were aware of me.

I asked to see the tree of life. At first, I saw an alcove filled with a strange mist. Slowly, the mist parted and I saw a very strange looking tree There was a gold and turquoise light shing behind this tree. I told my husband, Ken, that it sure was a strange looking tree, for the limbs looked more like roots than limbs and there were no leaves.

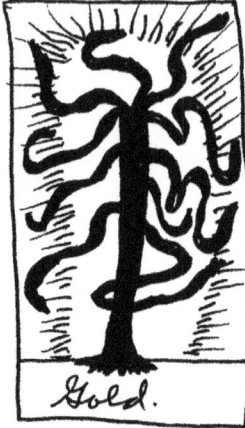
Gold.

I looked up the tree of life in Helena Blavatsky's books, the Secret Doctrine, and it described what I saw to a T. The tree of life grows upside down and it does have roots for limbs.

I asked to see the King of the World...(Rigden Jye-Po, Brahytma and Mataron are some of his names. I only saw his face. I seemed to be below him looking up at him. He looked at me and I felt he was studying me. I greeted him and he seemed to tell me volumes without words. I felt much love for him and I believe he felt the same of me.

I almost forgot: I also saw the second Adam. I had never heard about this before I saw the images

in the crystal. So using the images in the crystal I started piecing together the true story of the "Beginning". The Secret Doctrine provided the clues to unravel the symbolic meaning in those images.

The true story tells that in the beginning, there was a huge serpentlike being that came from out of the void of space and completely covered this earth. She was the great Cosmic Mother. The Earth Mother all blended into one Great life-giving force. Before she came, the Elohim, the God Essence had created the first Adam, but he was Etherial. He never had a physical body. I don't know for sure, but he may have mated with the Great Cosmic mother for she grew pods all over her body and out of these pods came the second Adam.

At first, he was round like a ball. He was bi-sexual, able to produce his own kind. He was also amphibian. As time passed, he began to try to appear in various places in the world. As he did, he began to develop an extension of himself kind of like a tail. In stressing energy in his need to survive and began to develop in that tail a body. Arms appeared and legs and after awhile he began to look like a man we know today. Then in doing this, he became male and female. It took a longer time for man to live independant of the Great Cosmic Mother. After she absorbed into the earth, she stayed there. Man was more able to act on his own. I still think that we need this contact, tho, for the astronauts, after being out in space a while seem to become weakened, and it could be they need this contact.

Well, there you have some of what I have seen in this crystal. There is nothing on earth like it, believe me!

Addendum: As with just about everything in the field of the unusual, there is some amount of controversy over Ms Willoughby's claims, pro and con. On looking into the matter, the only verification about the fantastic rock devices Ms Willoughby has found is through New Atlantean Journal editor, Joan O'Connell, who was sent one of Willoughby's "drinking rocks"....... Ms O'Connell placed the drinking rock in some water, but it didn't drink anything. Then she placed it in some beer and it didn't even hiccup, according to our sources. We sent some of her rocks to our rocktech, and his conclusions follow:

PURE BLISS

By BILL BLISS

Got the rocks in good shape, and scrutinized them. There are some low grade images, but the only definite one is the head of a bald fat man on one of the black rocks. Actually, I do very poorly at keying in on low contrast images or those almost lost in grain.

Just made some carbon tracings (which work best with a blunt stylus-- I used a small screwdriver handle) of ye Willoughby stones. Mrs Willoughby is unusually perceptive. There are two interpretations of the glyphs she sent you. An ancient form of writing, or image elements. If you peer at them at a distance of over 10 feet, images can be seen. The carbons and Mrs Willoughby prove to me that there are good images in those kinds of rock-- if only we can figure out how to transcribe them. I've found that if you have a field of identical image element, slight variations in any of the elements will change the images it generates. The elements can be spaced a bit and not connected-- if they are scroll, and scroll can simply be a very complex single image element.

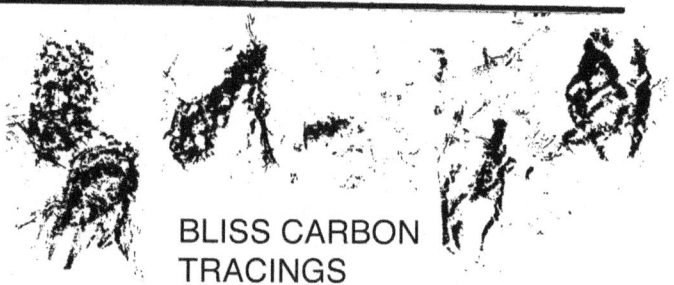

BLISS CARBON TRACINGS

The ELF system-- about a couple of decades ago, I read that mysterious signals were being heard on the extremely low frequencies-- below 300kc. I jury-rigged a receiver that went all the way down to 10kc. Somewhere below 90kc. (I didn't have it calibrated) there was an unbelievably strong signal, a continuous buzz. On the oscilliograph it looked like it was from an old-time spark gap transmitter...it never varied.

There's been scads of research on the biological effects of electromagnetic waves. Recollect that about 16 years ago there was a bit about (should have kept that klipping) the magnetic field from a power cable in an elevator shaft messing up the hemoglobin in some people. Biological stuff does have weak chemical bonds, so there would be good reason to suspect effects from 'em.

EXPOSED!
FANS WARNED OF CON-GAME
BIZARRE SHAVER MYSTERY SCAM!
STEELE PLAYS PIGEON AS DERO-DOINGS FLY -- SELLS OUT FOR "IMMORTALITY"!

MAX

When the curtain opened on this crazy drama we here at S naively imagined that we could sit back in the second or third row and applaud or hiss as the cast of characters stomped on stage.

As fate would have it, someone had written us into the script, whether we liked it or not. This made it necessary either to play along in the part we had been given, or to forge out into a spontaneous ad lib when our cue came.

We've decided on the latter, and here and now we've set the stage for a bizarre tale that, in reality, you are all a part of.

Our story began when many S readers received letters from one Henry M Steele, a former contributor to this mag. In these letters, HS claimed he had made direct contact with a certain tero cavern in Rainbow City, and more specifically, with our namesake, Richard S. Shaver, whom HS declared was physically alive and "having a fine time" in that tero mech cavern. Not only this, HS claimed that in this direct, divine contact, Shaver, in a fit of unusual sentimentality toward Henry, had appointed him the "official" spokesman for the Shaver Mystery.

To fill his new post more effectively, so the story goes, Henry was directly instructed to publish a newsletter/mag called the Richard Shaver Epilogue, to contain all future revelations, orders, and prophecy direct from RSS & teros. As Henry pointed out, those who followed his communications and orders "to the letter" would survive the holocaust of atomic war that, according to tero news sources, was imminent. He then informed breathless listeners of his sub rates (only $20 per year), and one further revelation: Bruce Lee is alive and happy in fabled Rainbow City. Beyond these wild exclamations, Henry would say no more, except that we should send in our money right away.

At first, we had to take these claims with a large grain of salt. After all, we knew people who had attended RSS's funeral who were quite aware of the fact that he passed on in 1975. What was he now doing alive, 6 years later in a tero cavern? Henry wouldn't say.

As time wore on, as it often does, Henry's letters began to take on a different hue. One, another "direct contact" message aimed specifically at your tainted editor, explained: "To answer the question as to why you were not chosen to be contacted initially, can be summed up in these words: Purity of Intentions. Eliminate the desire for personal gain through greed and you may find that your needs will be provided for." Evidently, this tero didn't know that S has always flown by the seat of its pants, and has never shown a profit at any time. It continued, nevertheless, and ended on a somewhat somber note: "To be accounted worthy, show yourself acceptable." Those who don't obey tero orders, S was told, get no help later on, when it really counts. Above all, your editor was instructed to co-operate with Henry on "his" newsletter or anything else of dire importance to the world at large.

In the meantime, after careful considerations and consultation with other S associates, we concluded that Henry's source of information was a con...a fake...a forgery. Not that HS wasn't getting orders from someplace-- but rather that his control was emanating from a negative source. We were still content to leave it at that, and we sent a warning to Henry to watch out for himself, but it did little good. We had no real documentation to prove our claim...until one day it came to us in the mail.

In a fleeting moment of free, clear thinking, Henry mailed S a frightened letter, despondent, and yet demanding as ever, along with an original hand-written letter from one Walter N. Rhodes, P.O. Box 518, Mail no. 432, Zepherhills, Florida. The letter from Rhodes was the "evidence" we'd been waiting for, and HS mailed it out of fear that it would be teleported away, and he would have no form of documentation to this weird situation he had gotten himself into.

HS is convinced that Rhodes is a Nelphi agent here on the surface to accomplish very secret and important work. It seems as though HS's role is that of mental slave, for, as HS admits, he is Rhodes' "front man"...also confessing he is NOT the one who will publish the RS Epilogue. Who will? Rhodes.

Another discouraging revelation in these letters was the fact that none of the information Henry had been sending out to fans had, in fact, been true. In reality, HS was NOT in direct contact with RSS or a tero in the so-called Rainbow City. All that HS had put into those letters to fans was directed by Rhodes. Why, we ask, did not Rhodes go directly to fans for his grand scheme of another zine dedicated to RSS? Why did he have to promise Henry a trip in a ufo to inner earth, where he would be changed into a "Nor-body" in which he would live immortally? Why all this secrecy? We think that S readers can guess.

In the interest of the truth, we're reprinting pertinent sections of Rhodes' letter...if anyone cares to read the entire transcript, just send $1 to S (to cover copying and mailing) and we will send it to you.

As we said before, HS was duped by this man ...but for what purpose? To sow confusion among everyone? To collect subscription money? As Henry worriedly explained: "First Rhodes told me his Nephlis wanted him to drive up here and take me to a waiting ship; this was put off, then put off again. Now its harped I'll be taken by him to a ship before the first issue of the zine comes out.. ...zine being put together by his group in Zepherhills, FLA. not here in Garland, Texas! Copies will be mailed up here for postmark--I'm the front man he says. All messages come via his letters. I am scared they shall now allow deros to get me.... Terrible, but I can't trust them anymore..."

The Letter

Hi Henry,

"You misunderstood alot of things that I relate--I never said you had to work or had to work on this zine. In actuality, you won't need much time to work on the RS Epilogue--and what needs to be done can be done in your spare time--we're talking about maybe 3 hours, once every week or 2. Understand? Most of your duties will be to answer and write letters--articles. A trip to the library once or twice a month or so. As far as putting together the zine, we (here) will take care of the main body of work.

"We will advise you on matters pertaining to Kelsoe ((HS's lawyer, who gives him his monthly allowance--Ed.)) and Sid ((HS's twin brother))-- be patient and you'll win out in the end. Kelsoe and Sid are out for the money. Keep this in mind always. We'll probably catch Kelsoe skimming money from off the top of your stock, etc. Do not let him catch on that you are aware of any of his actions. Just keep me advised on all matters. It would be wise to approach Kelsoe with the fact that due to inflation and the devaluation of the dollar, you need your monthly check increased. Write me a letter explaining exactly what stocks and interest you have-- exactly how much money is being held for you and I'll run this information thru the computer mech and keep tabs on the interest rates. You should not loan money unless we have advised you they are not dero controlled. Deros have many tricks to make you miserable. Listen to us and you'll prosper. Remember-- with us, you have hope-- without us, no hope.

"Now for business-- the RS Epilogue... Very few surface folks know as much about T's- D's- RS, etc as you do. That's why RS chose you. Write an article on the history of Richard Shaver--especially details as to your meeting with him at Arkansas for a few weeks. We want long articles in our zine, not TIDBITS like Richard Toronto puts out.

"Toronto is being rayed to help ((We think he is in for a big surprize--Ed.)) So here is what we do: you write everyone you know who may be interested in our zine and give some information about it. Send Toronto an article explaining about your zine to be printed in his no. 10 issue. You say everyone knows you have no $$ to start a zine, but the subscribers will be paying for it. It will just take a little time for you to show profits. As far as everyone else is concerned, you are making no profits.

"Whenever it is time for you to visit one of the under-cities, then if you become too frightened, you won't remember much because we'll put the memory in your subconcious.

"In your letter to Toronto: you were contacted several months ago (personally) by the teros, RSS and Nephlis and instructed to put out a zine by RSS. The messages to be relayed to readers are of DIRE importance and the zine makes no profit. THE RICHARD SHAVER EPILOGUE--Editor--Henry M. Steele, subscription:$20 per 1-year, $28 to Europe-- $23 to all foreign countries--back issues will be $2.50. Be sure to tell Toronto you were instructed to do this...

"Co-operation between both magazines will increase subscribers to each (important to mention this). This mag will be a monthly publication, that is why the increased price (also because of factual data and your sources). Whoever brings 3 6-month subscribers to us gets a free 6-month subscription. Do not advise RT we will have a pen pal section--we don't want him getting and using our ideas. Toronto washes our back (you can tell him) and we'll wash his! Got that? We will even share information to a degree but he can give us not much we don't already have-- except maybe RSS artwork or old photos etc. (Send me one of Toronto's lettersto you so I may have it analyzed--especially interested in latest one if possible). Tell Toronto you already have subscribers but the word needs to be spread thru his no. 10 issue.

"Send book of stamps. Keep this letter and do the best you can, especially involving Kelsoe-Sid.

> Your Friend,
> Walter

This letter speaks for itself. Would you send money to this man? It is disheartening to find that someone would sell out fans and friends for promises of immortality. But it is nothing new: "Just sign on the dotted line, Sir, and life eternal is yours..." says the dark stranger in the shadows..."All I ask is your soul". And if not that, then what??

In a recent letter from a correspondent, we've heard that Henry has been ordered to tell fans that S and your editor have been taken over by deros, and therefore should be boycotted. HS was specifically informed not to write to this zine. Also, Henry's trip in the ufo has been postponed once again, as the long-awaited first issue has been moved up to September now, instead of July as promised earlier.

We wonder at the intense interest that Rhodes takes in HS's financial affairs. Why does Rhodes wish to work through a front man who is under his total command? Why does he not think twice about lying to potential subbers, while he tells Henry one thing, and wants us to hear another? Finally, why don't we get to see a promotional issue (at least) before shelling out $20???

We say this to Rhodes: Don't bother us with your wool...your schemes to make dupes out of the gullible. We will expose you every chance we get.

We can only commend Henry (as we bid him Farewell) for sending this letter to us, and hope that some day he will find peace...

"I'm likely to get kicked out of my apartment by a dero set-up they allowed to happen, harping I'm not initiated yet-- which keeps get-

See Pg 16

MEET *the* AUTHORS

PRESENTING THE AUTHOR OF "JEWEL OF DEATH"

Would like to hear from
anyone that knows anything
about Albert McDonald and
his hollow earth society
newsletter. Also, does
anyone know the original
title, date and number of
pages in the full version
of the Hefferlin Ms? Please
write to: Frank Brownley,
29 McCall Rd, Rochester,
NY. 14615.

⬚⬚⬚

SD--please contact R. Ross
for info.

Writer would like to con-
tact ex-followers of The
Two, for a retrospect/
follow-up on their disci-
pleship. Anyone who may
know anything about The
Two is invited to write:
Annette Slave, Box C, in
care of Shavertron.

⬚⬚⬚

Mary LeVesque-- Good Luck
in Colorado. Hope both you
& the Hollow Hassle prosper
in all that fresh air!- The
Shavertron staff.

Researcher would like any
kind of info on the origin
of the "Admiral Byrd Diary"
that is being distributed
thru Missouri and Canadian
hollow earth groups. Please
send leads to the editor of
Shavertron. Thank you.

⬚⬚⬚

Anyone know where in the USA
I can purchase the new book:
"Subterranean Kingdom" by
Nigel Pennick? Write to:
Ken Meaux, PO Bx 189,
Kaplan, LA. 70548.

Chester S. Geier

WHEN not inquiring as to what I do for a living,
or as to where I get my plots, people frequently
ask me how I happened to become a writer. To
tell the truth, I don't know exactly myself. The truly
momentous decisions of our lives are those formed quite
suddenly, in a flashing moment of inspiration. I do know,
however, that I possessed a temperamental and intellectual background which made more or less inevitable
ready inclination toward writing as a career.

For one thing, I've always had vague creative urgings.
There was a period when I quite seriously considered
commercial art as a likely field. For another, I've been a
very heavy reader, especially of the brand of fiction
known as science and fantasy, since the age of 12, when
Fate gave me a kick in the pants in the form of an
attack of spinal meningitis which left me permanently
and totally deaf. Along with all this reading, I must un-
consciously have absorbed some of the know-how of
writing, which in combination with what I shall vainly
call my natural creative talents, left a gap requiring only
a chance action or remark to bridge.

As nearly as I can recall, such a stimulus was furnished by an introduction in my last year of high school
to William Lawrence Hamling, then the editor of the
school magazine. I learned that Bill wrote stories. What
process of idea-association followed, I don't know, but
the next thing I remember is that I was feverishly
scribbling atrocious yarns of my own, and that Bill and

I had become firm friends.

I was 18 then. A lot of time—according to my relative viewpoint—has passed. Time which, curiously
enough, I measure not in months or years, but in
story acceptances and rejections. There are some pro-
fessions that get into the blood and bones of a man, so
that he does all his living and breathing in its atmosphere
and all his thinking and dreaming in its terms. Fantasy
writing seems to be even more applicable to this condition.

My life for the past six years has been a sort of crazy-
quilt, patchwork affair. Upon graduation from high
school, I won a four-year scholarship to the University
of Chicago. I stuck it out for only two years, and this
because I wrote science-fiction and carried on various fan
activities at times when I should have been studying.
When schooling interfered with that, the schooling went
by the board.

Following this, I held a variety of jobs. I've been
successively a drill press operator, assembler, billing
clerk, order checker, stock clerk, and expediter of war
materials for a shipping firm. Like most people bent on
writing as a career, I've never considered jobs very
seriously. To me they always meant little more than
temporary stop-gaps between periods of full-time writing.
I'd work a little, save a little, write a little, and then
start all over again.

Somewhat over a year ago, Bill Hamling and I opened
up a writing office on Chicago's North Side. Bill had
then recently been retired as a lieutenant of infantry in
the army as the result of a little argument with a land
mine, in which he came out second best. We set out to
take the editors by storm, concentrating our attacks
mainly on the venerable Rap, whose defenses despite his
age were slowly and with difficulty beaten down. Rap—
or Ray Palmer, to the uninitiated—is a good sport,
though, and knows when he's licked. He began buying.
He's still doing so, I might mention. Neither Bill nor
myself knows why, but that fact alone is sufficient.

Bill and I still have the office. It would make interesting reading, I suppose, to say that a furious rivalry exists
between us, or that we steal each other's plots, or that
we constantly play clever jokes on one another. But the
disappointing truth is that we're both much too staid
to do more than get into an occasional mild argument
over some writing technicality or twist of plot.

I'm 24 now; 6' 4" tall, and weight around 160 pounds
more or less—usually less—which gives me somewhat
the general appearance of a broomstick handle; gray-
green eyes, brown hair, nicotine-stained complexion; and
married. My better half, a freckle-faced Irish lass with
mischievous green eyes, serves as my inspiration, in a
purely financial way, for the yarns I now write. Further
inspiration—also purely financial—is shortly due to be
forthcoming.

As to what I do when not writing . . . well, I read
science-fiction, putter around the house, bowl, and play an
occasional game of poker. I do the latter with even less
skill than the former. What keeps me going is the
knowledge that there's always room for improvement.

Some of you Shaver Mystery fans who used to read Amazing Stories when they came
hot off the presses will no doubt recognise Chester S. Geier: reknowned sci-fi
writer, and the first, original and only President of the Shaver Mystery Club.
We regret to report that Chet and his gall bladder had a fight to the finish.
Happily, Chet won the bout, and now his gall bladder must fend for itself. Glad
to have you back, Chet! The above feature is from December, 1945.(Cr. J.Wentworth)

Con't. from Page 14

ting put off too...I'm to lay at that de-aging stone-- some day. Fat chance!"

That's right Henry, Fat Chance.

RHODES = Deros with an H

Research Addenda

Derologists may be amused to hear that, just as we were typing up this final installment, the "d" on this ole typer up and flew out of the workings. A quick trip to the typer fixit shop, and a little solder took care of it...and so we continue:

From Our Man in Washington, we understand that: "A person whose address is a box within a PO box is obviously trying to conceal his whereabouts if not his identity. There is, or was, a postal regulation that said a customer or would-be customer has a right to find out from the postmaster the home address of a boxholder if that boxholder is running a business from that box." ((This may be why Rhodes is using HS as his front man, to avoid any direct statements in print, and thus avoiding any legal hassles--Ed.)).

From Charles Marcoux, psychic counselor, healer and medium of 35 years, a shocking statement is made in a letter to Bruce Walton:

"Here is something to consider: RHODES-- I am deeply impressed and sense that the name, Rhodes, is used as CODE, or a "symbol code", to recognise their organized center, or the Inner Circle, the selected group. Therefore, the code name is Rhodes. Their purpose is Dero activities. That is, they want to make you THINK that they have access to the Hidden World and the teros, but they really want to frighten off readers and investigators.

"Take the word Rhodes, remove the letter H, and you have Deros. The letter, H may be a code which identifies the real name of the person behind the operation. The letter H means HU (Hu-man, in the Mantong alphabet).

"Until now, the new movement of the younger generation who are investigating and searching for answers in the Hidden World, haven't, yet, really had encounters with the "unseen" in a direct manner, only from an indirect approach. So, they don't have the experience in how to protect themselves from the officials and yes-men that will do "anything" to destroy the movement. You, Bruce, Shavertron, Hollow Hassle, Crystal Ball and others are the new movement to which, I hope, I can pass on what I know, and be able to see it wisely put to use. My time is limited, and I pray that what I have been given will be passed on to the younger generation before I get my rewards and am freed from the prison of this world."

From pg 2-

led out of our Ufo Hamlin by malevolently-operated psychotronic devices (mech) hidden from our immediate scrutiny. Who owns and runs these fantastic mech?? Machines that Vallee says can create images in our minds, and alter our state of consciousness, our beliefs, our religions and social outlook! Here, Jacques falls silent. We kept waiting for him to shout out "Illuminati" but he didn't. We wondered if Jacques had ever read Shaver, as this "new line" of Vallee has long been expounded upon by the SM, John Keel and others.

Jacques asks: "Are the manipulators...nothing more than a group of humans who have mastered a very advanced form of power?" The ufo's, he says, are real, no doubt about it, but they often act more like holographic constructs than nuts and bolts machines..."They are an application of psychotronic technology, that is, they are physical devices used to affect human consciousness".. (Shaver used to call these holograms "Tri-dis" projections). We say, " Good for you, Jacques, you have uncovered a key element of the Shaver Mystery: so what else is new?"

Vallee seems unsure of where to cut off his warnings of divine revelations that lead to irrationalisms. According to his book, the Bible would fall in the category of social and psychic manipulations, although he shies away from discussions about the validity (or threat) of Christianity.

We thought that Vallee's previous effort: "Passport To Magonia" was excellent. But on this book, we advise Mr Vallee to read Shaver, and stop acting like the rock star ufologist he seems to imagine himself...

One final note to this (again) overlong editorial: Mary LeVesque pointed out that we cut off part of our review on Floria Benton's book, "Hollow Earth Mysteries and the Polar Shift"...here's the part that got lost in the shuffle: "The real secret is the pole shift, she says, and Alternative 3 is a '...trick engineered by ufo agents to make us blame ourselves for something that is bound to happen anyway'. At the end of the book is an impressive bibliography. "

SHAVERTRON

Only Source of Post-Deluge Shaverania

c. Richard Toronto

$2

SPRING 1982   ISSUE 11

S

SHAMBALLA

CAPITAL OF AGHARTA

MAX FYFIELD

INNER EARTH CITY

CITY OF LEGEND -- OR REALITY?

Will this be your last issue of Shavertron ???????

Before wallowing into the shocking statement above, we want to thank all of you kind readers who sent in your survey slips from last issue. You will be happy to learn that the consensus was unanimous (well, almost): no one wants to see any major changes in S, so we must be doing something right! We're glad to know that Richard Shaver has found a permanent spot in everyone's heart.

Now on to serious business...if one can take anything seriously these days. As you've already been quite aware, there is much gloom & doom going around. Ronnie Ray-gun was flying around in the doomsday plane a few weeks ago, contemplating his button (and we don't mean belly!), while Attila the Haig was talking about dropping a demo-bomb in Europe somewhere. Lately, not a day goes by that your editor doesn't read or hear a media report on OIW (Our Impending War...you know, the Big One -- WWIII), and what things will be like after said war. Either the Pentagon is being very optimistic, or they have big plans to split from this planet a la Alternative 3.

Many S readers subscribe to other "underground" publications that are also gloom-ing and dooming...Cosmic Awareness Communications has been pushing their prediction of a nuclear "first strike" by the USA against the USSR in the spring of 1982.

You'll note that this issue of S is dated Spring, '82. In case of nuclear war, your subscription to S will automatically expire, due to the fact that S headquar-ters is located on Ground Zero. We have an A-sub base here, you see.

notes from the underground

Even our resident psychic counselor, Charles Marcoux has little to say that will cheer us up: "In my interpretation of numbers given by Daniel, the number '8-10' is the hour. As far as I can figure out, this hour takes us to Dec.7,1981 -- add 3 weeks and 3 months, and it would take us to late March or early April of 1982. There are 2 signs, Fire and Saturn (fire means Aries sign, 3-21 to 4-21) so there should be some political upsets, or tribulations should occur between Dec. 3, 1981 and April of '82. This may be WAR, or the beginning of a great war..."

Readers may not be aware of the "war" that raged between Cosmic Awareness Com-munications and Riley Crabb of the Borderland Sciences Research Foundation. Riley pubbed a letter from an associate who claimed that Shockley was in fact an evil follower of the Left Hand Path, and a Vampire, to boot. The associate then related a series of events that explained why he believed this to be true. Shockley thun-dered out an irate demand to Riley, threatening him with a Huge Lawsuit -- a battle to the death was intimated. Neither party has really backed down, in essence, al-though Crabb printed a retraction in his Round Robin. Both men are sticking to their guns. We're sorry to see such goings-on, but then, we've had our own hassles too... will truth win out? Well, if WWIII doesn't hit us next spring as CAC has claimed you can write to them and demand a refund! But hang in there, gang! You have alot to look forward to in issue 12 of Shavertron...it's our special rock book ish, with help from Bill Bliss -- the only surviving rogfogo expert in the world.

Jim Wentworth has come up with a great new column idea, called RAP's CORNER, premiering this ish. It will spotlite some of RAP's formerly pubbed gems. This particular column presented herein is timely in the light of recent Shaver Mystery scams promulgated by so-called "supporters" of S and the SM.

If you're looking for Bill's column this time around, you won't find it. We are initiating a "round robin" of 4 different columns, which will include another new item from Ray Archer titled "Rays From the UK". This one will cover various Fortean and ufo topics from Britain. Its column-mates are GIANTS IN THE EARTH, PURE BLISS and, as mentioned, RAP's CORNER.

So many readers have written in complimenting on the fine artwork in S lately, especially the now collectable cover on the last ish, that we want to make some formal introductions. In this issue, you will meet Max Fyfield, S's art director, face to face. In fact, this issue is dedicated to Max! S is fortunate, indeed, to have the likes of Max on the staff.

S readers are no dubt aware that Richard Shaver was one of the first proponents of the Devolution theory, as well as one of the first denouncers of atomic energy and the Bomb. If you combine these 2 elements-- proliferation of the Bomb and Devo-lution, you can see why Shaver spent alot of time worrying about the shape of things to come. So, we'll end this epistle, dear readers, with the lyrics from one of the most devoluted rock groups we know...Devo: "It's a wonderful time to be here/It's nice to be alive/Beautiful people everywhere/See the way they comb their hair/It's a beautiful place we live in/A sweet Ro-man-tic place/Beautiful people everywhere/ See how they show they care/It's a beautiful world..." Merry Xmas everyone...

SHAVER TRON

Editor/Publisher
Richard Toronto

Associates:

Literary Research
Jim Pobst

Art Director
Max Fyfield

Psychic Advisor
Charles Marcoux

Bibliographer
Bruce Walton

Rogfogo Tech
Bill Bliss

Moral Support
Mary LeVesque

SM Consultant
Jim Wentworth

Our Man In:

Britain: Ray Archer
Rome: Francesco Savorgnan
Washington, DC:
"The Librarian"
Private Idaho: R.Finley

Shavertron is quarterly at $8 per year domestic, $9 overseas via surface, $13 via airmail. Make out all checks or money orders to the publisher, not to the zine. Address all mail, including mss. to 309 Coghlan Street, Vallejo, California, USA 94590.

Make out checks, money orders, etc to the Publisher! RICHARD TORONTO!

2

(A few notes after reading <u>S</u> at 3am...)

A friend of mine knew a fellow in Monterey who claimed he knew of tunnels leading from Peru to Easter Island. Those serpent people mentioned in last issue interest me <u>greatly</u>. I've been trying to crack that enigma for years. From archeological research I've done (which has nothing to do with the SM) I've often come across the worldwide "dragon-slayer" myths found in just about everywhere. The NAGAs (serpent people) of India created the 7-headed cobra symbol used by the SLA ...there's an unpublished story there. NAGA priests were the ones who showed Churchward the tablets he based his book "Lost Continent of Mu" upon. The NAGAs and the NAACALS (Mayan Tribe) were the same people. Indian mythology (east & west) are full of stories about the snake people who could fly or go underwater. Have you seen STONEHENGE VIEWPOINT? It has alot about snakes in the sky. In the August "Sunset" mag, is a map of the Mohave which shows CIMA. Refer to early AMAZINGS for story about the giant CIMA caverns. I believe these exist, but were bought up by the Kaiser Corporation. <u>Alot</u> of weird stuff in this area--actually part of Death Valley...Von Daniken says there is a melted city there. Alas, there is no <u>there</u> there. Last issue was fine as is-- dont change it. <u>Good illos</u>.
Cheers,
Vaughn Greene

Dear Richard Toronto,

For your readers who would like to study the serpent rocks further (see article in <u>S</u> 10) I have gathered quite alot of these ancient stone carvings & if anyone is interested I would send them some if they would pay for the postage.

For the last few nights I have watched a huge ufo fly around in this area. It doesn't make any sound & it flys real slow. It goes into the area where I rock hunt.
Sincerely,
Cosette Willoughby
Box 317
Fairacres, New Mex.
88033

Letters

SCRIBBLE BY SHAVER

Dear Richard,

I write to inform you and your readers that I have decided to cancel NEW WORLDS. It is too much to spend all my time on. It is costing me far beyond the amount it makes. Please let others know...it is bankrupt.

Also the other night I was on board a spacecraft and have made interesting arrangements with them, a master from out there to study under while here. The regenerative process I went through is having its effect on my system now. Can't hardly touch food now it seems so horrid. I must go to higher levels now of more non-material things under them to be a student.

We are just going to have a small group here under this space master from the Space Temple, the same one Ezekial was on. To learn new ways and then help people through it.
Yours Sincerely,
Ivan Boyes

Dear Richard,

The thing that always amazes me about sci-fi people, (Phil K Dick is one exception) is how <u>conservative</u> they really are when it comes to "speculation", "new ideas" etc. I do feel sure that as time goes on and the final assessments are toted up, Ray Palmer is going to be seen as important in his own way as John W Campbell, Jr. I find the late-'40's AMAZINGS as regards the impact of the a-bomb to be fully as revealing as the late-40s ASTOUNDING. I think RAP was the champ when it came to writing enthusiastic editorials. I <u>know</u> that the lettercols of AMAZING during the reign of the SM are easily worth a psychologist's doctorate. And though it must be over 35 years now since I first came across them, I'm sure that those letters re. The

Mystery have yet to be equalled. The one that sticks in my mind best was from "Laurel McElwain. I wish somebody who knows the score would find a publisher & collect them, collect them all!
Dr. Al
Ackerman,
CASFC
R--We couldn't agree with you more.

Dear Rich,

Re. Henry "Hankus Pankus" Steele and forthcoming somewhere-way-down-the-road SM zine effort: well, to begin I don't think those so-called Teros (W. Rhodes & co.) busily harassing the poor guy have their heads screwed on right (note I said 'heads', because they got 2 each no doubt).

RS alive in R.C.(??) SURE! Yeah. And I believe that Superman and Robin Hood are alive in Hollywood. To what purpose was Shaver killed only to be resurrected (teleported too) in Rainbow City? Pray tell.

When dear old Henry tried to hook up German Nazis with RC all in one fell swoop via his numerous & often lengthy epistles to me (mis-directives to one of the 'lesser-evolved'-- yukk--lowly slob disciples, if you will), I sez to meself: 'Uh-oh, this is where this hyar ol' bird has to be takin' off (for heap more productive happy hunting ground! ugh) I mean, this super-evolved special privilege class jazz you try to hype, Hank smaks too much of one herr Goebbels unending line of classic b------it (Tell a BIG LIE enough times & ANYONE WILL BE-LIEVE IT FINALLY remember?)

It'd be funny were it not instead very decidedly devisive (<u>DE</u>-vise) Let's give no priority to devisiveness!

Best wishes S & Co! And, Henry, GOOD LUCK--I mean it because I do very strongly suspect YOU ARE GOING TO NEED IT.

All For Now,
Al Wiseman

Don't forget to subscribe

THE MUDMAN OF PEGWELL BAY

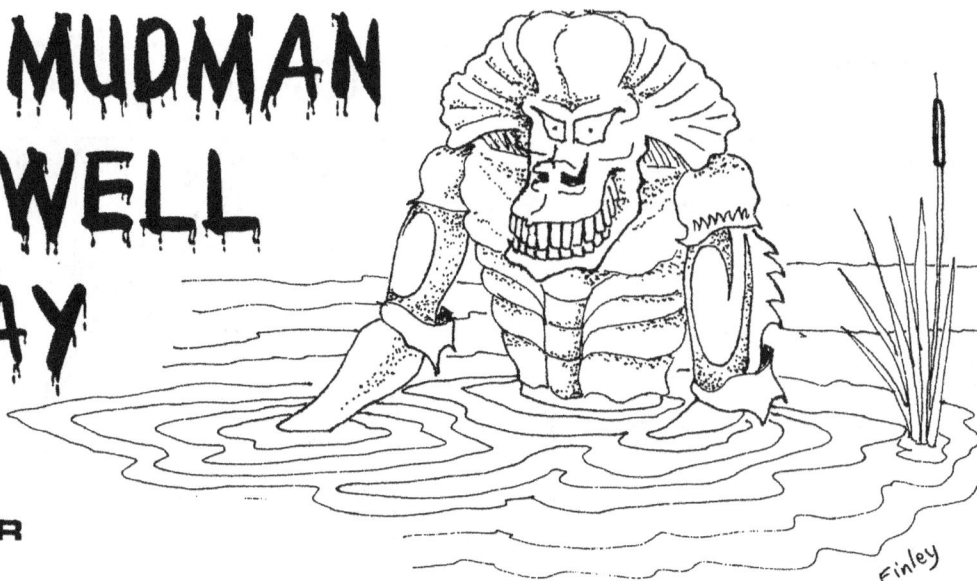

Finley

By RAY ARCHER

On July 1st, 1970, an unusual account appeared in the Daily Sketch newspaper with a rather sensational headline: HUNT FOR ABOMINABLE MUDMAN! According to this press item, night workers at the International Hoverport (for hovercraft) Pegwell Bay, Ramsgate, Kent, were worried about a "strange Yeti" creature that was prowling the lonely mudflats nearby. Two men claimed they had discovered odd claw marks over 6" across leading from old smugglears' caves into the sea.

Both men, Keith Walters and Trevor Burgess, were hoverport engineers and had also managed to obtain plaster casts of some of the prints. The larger ones allegedly had a distance of four feet between them. This, then, is the gist of the account from that time. I was determined to find out more about the mystery and just over a year later I took advantage of an holiday and spent a week in the area.

I was accompanied by a friend, Theo Price--now, unfortunately deceased. During this week from Saturday, August 7,1971 to the following weekend of the 14th of August, we investigated the strange incident.

On Monday, we paid a visit to the East Kent Times news offices in Ramsgate, and managed to obtain the pertinent papers of the time, with the original account.

The next day, after several enquiries, we managed to interview Mr Walters at his home, which was then in Ramsgate. He gave us more relevant details on the finding of the prints. He said that the claw prints were found in the sand, between the hoverport and a man-made tunnel that passes through the cliffs-- apparently used at one time to transport fish inland from the beach. This was at night, and both he and his friend decided to have a breath of fresh air during the customary tea break at work. The prints were indented quite deeply and even he himself could not duplicate their depth with his own feet.

They pointed out the trail of claw marks to others at the hoverport and everyone was baffled. This all happened on the night of the 25th of June 1970. The following day, he said, they plucked up their courage and returned to the same spot as the night before and found fresh tracks in the mud.

Some "polyfilla" was obtained and two casts were made from these prints to show to others on the night shift, who had been rather skeptical of the affair. Mr Walters being a family man became concerned about the children who often played in the old smugglers' caves. The press was then brought into the case. Mean while, Walters watched when possible for signs of the elusive creature roaming the foreshore.

Although nothing was observed more tracks were found--and this time photographed. The film still in the camera was given over to the East Kent Times who developed it for him, ruling out any faking on his part. But following the processing, they kept the negatives, he said. After the accounts appeared in both the local and national press on July 1st, 1970, cranks began plaguing him and his family, and worse, people started ringing up the hoverport putting his job at risk. Jobs being hard to find in that area, understandably he got fed up with the whole thing. We visited Mr Walters again on Thursday just to clarify some of the points already raised.

His answers to our questions were completely concise as on the first occasion, and he seemed sincere in everything that was recounted to us. On this last visit he handed both the photographs and the casts over to me, saying that I could keep them. But I'm jumping the gun! After leaving Mr. Walters home on Tuesday we called at the house of his friend, Trevor Burgess, but were told by a neighbor he had gone away on holiday.

On Wednesday afternoon we visited Pegwell Bay and many colour photos were taken of the area. The foreshore was quite thoroughly explored with the rock cliffs and caves being looked over in turn, as also was the tunnel mentioned previously. We had also decided on having a vigil one night on the cliffs overlooking the bay, with a chance, though slim, that something might be seen.

In the meantime we made enquiries regarding large dogs or other animals owned by people in the Pegwell area. On Friday we paid a visit to the proprietor of one of the large hotels in the vicinity who owned a Great Dane dog. This man was very cooperative and even assisted us in obtaining a plaster cast of one of the dog's paws. From this new cast, we concluded that the dog print was smaller than the mystery animal cast and the latter also had very sharp claws in relation to the former, so it seemed the mystery was still not cleared up.

That afternoon, we made our way to Pegwell Bay. We had our cameras, plaster of paris, and torches for a late vigil on the cliff top. The first indication of rather odd goings-on was late in the afternoon, while we walked below the cliffs on the sands. In skirting some bushes there was a slight rustling sound heard in the undergrowth. On looking in the direction of the sound, what appeared to us to be a cave entrance in the rock was noted. I climbed the cliff in this area towards the cav -

ity in the rock, finding a crude path. On reaching the spot I found an oval cleft--rather like a door set into the rock. In looking at the flat area before this crevice I was startled to see a large clawprint similar to the ones allegedly found and photographed by Mr Walters. Here was proof and I intended to get both casts and photo-

graphs myself, making my way down to Theo below. We grabbed our cameras and ascended the few feet to snap the clear claw mark. When we reached the area, there was no clawprint visible where I had seen it! Now this was against all logic, prints just do not disappear in a few minutes! And how did it get up there anyway? I was baffled, and would soon be more so later that night.

After more explorations around the foreshore, and further pictures taken, including an hover-craft sitting on the mudflats, we made our way to a good vantage point on top of the cliffs over-looking the bay.

By this time, it was getting quite dark with several stars clearly visible. At about 9:30pm we both noticed a bright star-like object in the distance across the bay. There was a lighthouse also a fair way out and every time the beam from this swept round, this slowly moving object in the sky would blink out as though avoiding it. Soon after, clouds obscured it and we never saw the thing again.

A short while later an hovercraft, its ports ablaze with light, noisily plowed its way across the bay from the hoverport on our right. It seemed to shake the cliffs we were standing on, until at last all was quiet again. Soon after this, I became a-ware of a luminous cylinder-like object, a little ways out from the beach below us, so I pointed it out to my friend. Whatever it was, the thing appeared to move standing on end, sometimes sticking out from the water and other times floating on the surface. It reminded me of the periscope on a submarine as it kept emerging and submerging. It could also be likened to a faint vertical neon tube with a golden coloured glow around it. We shone the beams of our torches at it and it definately dimmed in brightness. Both of us tried to get it on film, but for some reason our flashes would not fire and so as a last resort, we tried photographing it with the aid of our torches. Only two small lights reflecting in the water showed up, which could have been anything.

While watching the odd object below, our attention was diverted from this to a loud crackling noise-- as if hundreds of twigs were being broken at once-- appearing to come from from the bushes to the left of us. Moving away from the cliff edge, I caught sight of another cylindrical light on the other side towards the hoverport. On stepping out from the grassy area used in our vigil onto the path that leads into Pegwell Road, we saw a figure

in dark clothing-- a man at least 7 feet tall standing beneath a tree! He had a rather odd man-ner and when we shone our torches at him, he just stood and stared back at us without saying a word. Naturally, this made us feel uneasy...what with all the other goings-on as well, we decided to col-lect our gear and depart. On leaving we looked back to find the man was gone. In all, the vigil on the cliff lasted about 1½ hours from 8:30 to 10pm.

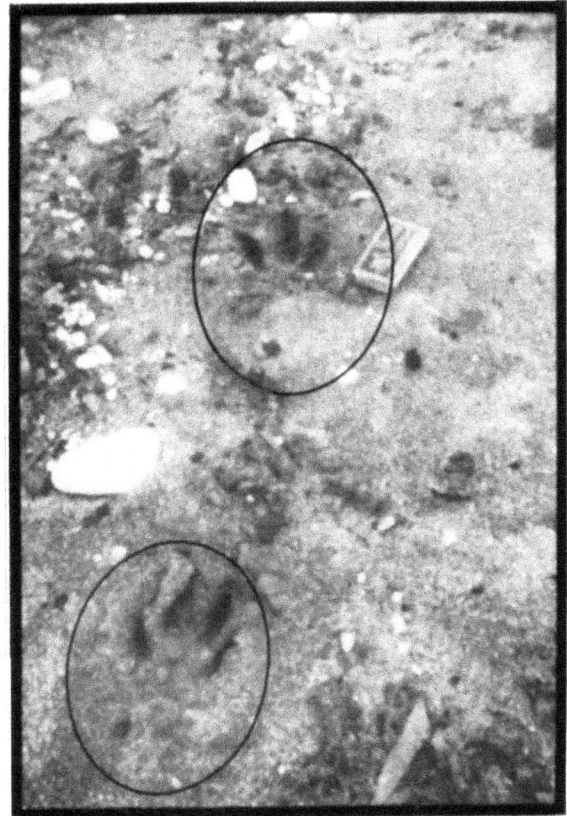

Mudman prints, photographed by Walters

A few months following our interesting time spent down at Pegwell, an item in a newspaper came to my attention. The story was that two coastguards appar-antly found that a grill cover in one of the caves on the Ramsgate coast had been removed. They decided to investigate the uncovered shaft and followed a maze of interconnecting passageways not realizing until it was too late that they were lost. Eventu-ally, after looking for a way out of their dilemma, they saw above them daylight streaming through a man-hole cover, and emerged into a Ramsgate street.

This account, amusing as it may sound, could well have a connection with the earlier incident we in-vestigated. The idea of "things" actually coming up to the earth's surface through caverns and on into our sewer systems is not entirely without support. A possible confirmation of this are the two alleged cases reported from Cabbagetown (Shavertron 1) and from New Kensington, PA recently (2). The latter incident briefly, concerns an alleged sighting of a green creature by a sewer drain. Four boys claimed they saw this "thing" and one lad even said to the police, who were called to the scene, he had "grabbed

RAP's CORNER

by JIM WENTWORTH

'((From Flying Saucers, July, 1959))

The demand was made by a reader that Ray Palmer reveal a long-held secret -- his Fact -- that enabled him to know instantly if a person claiming to understand the truth of the Shaver Mystery, Ufos, etc., was really telling the truth, or lying. His Fact was "Tradition" or "Traditional Behavior". Following are five quoted paragraphs of Ray Palmers reply:

"Shaver gave a small part of the Tradition, when he said it was 'traditional' in the Cavern World to adhere to secrecy. Under no circumstances is the secret (of their actual existence) to be disclosed. Always it must be made to appear something else. If you hear voices, for instance, you are a 'medium' and are hearing the voices of the dead. If you see a 'projection ' from some visi-ray machine,

it is only a 'ghost', and not real at all. Actually, it isn't, but you must also be kept from knowing it is an unreality produced by a REALITY, the machine that does the projecting.

"If you see a space ship, you will see others most likely, and these will be readily identifiable as illusions. If you do not see a space ship, and one is there, you may be caused to look in the other direction by an illusion, deliberately projected to distract your attention.

"Secrecy is only a small part of the Tradition, however. It is no longer possible to maintain secrecy. But as long as you can create something to becloud the issue, the more that comes out which is distorted...the better it is, the greater the confusion ...if total confusion can be achieved, progress is halted toward solution by actual disgust and despair, and abandonment of the whole thing as 'a mess'. ((Editor's underlining))

"Bender invented his three men in black to give him a reason to shuck the whole mess, which would have backed him into innumerable inescapable corners. He knew they had him completely frustrated, and to go on would have only landed him in the nut house.

"Oh, yes, Bender has a secret. He knows. But his knowledge is useless. If, for instance, while seated alone on his front porch, he were to see three men in black, walking toward him down the street, he would only groan and say: 'Don't rub it in!' He wouldn't bother to get up and go into the house, because he KNOWS they aren't actually there."

Mudman track next to matchbox for scale.

the short creature from behind, but it squealed and escaped".

So just what are we to make of such cases? No doubt many laughed when Shaver said deros are tucked under our cities. Will time prove him right? Is it not conceivable that the Kent region of England holds more than a few mysteries of its own? It might even be a window area as John Keel termed them-- a gateway into another dimension, from where strange creatures, even mysterious craft enter our own world. This is not the only time the calling card of a creature of unknown origins has been found. In February 1969, a naturalist took casts of large prints-- again leading into the sea--at Flint, North Wales (3). In a fascinating book (4) by the late author of unexplained phenomena, Harold T. Wilkins, is yet another mystery creature reported in the Ramsgate region...this time reported by a policeman. This "weird beast" he states was seen in "Dumpton Park, Ramsgate, Kent, in the early morning". The officer described it as follows: "The thing was covered with quills, had a long snout and short tail. It was as big as an Alsatian dog, and had large claws. You might have thought it was a walking fir-cone".

In our world, then, concepts of reality often have to change-- especially when faced with something entirely alien. Can we really be sure what reality is anyway?

FOOTNOTES:
1. The Sunday Sun, Toronto, Canada-- 25/3/79
2. Valley News Dispatch, New Kensington, PA--5/3/81
3. Daily Mail, London, UK, 28/2/69
4. Flying Saucers Uncensored, HT Wilkins, 1956

6

EMPRESS OF AGHARTA

SYNOPSIS OF A MOTION PICTURE -- TO BE!

Sequel to "The Busy Pyramid"

by MAX FYFIELD (alias MAXIMILIUS)

There is a large subterrainean hall 1800 feet below the Great Pyramid of Giza. MAXIMILIUS and GIN-A-LOH have just gone through their initiation in the pyramid above, and now they are shown this secret hall. With a group of Initiates they enter the tunnel-vehicles, and soon they are speeding down through a narrow tunnel -- faster than an ostrich can run (Gin is thinking)...

Hours later they stop in a huge cave, large enough to contain a city like Baghdad. There are tunnel openings at various places, many of them were constructed by Lemurians and Atlanteans to escape solar radiation, bacteria, floods -- and ATOMIC BLASTS!!! While they continue downward, Max explains how the tunnels were constructed by SUPER-HEAT-DETERIORATORS which could blast a city into nothingness, all molecu--- He is interrupted when the vehicle comes to a sudden stop. The tunnel is blocked by large stones, they step out and ch--- Suddenly, they are attacked by a group of creatures, half human, half monkey, that is dragging a large machine along. Max quickly explains: They are DEROs, degenerated humans who steal flying saucers and equipment, there is only one thing that will scare them away -- LAUGHTER, so start laughing! It works, the deros flee, and the machine is left behind. Fortunately, the machine is a "Deteriorator", so Max's party blasts its way through and continues...

Suddenly they feel weightless, they are passing the center of gravity 400 miles below the surface, and soon they acquire a new upside-down. They pass through large man-made city-caves built by THE ELDER RACES millions of years ago, now inhabited by a Blue Race who maintain life simply by inhaling the nourishing AIR! (See, it can be done!)...

At last they emerge into the HOLLOW INTERIOR of the Earth and see THE CENTRAL SUN! They pass through a city of friendly giants, they are taken in a flying saucer to SHAMBALLA, capital of the empire of AGHARTA. The ruling council shows a great interest in GIN-A-LOH because they know she has been there before in former lives, with Max. They see THE STONE OF LIFE which rejuvenates all citizens of 50 -- to the age of 20. Max explains: We have an empress called LOLIX THE MEAN ONE, and that's where you come in Gin, since you look like her twin...

Max and Gin settle in Shamballa, they gain occult power, in secrecy Lolix is exchanged with Gin-a-loh...who thus becomes EMPRESS OF AGHARTA. Max is really an inner-earth being who went to the Giza pyramid to get his beloved. At last they are allowed to visit the most secret area of all Agharta: The SPACE SHIP BASE for visitors from other planets!!! They come and leave through the North Polar opening!

So, perhaps the combination of these Space People and Inner-Earth People will be THE COMING RACE with a few Surface-Earth People joining in-- perhaps you will be one of them!

7

MAX FYFIELD -81

SHAVERTRON
INTERVIEW

Lucius Farish will be remembered by most S readers as the author of numerous magazine articles on such specialized aspects of the ufo enigma as the 1897 airship flap. He is currently publisher of one of the most comprehensive newsclipping services on ufos worldwide: the UFONS (Ufo Newsclipping Service), Rt. 1--Box 220, Plumerville, Ark. FATE readers may also recall Lou's obit that appeared soon after Richard Shaver's passing, for Lou was a friend (among many) of RSS.

Toronto: I know that you used to visit Mr Shaver at his home in Summit. What was the purpose of your visits and did you discover anything that you didn't expect?

Farish: Well, my purpose was simply to learn as much as I could about what Shaver had been talking about since the 1940's when the Shaver Mystery was first publicised in AMAZING STORIES. And of course in the later years, to find out about the rock books.

Did I discover anything I didn't expect? Well yes, I guess I did. I didn't really know what to expect from Shaver himself, having never corresponded with him before I met him. That was around 1962-63, somewhere in there. I didn't know what to expect. Victor Johnston first introduced us. Vic used to visit with me quite a bit when he lived in the Oklahoma City area. He had visited Shaver around 1945-46 or so...well, it may have been the mid-1950's...at any rate, Vic did know Dick Shaver and Dottie, and so when he came down to visit with me, we went up to Summit and that's when I first met him. I visited him on several occasions with Vic and with friends of my own who would visit me.

I soon discovered that, as I have said elsewhere in FATE and other places that Shaver was not by any means the uh, fanatic one may have expected. ...not from his stories, but from what others had said about him, which is usually not a very reliable criterion. I think he deliberately gave the impression of being gruff when various people met him, but he had his reasons for doing so. He firmly believed in the dero/tero philosophy. He was convinced these beings did exist. Now, personally, I simply don't know whether they do or did or whatever, but he believed it and also that there was a possibility that people might undergo some kind of harassment from the deros if they had a close friendship with Shaver. So for that reason whenever a camera was pointed his way he'd put on his most demonic expression...purposely. I remember one time he said (when we were talking about the Kennedy assasination) that he thought the deros were responsible for it because it was the principle of dero activity...the backward principle. Kennedy was loved by so many, they couldn't stand the thought of him being loved. Therefore they had to kill him. And then Shaver said: "I don't want anyone loving me...it's dangerous for everyone involved"! I think he stuck to that principle.

Underneath that he was one of the most delightful people, one of the most well read and articulate people that I have ever met, and certainly a truly gentle and kind man. Considering that the first visit was nearly 20 years ago now, it is hard to pick out certain things. I always greatly enjoyed the visits with him. As I say, I never knew really, what I believed as far as set ideas about deros/teros or rock books. They were all interesting, but I was never able to make up my mind definitley one way or another. It was simply a pleasure to be in Shaver's company, and also I enjoyed talking with Dottie. She would often be gone when we were there, as she was busy with other activities. I remember the ceramic work she did. She made some beautiful pieces.

Toronto: Lou, what's the state of ufology right now?

Farish: Sad. If, by ufology you mean the work of organizations and today's publications. I'm not very impressed with ufology today. They dont study ufos. I am interested in ufos, not politics and all that falderall. I strongly believe that the best course of action for any individual to follow is to be independent...not to be affiliated to any great degree with organizations. To consider the information they have to offer, yes, but getting involved in an organization is very time consuming at the expense of actual research.

Toronto: Then do you disregard the viability of ufo organizations and their ability to solve the ufo mystery? I'm sure that you know that European ufo researchers are going for more and more organizations and group projects. Project URD in Sweden recently got off the ground, and MAPIT in England is working on a ufo library tied together with computors. European ufologists (some) are suggesting that ufology should take up the language of science in order to be accepted into the scientific community. Are these people headed in the wrong direction?

Farish: Well, that's supposedly what they plan to do. Alot of these groups get grandiose schemes of what they're going to do, most of it involving computors, and most rarely does it materialize. I do not know if that's the case of Project URD or not.

>lucius farish

I'm just leery of such claims.

As for the rest of your question, I couldn't care less if the scientific community accepts ufology!! I'm not at all impressed by the scientific community! So what do I care? I'm more interested in learning about ufos than I am in having scientists recognise there is a ufo "problem". They've had 35 years to realize that and if they haven't by now, to heck with 'em. Go out and collect your own information whether you've got a computer or not, and make your own decisions. Don't wait for scientists to do it or you'll be waiting a long, long time.

Toronto: Then what kind of progress has ufology made in those 35 years?

Farish: There are some days when I think it hasn't progressed at all! I don't know...it's hard to assess the whole thing. It has progressed, I suppose in the sense that we have more evidence if not solid conclusions or hard data now than we did in 1947. We know quite a bit more about the different types of craft, we have all the abduction cases, the contactee cases and so forth, and that must be taken into consideration and evaluated as best one can. So, yes, I suppose there's been progress, but I do think that ufology in general (primarily the ufo organizations and magazines and so forth, as opposed to the individual researcher) has gotten off the track somewhat. It always tends to happen with organizations-- they get bogged down in their petty politics and intra-organizational arguments and then ufo research goes by the board. It gets neglected and takes second, third or forth place behind other matters which really aren't getting anyone anywhere. If ufo groups would stop all the bickering and get down to investigating, we'd be much better off. Of course, I don't expect that to happen, but that is one of the places I think ufology has gotten off the track-- another is the profusion of what I consider non-sensical theories to "explain" ufos.

Toronto: What do you consider to be the "non-sensical" ufo theories?

Farish: I refer to such things as the parapsychological 'explanation' for ufos, the 'planetary poltergeist' theory (a la Clark and Coleman), a large portion of Keel's writings, the Persinger theory of piezoelectric effects being responsible for ufos, etc., etc. Not that all these theories might not be partially true, but there is no way they can account for the total ufo picture.

Toronto: Isn't there anyone who could be considered to be "in the forefront of ufology"?

Farish: Humm...that's a pretty tough question to answer. First we have to decide if this field has a forefront! I don't want to go naming names, because I would probably leave someone out that I should put in.

I have been impressed by various things in the past year or so. Missing Time, by Bud Hopkins, is an outstanding book in my opinion. It's about ufo abduction cases. In another area of ufology I've been impressed by a book by Dr. Harley Rutlidge, titled Project Identification, published by Prentice Hall. It's the story of his investigations between 1973 and 1980 in South-Eastern Missouri. These two books are exceptional.

I'm also impressed with some of the research being carried on by Wendelle Stevens and his associates in Arizona. Of course, Wendelle and his friends are some of the most controversial, I guess. ...but for no good reason that I can see. Their conclusions are their own of course, I have not done what they have in the way of research, specifically on the Meier case in Switzerland. I respect what they have done-- that they are willing to take the time and money out of their own pockets to go to Switzerland and try to investigate this as best they could...which no one else has bothered to do. I think the reactions to their research has taught me quite a bit about the motives of alot of the people involved in ufology.

Toronto: At least one magazine in an article by Kal K. Korff has called the Meier case "the most infamous hoax in ufology".

Farish: I'm not at all impressed with Korff's writing on the Meier case and I'm willing to give the benefit of the doubt to the people who went there and investigated it at their own expense.

Toronto: Do you think that belief in ufos can eventually leave one open to manipulations by totalitarian masters, as Vallee claims?

Farish: Well, belief in anything can leave you open to manipulation by a variety of people. I don't like to talk in terms of belief-- I don't believe in ufos. It does not require an act of faith to accept their existence. Ufos exist! Whatever they are.

Toronto: How deep has CIA tamper sunk into the actual ufo scenario?

Farish: I don't think the CIA is as involved as for example, Leon Davidson thinks they are--that they were responsible for the experiences that Adamski, Fry, Betherum and others claimed to have had. I think that's going too far. On the other hand, I wouldn't be surprized at anything the CIA tried to do. That they had their finger in the contactee pie would not surprise me in the least, but to what extent, I don't know.

Toronto: Many writers, such as Keel, Vonnegut and others, suggest that the ufo enigma is a cosmic joke being played on us stupid humans...that its a device to, well, drive us nuts. A big game.

Farish: If it's a CIA con game, its a very extensive one and has been going on longer than the CIA has. Who says that humans weren't nuts before the ufos came along? I seriously doubt that the ufo phenomenon, whatever it is, from wherever it may come, is designed solely for the purpose of driving us nuts. What it all means, I don't know, but I hope to find out.

I think alot of people regard the ufos as a manifestation of one particular race of beings or whatever-- I don't. I think it is extremely complex. We may have visitors from another physical planet, or other so-called dimensions or realities, planes of existence, etc. and a number of other things. There are no simple answers to ufos--at least if there are, I haven't run across them.

The only thing we can do is continue to study the data, to investigate as best we can and try to make some sort of personal decision or philosopy about what it all means to us individually. You'd better decide what ufos mean to you. It's not my place to tell anyone else how they should think or what they should think about ufos.

Toronto: When you say, "decide what ufos mean to you" do you infer that ufos will be different things to different people? If so, this reminds me of Carl Jung's statements about racial mind projections in times of strife.

Farish: Absolutely not. But let me frame my answer here: I accept that some ufos are physical craft from.....where-ever. That doesn't necessarily mean that they stay physical all the time. And that's not all I think ufos are. I think there are some that may very well be the space animals that you, Rich, and Trevor Constable apparantly photographed. Ancient civilizations is another possibility.

Everyone has to interpret it, has to...come to grips with the fact that ufos exist, and then determine what that means to them personally. It's not at all like Jung's theory. I don't go along with all this "our minds project our turmoil onto other things" as Jung believed. Of course, there's been a great amount of misrepresentation of what Jung believed or thought or said about ufos. You'll remember, Rich, that one possibility that he regarded highly likely was that ufos are entities, beings of some kind, presumably from E-T sources. So if there's one man who's been grossly misinterpreted in ufology it's Jung. But I am not an advocate of Jung's ideas.

Toronto: Let me give you a new term (I just made it up for this interview): IGO, or Intergallactic Overlord. This I define as a "cosmic" or "universal" data source that is channeled through earth individuals. Many churches and other "occult" groups flourish on this channel. Ashtar is a space overlord that pops up throughout ufo literature. Cosmic Awareness follows the teachings of It or the Awareness, another "space channel". Do you run across this kind of material in the thousands of ufo clippings you are constantly reading through? Is this IGO phenomenon widespread?

Farish: Let me just say this. My impression is that people who channel messages from "wherever" are obviously getting something. Whether it is from their subconscious mind or intelligences of some sort (e-t or e-dimensional, whatever) I don't know. I don't run into too much of that in the clippings I go through, but then there's

plenty of it around in various publications. The clippings I get mainly relate to phenomena and sightings. Obviously, these channelings exist but there's simply no way, as far as I know, that you can check out the source of this information, and determine whether you're being given reliable information. In some cases, you will be given reliable info that can be checked out, prophesies that do come true. But, at the same time you may be given some absolute nonsense, along with it. Sorting it out is the problem.

Toronto: Do you think that people should be paranoid when another MIB story makes the rounds? Or is it that MIBs are a necessary part of the ufo enigma?

Farish: Paranoia shouldn't be spent on anything as far as I'm concerned. If you're asking me if some of the MIB stories be taken seriously-- YES. I don't know if they're a necessary part, but they are a part for some people, according to stories I've read and heard. I do not dismiss all the MIB stories I've heard. I think that some of the stories are attributable to various intelligence agencies...CIA, NSA, who-knows-what. But the others seem to have a direct link with ufos. As to what it all means, I don't know.

Toronto: Is the concept of the inner earth, in your opinion, with all its races living down there, any more or less credible than the concept of ET's from space?

Farish: That's a hard question to answer. I think its entirely possible that there are inner earth inhabitants in the sense of bases created by ufo intelligences. By inner earth, I do not mean hollow earth. I find it rather hard to accept the notion of the holes at the poles, the doughnut-shaped earth and all that. But-- I do think it is entirely possible that there are subterranean bases, maybe even native races, who knows? I do not exclude the possibility of underwater bases for ufos. I don't know whether these beings would have originated there as original inhabitants of earth, or if it is a case of them coming from somewhere else and basing themselves here. I suspect the latter, but really it doesn't make much difference, does it?

Toronto: Well, I began this interview with Shaver and I'll end it with Shaver...just what were your discussions with RSS like? Did you argue, discuss history, art, his days during the Depression? What did he show you in the way of rock hounds?

Farish: It's really hard to summarize my discussions with Shaver, partly because of my faulty memory and partly because there was such a wide range of subjects. He rarely argued if someone disagreed with him, so you couldn't say he was dogmatic in his beliefs. He was sure of his beliefs, but he did not try to convert you, you know. He believed what he believed and if you didn't believe that, well, ok, that's your business. No, he wasn't an evangilist. Just matter of fact about it. You weren't going to talk him out of his beliefs, not that any of us ever tried, but that's certainly the impression one got.

Yeah, he liked to talk about history, his life as an artist. We talked about everything from the core of the Shaver Mystery itself (ie. the deros/teros/caverns) to mundane things like pet dogs and hunting and fishing and raising cattle. We didnt sit down with Shaver and talk about strictly deros and teros. He was a fascinating conversationalist on just about any subject you could name.

Yes, he did try to explain what he saw in the rock books...and I don't know if you should put "saw" in quotes or not...but he would take a rock and show me what he did see in it, and I must say he had some very unusual rocks there, some that I had never seen anywhere before. Some of them did look virtually artificial to me. And in some of them I could "see" what he was describing--I could not see as much as he did, but I could certainly see what he was talking about. I'll tell you one thing: its much easier to see things in the rocks when you look at the rock itself, rather than photos of them. In photos they just don't reproduce the same effect. And of course, you feel the rock...its texture, you can see the color. The rocks themselves are much more impressive.

I guess alot of people had the idea that Shaver was some kind of nut, well he wasn't as far as I could tell. I mean, in something like this, Richard Shaver was the only man who knew what he was saying was true or not, we can all have ideas about it, and opinions about it, but none of us really know unless we experience the same thing he did. And I haven't. I don't doubt his sincerity in his belief that he was telling the truth. I only wish that I could have sat down and talked with him for many many hours and got the whole story on tape.

Toronto: That's the recurring dream of every SM fan, including me. Thanks, Lou for taking the time away from the UFO Newsclipping Service to do this interview for S readers.

4-21-81

Easter Bunny Burned as Pagan

Niles, Ohio

Three church members were charged with disorderly conduct and violating open burning laws yesterday after a five-foot stuffed Easter bunny was burned as a pagan idol on the church lawn.

Police in this northern Ohio town said the elder of the Truth Tabernacle and two members set the stuffed rabbit ablaze in an afternoon ceremony on Easter Sunday.

Timothy Cayten, 20, of Warren and Danny Chitwood, 32, of Niles pleaded not guilty yesterday to charges of disorderly conduct and violating city burning laws. Vernon Cayten, 32, the elder, pleaded not guilty to disorderly conduct and obstructing official business, and pleaded no contest to violating the open-burning law. He was fined $50 in Municipal Court.

Police said the white bunny was seated on a chair on top of a table decorated with colored eggs and flowers. They said that when they tried to arrest the three men, they ran around the table, chanting and yelling.

During the ceremony, police said, Cayten called anyone who had Easter bunnies "heathens and dummies who worship pagan gods."

Associated Press

On the Track of Italian Contactees

I was quite disappointed when I called Germana Grosso on the phone, only to find out that she knew nothing about Inner Earth...although she knew about UFO bases under the ground and under the ocean--she only mentioned that those fertile green lands spotted by some Luftwaffe planes during the War (close to the South Pole) should be connected with extra-terrestrials.

I agreed to meet her 2 days later for a short interview. I found a very kind, but nervous woman trying to avoid most of my questions. What she did tell me though, talking about hollow planets, was the fact that Jupiter, not Earth, was a hollow planet! But no living conditions are to be found on Jupiter--at least on the icy, gas-covered outside crust.

Not so inside the planet! Jupiter has a central rocky nucleus, where life is possible by means of high technology (the energy of positive atoms coming from the outside crust.)

So life, just as we know it, is indeed possible out there, flowers, plants, light, clean air, are all available in great quantity. Who made all this possible?? The common effort of 3 advanced races:

Etruscans, Atlanteans, Egypitians...three races we have always connected with mystery and whose origins (and in one case whose disappearance) are still without a clue. These 3 races live in peace with each other and often visit earth with their spaceships. They've been following us very closely. Apparantly we have blown up one planet already, because of nuclear warfare, and they are very worried we could do the same here. Kozmic laws of evolution limit interference from other space inhabitants (Are we not space dwellers?) In other words, it is highly recommendable we solve the nuclear warfare problem ourselves, even though (on the verge of disaster) we might get external help. By the way, Jupiter's name is ETONYA...

More to come over the next issue...
Francesco Savorgnan, Via Barnaba Oriani 91, Roma, Italia 00197.

El Cajon, San Diego County 10-16-80

Ruth Norman says she is getting signals from outer space that spaceships from 32 planets are heading for nearby Jamul, and she has rented a theater to help prepare for their arrival.

The news is especially good for people with heating problems because the outer-space ships will form a tower of power to supply all the energy needed on this earth, says the 80-year-old Norman, who also goes by the title of the archangel Uriel.

Arrival time is only three to six months away, she says, so her group, called Unarius, the Science of Life, has rented the 1200-seat East County Performing Arts Center in El Cajon for a 12-hour readiness briefing on October 21. She says a staff of more than 60 persons, including scientists, engineers, composers, artists and film producers, is helping her prepare.

"The spacecraft have been configured and built in special sizes so that the biggest will land first and the others will land on top in descending order of size to create an energy tower," she said in an interview. "They are planning to teach the Earth World people and to help them."

Not Again !!? Note date

Associated Press

11

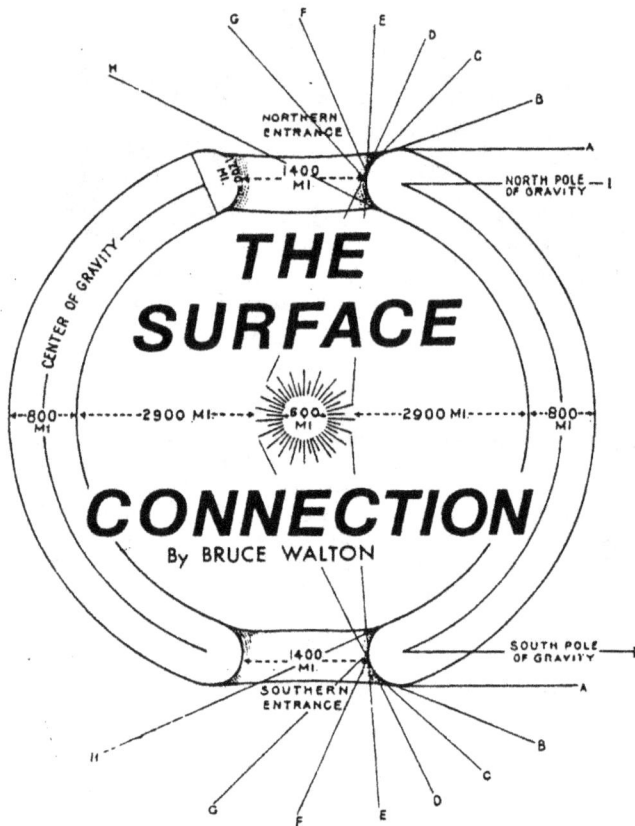

THE SURFACE CONNECTION

By BRUCE WALTON

DIAGRAM II

In the May, 1967 issue of the HOLLOW BULLETIN was printed portions of "The Messerschmidt Manuscript". A French woman, thought to have been killed, returned to her home in the suburbs of Paris with a frightening tale of being kidnapped and taken into a dero's lair. The story also appeared in Warren Smith's book "THIS HOLLOW EARTH". An edited version of her statement follows:

"...I was a young woman of 19 years of age in 1943, proud of my ability as a student, and eagerly looking forward to marrying a young man who planned to be a physician. One night we planned to meet in my fiance's office building, join another couple, and have dinner in a small cafe. We were not worried about the Nazi's. I arrived a few minutes late at my fiance's office building and the old man who ran the elevator had left for the day. I decided to operate the lift for myself. I stepped inside to inspect the controls. There were no symbols to indicate whether the lift went up or down by moving the lever one way or the other. Light-hearted and in love, I decided that if I ran the elevator into the basement, I could reverse the controls and go up to the other stories...I made an error and the elevator stopped in a dark basement. I reversed the controls, but my hand slipped. I pushed the 'down' control. The elevator suddenly plunged down below the basement, falling through space as if the cable had snapped. After a rapid drop, perhaps several hundred feet the elevator stopped with a sudden lurch. I was so frightened as I fell onto the floor of the cage, sobbing and screaming. Through my terror stricken mind, I heard a loud, guttural noise on the other side of the elevator door. The door was torn open with a vicious slam and I saw the most horrible beast in the world...His face was

the most terrible feature. It was much too large for his body, totally devoid of hair. The skin was scarred and wrinkled. His nose was fashioned more like a snout. It was at least seven inches in length, hanging down over his lipless mouth.

"He was nude. His body looked as if he had never worn garments. A filthy, animal smell filled the elevator. Mercifully, I fainted. I never knew what happened in that elevator. Did they use it for an entry into the outside world? I have never thought about it and those elevator shafts may go down far into the earth at certain points. When I came to, I was lying on the polished floor of an immense cavern. There were several other women standing around in a dark corner, and as my eyes adjusted to the dimness, I saw that we were caged into one corner of the cave...There were about 20 women crowded into the cave. Most of them were totally mad, insane creatures who had lost their minds...their emotions and human feelings destroyed by the horrible existence in the caverns.

"The devil man who pulled me from the lift grinned wickedly through his lipless mouth. I moved farther back into the cage. He grabbed me. They pressed me against the bars of the cage.

I passed out again as the devil man placed a dirty palm on my breast...I regained my senses once more that same night. I remembered that 7 or 8 of the devil men chased me around the cavern. They tossed me back and forth between each other, fondling my body, and -- as they wished-- carried me off into a passageway for their amusement...I must have been a captive of these creatures for two weeks, perhaps a month, when the grey men appeared from out of the tunnels. The devils scrambled in the opposite direction, grunting with fright, as the grey men shot them with gas guns. Several of the bestial men-animals were killed. Prisoners were released from the cages, given a toga-like robe for clothing, and taken through the tunnels for medical attention. They had a strange sort of vehicle, not like our automobiles, that was parked in the tunnel."

She was taken into one of the vehicles, a mobile laboratory, which contained a large number of machines. These strange men spoke perfect French, but with an odd accent. They were about five feet tall, their faces more elongated, thinner, than those of normal human beings, and was of a greyish color, almost like the cast of old baking dough. After being treated in another vehicle which looked like a combination hospital and computer room, she asked one of them about themselves, who they were and who the devil men were.

She was told "It would take many years of time, as you measure it. The machines implant information in your mind without error. The data is not filtered through your mind, but remains purified."

From these machines she learned the following: Many millions of years ago the earth was devoid of human life. The "starmen" selected our planet as a space lab, transplanting dominant species as our aggressive, war-like characteristics drove the species from us. Some species became extinct. Others vanished and even the "starmen" don't know what became of them. As the human race continued to grow, many of the species were driven underground to caverns for their survival. They adapted themselves to the life beneath the surface and, in time, created the tunnels and cavern cities.

There were problems among some of these species relating to biological mutations and the necessary

Retrospeck:

By Raplh M. Holland

((Continued from last issue))

The science of the Elders was so far beyond the understanding of these early ancestors of m man that they were regarded as supernatural beings. They were the "Gods" of classical mythology, and the prophets of our own Bible. The earliest parts of the Bible are, in fact, regarded as distorted accounts of the Elders, the ancestors of present man not being far enough advanced at that time to be worth writing about. The Biblical account of the creation of "Adam" is regarded as a symbolic account of their actual creation by the Elders; the "lump of clay" mentioned in some of the accounts symbolizing the base brute from which man was made. The

Elder Race is mentioned in many places in the Bible, beginning with the passage in Genesis: "There were giants IN the earth in those days."

These early humans were apparently quick to pick up knowledge from the Elders, who feared that they might also learn the secret of indefinately prolonging their life. They did not want them to know this at that time because they considered the human race to be in a low state of developement, and did not wish to "fix the type" at that stage. The name Adam when analyzed by Mantong, reveals their opinion of the early humans: "A de animal-man"..."de" in Mantong having a meaning of defectiveness. So the humans were sent up to the surface, away from the mech. "Behold: the man is now become as one of us...now lest he take also of the tree of Life...and live forever...the Lord God sent him forth from the Garden of Eden."

The Elder Race finally began to die at much earlier ages than formerly and a particularly vicious form of insanity, marked by sadistic orgies, began to appear. Their scientists determined that both of these symptoms were being caused by increased radioactivity in the solar rays, which penetrated even to the great depths of their cities. A more benevolent sun was discovered in far space, and the "Gods" left for their new home on a distant planet which they called "Heavi 'n".

Continued next issue...

---

evolution of the species to survive the environment of the caverns. In time, some of the original colonists degenerated into the brutal animal men...The constant tests of nuclear weapons have destroyed, or cracked many of the great tunnels. The men in the metallic grey uniforms are what we would call a biological team from the far reaches of space. During a routine check of the earth, they learned of the mutations that had occured, and began establishing bases and stations, notably under oceans and seas, from which they would observe the future happenings on this planet. The woman's story continues:

"After the treatment, I was taken to another section of the tunnels. Some of the men in metallic uniforms were sealing off the tunnels. The leader designated a man to lead me back to the surface world, and in another two hours, we were in the sewers of Paris. I was back on the streets shortly thereafter. I must have looked very odd, walking barefoot through the streets in winter.

A gendarme stopped me and I was taken into custody and eventually my family was contacted. I spent many weeks in a mental hospital and today I am in a sanitarium trying to recover from the experience".

After the Hollow Earth Society learned of her ordeal, their representative in Paris checked her history and background in great detail. She disappeared for about four months, at the time indicated. He checked the elevator at the office building where the kidnapping allegedly took place. The shaft ended at the basement but-- strangely enough-- there were signs of fresh masonry construction at the bottom of the shaft. The Society asked for permission to test the shaft for possible proof of her story, but the building owners refused.

Two other accounts which have already appeared in Shavertron may also be considered among the stories that fall into this catagory. The first case appeared in the first issue (back issues now

available in Xerox form) and concerned a tunnel with an entrance in a blind alley between two buildings on Parliament Street in Toronto, Ontario. ..in which was observed a strange human-like creature which was seen to scramble down a steep cross tunnel into the depths. The other case concerned a letter which appeared in the Purdue University Exponent, from a student who claimed that "there are men who walk the tunnels beneath Purdue", and who maintained that certain forms of activity were spreading across the campus in Lafayette, Indiana. (p.11 issue 7).

Another confirmation of this appeared in a Special Report published by the Cosmic Awareness foundation of Olympia, Washington called "The Web of Conspiracy" (Part 2). This report consists of "messages" received through trance-interpreter Paul Shockley from a "force" which exists on a higher plane of consciousness, and which calls itself "Cosmic Awareness" or "It". During one of his sessions, Paul Shockley received the following message:

"...this Awareness indicates that there are many types of entities beneath the earth...that those closer to the center itself are of a highly evoled nature, whereas those who are subsurface entities, these are somewhat demented by the effects of living underground for so many thousands of years. This Awareness indicates that occasionally these entities surface, particualrly through certain buildings which are often built in a way to allow an opening into the subterranean levels, and occasionally these entities walk around on the streets of your cities, and have been known to kidnap others..."

If you are still not convinced that this "surface connection" exists, dear reader, stay tuned for further evidence in future issues of Shavertron! (Ed. Note: Yes! We have more on those suspicious elevators which might prove interesting to some S readers).

FEAR & LAUGHTER ON THE UFO TRAIL

by MAX FYFIELD
& INNER EARTH

A NOTE FROM MAX:

This article is written on a request from your editor. He asked my opinion on the Rhodes affair, which I answered in a personal straightforward manner (not to be published), adding some of my own experiences with some notable correspondents...Pillars of the Ufo Society. Some names are slightly changed to protect the innocent... even the guilty! So, if anyone wants to call me Pax Myfield, I can take it!

HOW TO SURVIVE.

One man told me the answer to this question: "As you know, Max, in America one has to measure one's time with care to survive".

To survive or not to survive...that was what started it all in 1966, while I was still living in Hollywood. I decided that I had to study the survival possibilities offered by the Ufo/occult groups, in case, as everyone is predicting, the Holocaust is just around the corner. My plan was to write to all the ufo "pillars" of society... personalities who could get me in touch with the spiritual side of things. I imagined that soon I would be in touch with the highest intelligences (HI's) in the world -- perhaps even the space people (SI's). I envisioned a kind of team work

that would develop between me, the HI's and the SI's -- life would be most exciting and meaningful, at last! But wait -- not so fast!

I returned to Denmark minus my wife and tv set, giving me more time to continue my Quest. In the beginning, I wrote long handwritten letters to some of the Pillars, telling them about my ideas for motion pictures. First thing I did back in Denmark was to have my long letters typed and printed, calling them Letter 1, 2, 3 etc. and always including lots of my own drawings when I sent them.

One of the first I wrote to was Gray Barker, who was most kind and encouraging. He liked my film ideas and told me more about Raymond Bernard (but not more than the readers of S already know). My elation was short-lived. Next day I got a letter from a society called the Dark Age, and that was a dark day indeed.

First off, they told me that they had their own film ideas -- much more correct ideas than mine. I was much too frivolous in esoteric matters, besides being all wrong. Regardless, films such as mine they said, would never be made until the Masters permit it -- which would be OK with me, if the Masters just put up the cash for the production! Nevertheless, the Dark Age disciples had a dozen writers who had written almost

14

the same thing, so there was nothing significant about my stories. They made me feel like a nerd. They even offered to return all my letters, or BURN them, as their vibrations were disturbing their files! This letter was signed, "Love In Action".

Somehow I got to thinking about deros when I remembered this affair. As it turned out, I got a letter from a former Dark Age member who had to leave the group due to many disagreements. He also claimed to be the reincarnation of Dwajl Khul, one of the Masters, and he said my film ideas were most unique. I continued onward...

The Tampa Story: Then, on a Tuesday came an odd letter from a most controversial figure, Dr. Tampa. He had read my first letter with great interest, but he had a "message" for me: "If Mr B was my co-worker in any way, he would not have any part of my ideas. Mr B, it seems, owed Dr. Tampa royalty money. Not that the good Doctor needed the money...no, not an enlightened being as he: "All profit from my books goes to the Save-A-Cat League in New York", he said. "Also, maybe your Mastermind group will be the most wanted by the police if Mr B is involved... and finally, I will be unable to write to you anymore as I am very ill (a sick yogi?) and I am very busy writing my 13th book."

At one point I got many letters from a Canadian engineer, Bartur H. Cashews (again a psuedonym) who knew Tesla and had the formula for the Tesla rays. He called me C.M.W. (Christ Mind Working). He got copies of all I have, sent me color slides of his paintings, and his book, "Wall of Light". Most exciting. It tells about his contact with Space Ship X-12. Once he offered the Tesla rays to the government, but was turned down. He had also invented a machine that could produce Gold, but didn't use it, and then told me he didn't eat much except an occasional hot dog.

Another group here gave me the address of Mr. Gone R. Swirl in England, who had invented a flying saucer which flies by using Free Energy. With great excitment I wrote to him. He answered like a shot, offering me the "position" of Art Director in his PR department. WOW! By a unique twist of synchronicity, right away they needed new stationery and posters of full-color space ships and airports. In fact, he offered to fly over here in his private plane (what happened to free energy??) if I could only put him and a friend "up for a night or two". According to Swirl, I could "work in my home in Denmark in my spare time". And because it was my duty to tell Mankind about ufos, I could forget about any financial return. There was no mention of my own ideas -- yet I do have some. I declined his kind offer.

And this brings us to Mr. N.O.L. Greet, who sent me 3 names of my former lives. I have been a beautiful blonde woman in 11th century France, popular with men. Then a 16th century Gothic painter, very eccentric, misunderstood, but popular with WOMEN. And then Hector McDonald, an 18th century Scottish clan leader, nicknamed "Fighting Mac".

One of my brighter mail days came from America and George Van Tassel (via Dorris). They liked my letters and encouraged me and told others about me. Van has a very direct way of expressing himself...for instance: "It seems that today, the people who know how to do things are stopped in their tracks by laws and opinions from authorities

who don't know how to do things". And best of all, Van and Dorris didn't ask for a thing.

A letter followed soon after that did ask... It was from Dr. Ranges, who wanted me to open a branch office of his ufo club here in Copenhagen. I was to put ads in the newspapers, find a group, sock each person for $20 and then send everything to him-- minus my 30% for expenses. Voila! See how easy it is when you get someone else to do the work for you. And what about translating it all into Danish?? Good grief, I just had to decline the kind offer.

Another depressing day: I got a long detailed letter from Mr. John What? He had written a book about his Trip to Venus, which I had thanked him very kindly. He answered me by giving a critique of my letters. He tore me to pieces. Sentence after sentence he 'proved' me wrong, but I was getting used to it by this time.

He advised me to "stop trying to rule God's world"...when in reality, I'd much rather be a movie director! "Never criticize others", he continued, "You need to read a good book on meditation". He also told me that he believed my landlady was right when she told me to work for a living instead of writing -- writing isn't work? I was deeply depressed by this time. As a parting shot, he added: "Always leave the reader in a state of OPTIMISM".

SUNSPOTS: If you say Sunspots, you must say Naura Sundo. She wrote a very nice "open letter" answer to my Letter 1 in her newsletter. According to Naura, my attitudes project an Ultra Protonic personality with an influx of negative ions when sunspots are increasing. Beware of those sunspots! She asked me: "What are you doing about the sunspots??" And I answered, NOTHING! What's to do? She added: "Don't work against the Plan - work with it". So now I did my bit about mentioning sunspots, OK, Naura?

Brat Geiger wrote 40 or 50 books -- some say 60 -- I lost count. I believe he is 40 years old so that would mean one book a year since his birth. Well done, Brat! Nevertheless, he is a true Pillar of Ufo Society having made his own pillar of books, (see drawing). He wrote me a kind letter -- he also liked a drawing I sent.

There are many more whom I contacted, people like Helen Hoag, Harold Serman, Dick Sutphen, Will Sox and his pyramids, the Stelle Group and so on, not to forget all those who didn't answer, two of them being Ray Palmer and Doc Anderson.

At last we have "our own" group closer to home. Our friend, Frank Brownley wrote many long kind letters and helped put me in touch with others, like Charles Marcoux our spirit-photographer and also Christine Hayes. My final praise goes to Bruce Walton whom I thank for his 5 volumes of inner earth entrances. Forgive me, Bruce for not putting you on a pillar, but all pillars were taken when I got your photo.

You might be wondering what my conclusions were after this experience. Well, I used to think that there were two kinds of people: New Age People and then the others. Now I'm not so sure. They all seem to blend more or less. Differences are harder to distinguish if you make personal contact. You may discover that people are people with all the human traits of strengh and weakness...myself included of course!

Your surviving friend, Max...

15

MAX FYFIELD

Profile of an ARTIST

I was born in Copenhagen, but since I spent 20 years in north America I'm not a true Dane! I went to school in Denmark and I hated it. What I remember most is the noise and waste of time (kids are alike everywhere). Then came art school--I was to become a commercial artist. I should have chosen an acting career, as I almost did. Who knows, I might have become another James Bond by now-- well, maybe next lifetime!

My childhood and youth were quite uneventful, except for the German occupation of Denmark during WWII (a clue to my true age). I still had dreams of becoming a MOVIE STAR in Hollywood and I made plans no human being could live up to --but at last I took an ocean liner to Canada (via New York) where I arrived as a naive immigrant and soon was sent "up north" to a lumber camp.

After 2 weeks it was obvious that I was not cut out for that kind of work, therefore I returned to "civilization" in TORONTO (my first acquaintance with the name TORONTO) where I soon got various degrading jobs-- but at times some art jobs came my way. I learned to speak English as I went along, and soon I could ask for a cup of tea without getting a cup of cheese! (smile)

Up til this time nothing of an OCCULT nature had entered my life. Then it happened-- I met a beautiful redhead who was a time-bomb with big ambitions (like me) and soon we went WEST to Vancouver, BC where I found work with a big advertising agency, while she was preparing for a career as a SINGER and ACTRESS. She also had a good knowledge of all occult subjects (except for flying saucers and hollow earth--forgive her).

At last we went to HOLLYWOOD! Oh, by the way, we got married on the way down to CAL.--in Frisco. Now I worked as an artist all the time, except when I was unemployed. I was an extra in many movies (not an actor, darn it). Her career moved ahead fast, she became acquainted with several STARS, like David Brian, Ty Hardin, Roy Rodgers and others. Soon our apartment was invaded by actors, extras, stuntmen, spiritualist-ministers,

magicians, free-loaders and a Hindoo astrologer.

Just as she was offered a real big part she died! I almost died too. The first 3 years after that I became a regular visitor at most of Hollywood's bars, nightclubs and burlesque shows, including the PINK PUSSYCAT! (We are still far from Richard Shaver, I know).

During the years that followed, I wrote a film script called "Free of the Past" which is the story of my life-- both the past and the future! In this script I had to incorporate all kinds of subjects, like ufo's, reincarnation, air pollution, the future of the world and much more. This is where my occult study really began, because my script had to be absolutely authentic! I got books from all over the USA and made contact with many personalities like Gray Barker, Dan Fry, Van Tassel, Gabriel Green and many more.

In Raymond Bernard's books I read about the Inner Earth for the first time-- and soon after that I got the idea to write a sequel to my first script and have the same characters make a visit to AGHARTA! (that will include myself, see?) Perhaps there will be more about my film ideas in future issues if space and editor permit.

Then, as can happen to any man (?) I fell in love with an actress in Italy, and this partly caused me to leave the USA and return to Denmark. During the following years I tried to sell my script and other ideas to Italian producers, and I made trips to Rome--but no luck. At the same time, I continued to contact still more ufo personalities and societies in the USA--ending up with one of my most interesting contacts: Richard Toronto and Shavertron!

Maybe I am an artist, but now I also consider myself a writer of screenplays, and in the near future also a FILM-MAKER. About a year ago I got the happy impulse to send copies of all my work to an American producer who is most interested in making what he calls "New Age Motion Pictures". He has sent me a positive reply-- so, films about the Inner Earth might soon be in the making-- and I might have to return to Hollywood to work there again-- see you all soon!

Your devoted friend

Max Fyfield

Dinosaurs As 'Old' Relatives Is Probed

BERKELEY (UPI) — But for a twist of evolutionary fate, dinosaurs rather than apes might have been our ancestral forebears, according to a Canadian scholar who has developed a model of the imaginary reptilian creature.

Dale Russell, curator of fossil vertebrates at the National Museums of Canada in Ottawa, has developed a theory that intelligent life forms could have developed from the large reptiles that roamed the earth millions of years ago.

Russell calls his imaginary creature a "Dinosauroid" which would look like a hairless, green-skinned reptile with a bulging skull, luminous cat-like eyes and three-fingered hands.

Russell, a sober expert of evolution who is a visiting scholar at the paleontology department at the University of California at Berkeley, calls his imaginary creature a "dinosauroid."

All it would have taken, he thinks, was an adjustment in the Earth's history that would have kept the giant dinosaurs as the dominant form of life on the planet.

Strange as the theory may seem, Russell says his lizardman has a serious message: high intelligence may be a natural result wherever life evolves in the universe, and perhaps man's general body form is no fluke.

In developing his creature, Russell followed evolutionary trends he believes were already under way in one line of dinosaurs 78 million years ago.

The stenochyosaurus, a long-tailed carnivorous forest dweller that stood about five feet tall, had many of the attributes that man's own ancestors possessed three or four million years ago, Russell said.

The creature stood on two legs, had thumbs, binocular vision and a large brain, for a dinosaur.

The result of his conjectures. Russell admitted to science correspondent Charles Petit of the San Francisco Chronicle, made even him nervous while he was evolving the theory.

"When I saw the direction it was going, I started having second thoughts,"

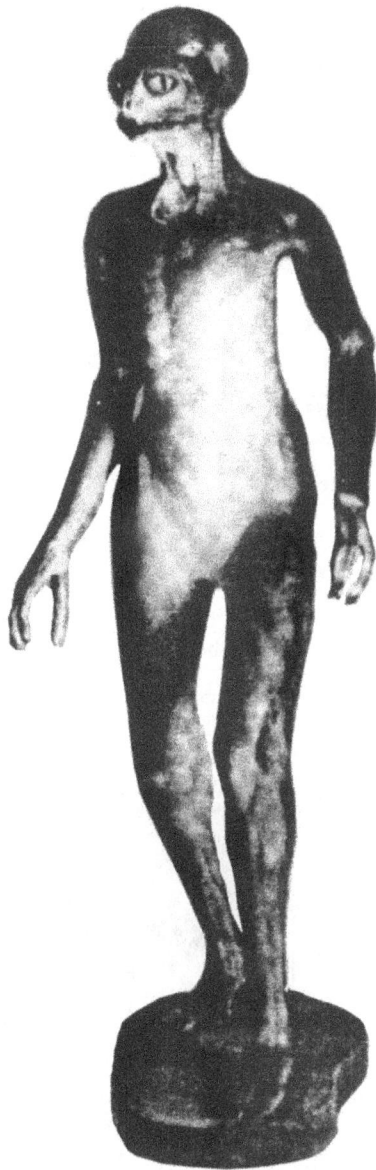

DALE RUSSELL'S DINOSAUROID

he said. "This is not the kind of speculation most of my colleagues are comfortable with."

"Can you imagine the reaction from Biblical creationists to this?" he asked.

So far, the reaction at Berkeley has been positive.

"Most of the people are absolutely fascinated," he said. "Nobody has started avoiding me in corridors."

The intelligence of humans today, Russell said, is in accord with a trend established more than 200 million years ago. The first creatures that began developing along the natural line toward

dominated by the dinosaurs before extinction.

When the dinosaurs abruptly disappeared along with half the species of life in the world 65 million years ago, mammals underwent an evolutionary explosion to fill the void. And, according to Russell, mammals picked up the natural line toward developing intelligence right where the dinosaurs left off.

Russell's dinosauroid, designed from complicated scientific calculations, has no external sex organs, in accord with standard reptile form: He doesn't even regard a sculpture made of it as

---

Mom of last Berkowitz victim beaten, warned to keep away

The Herald Statesman 3/25/81? Cr: Tellurie Ric

By ED TRAPASSO
Staff Writer

The mother of Son of Sam's last victim was roughed up Tuesday night in her Brooklyn home by two tall assailants who commanded her to keep quiet about new information linking the murders to a Yonkers-based Satanic cult.

Meysa Moskowitz, whose daughter Stacey was killed in the mass murderer's final ambush, was rocked by powerful backhand slap to the face after being told: "Stay away from Berkowitz. This is a warning."

Brooklyn detectives said late Tuesday night they were investigating the attack, but offered no other information.

The attack came less than one week

after Gannett Westchester Rockland Newspapers reported that David Berkowitz, who had long claimed he was the lone Son of Sam triggerman, now says he was aided by Satanic cultists in carrying out the murderous spree that clamped a stranglehold of fear on the New York City metropolitan area in 1976-77.

It also came three days after Mrs. Moskowitz appeared on a nationally televised newsmagazine show, "What's Happening, America," which explored the conspiracy theories in detail.

In an interview late Tuesday, Mrs. Moskowitz, who believes Berkowitz did not act alone, said her nose was bloodied and her neck stiffened by the attack. But she said she was otherwise unharmed in the assault

that occurred at about 7:30 inside the foyer of her Flatbush apartment.

The intruders were both men not more than 6 feet tall, she said.

Mrs. Moskowitz said her husband reported the attack to the police after she phoned a nearby pharmacy where he was working when the assault occurred.

"They were very plain looking," Mrs. Moskowitz said about her assailants. "They

---

Mutilated dog found in Yonkers

Earlier in the day, Yonkers police reported that the carcass of a black Labrador retriever was found near Greystone Railroad station.

The dog's left ear had been cut off and its right eye gouged out, police said.

A police officer found the dog near the railroad tracks after being alerted by a passerby.

Several dogs, including black Labradors and German shepherds, have been found slaughtered in Yonkers and Minot, N.D., the two locations that the Satanic cult that allegedly carried out the Son of Sam murders has used as home base in the past.

The reports published in Gannett Westchester Rockland Newspaper last week

looked like store mannequins."

featured letters written by Berkowitz from his prison cell at the Attica Correctional Facility where he is serving a 300-plus year sentence for the bloody rampage that left six dead and seven wounded.

In the letters, the former Yonkers resident admitted he had accomplices, saying authorities covered up his case and, "would have to be idiots to ignore the overwhelming evidence" demonstrating the involvement of others that left six dead and seven wounded.

The Queens District Attorney's Office, spurred by earlier Gannett Westchester Rockland Newspaper investigative reports on the Son of Sam case, reopened its investigation of the killings last year. That probe is continuing.

Heavenly Guidance for a Bus Driver

Leon, Spain

Spaniards returning from a pilgrimage said yesterday their bus driver shut his eyes and took his hands off the steering wheel for nearly 20 miles of night driving.

The national news agency EFE said a priest returning with the pilgrims from the Portuguese shrine of Fatima affirmed he sat next to the driver during the incident.

The driver put his right hand behind his head, shut his eyes and smiled, then took the left hand off the wheel, the priest told EFE.

The lights of the bus signaled to other cars on the road, although the driver, identified only as Juan, never touched any switches, passengers said.

After a 20-mile ride, the bus stopped. The pilgrims said they heard a voice speaking through the driver's mouth:

"I am your brother, Archangel Michael. God had the grace to drive this bus himself as a test of faith for our brother (the driver)."

United Press

10-19-81 S.F. Chronicle

Mountaineers spot UFO

KATMANDU, Nepal (UPI) — One of the world's foremost mountaineers says he watched a UFO "the size of a full moon" for nearly three hours while climbing in the Himalayas.

Italian Reinhold Messner said he spotted the unidentified flying object as it drifted south into Nepal from Tibet over the mighty snowcapped mountains, as he was descending Mount Chamblang.

"It was moving very slowly," he said. "It moved eastward and then went again southwest and drifted finally north into Tibet."

His climbing partner Doug Scott, a British schoolteacher, also sighted the object, he said, as did a nearby joint Polish-British expedition, but at a different time.

10-12-81 – TORONTO STAR   CR. Jim Wentworth

Jim Jones Called Agent of the CIA

S.F. Chronicle
Nov. '81

By Erica Goode

A group of Jonestown survivors and the parents of a 19-year-old Guyana victim filed a $63.4 million suit against the federal government yesterday, charging that People's Temple leader Jim Jones was a CIA agent.

The suit, filed in U.S. District Court, also accuses U.S. government agencies and officials of conspiring with Jones in a macabre plot to control political dissidence. Government officials knew about Jones' plans for the mass murder-suicide of his followers as early as seven months before the November 1978 tragedy, the suit charges.

"I want some disclosure, I want some changes," said Robert Bockelman, the attorney who filed the suit for the group. "Jonestown occurred, and a thousand people died and nothing changed in our society."

The seven plaintiffs seek $50 million in compensation for violations of their civil rights and another $13.4 million in personal injury damages.

From 1963 until November 18, 1978, the suit alleges, "James Warren Jones was an employee, servant, agent, or operative of the...Central Intelligence Agency."

The suit also charges that former Secretary of State Cyrus Vance and former CIA director Stanfield Turner took part in a conspiracy to "enhance the economic and political powers of James Warren Jones," in order to gain control over "persons tending toward a socialist perspective."

Vance, Turner, the U.S. State Department, the U.S. Department of Justice, the U.S. Customs Service, the House of Representatives and several other past and present government officials are named as defendants in the action.

Attorney Bockelman, conceding that the evidence he has collected against the government is mostly circumstantial, said he hopes the suit will bring to light previously hidden information about the government's complicity with Jones.

Monica Bagby, who was wounded in the ambush at the Port Kaituma airstrip that left San Mateo Congressman Leo Ryan and four others dead, claims in the suit that she was "falsely imprisoned for three months in Jonestown," and that she was "the victim of fraud and deceit..."

Bagby was a witness in the recent trial of Larry Layton on charges of conspiring to murder Ryan. It was declared a mistrial, and new proceedings against Layton are scheduled for December.

Joining Bagby as plaintiffs are four other former temple members: Thomas Bogue, James Bogue and Teena M. Turner of San Francisco and Juanita Bogue of Burlingame. Robert and Virginia Richardson, whose daughter, Kathy Purifoy, died in the Jonestown tragedy, are also plaintiffs in the suit.

MYSTERY

Nightmares that kill . .
by the communist Pathet Lao six years ago.

IT'S called "the Oriental nightmare death syndrome." And it has claimed the lives of 25 people scattered throughout America.

The symptoms are always the same, apparently healthy victims literally frightened to death by nightmares. Victims are always the same, too—primitive Loation mountain people called the Hmong.

The 35,000 Hmong in America fled their homeland when it was overrun

Suddenly they've started dying in their sleep in the early hours, their death preceded by heavy breathing, wild thrashing about in bed and nightmarish screams.

Mystified doctors have scoured medical books for an explanation.

NIGEL NELSON
Daily Mirror 10-27-81 New York.

Cave body mystery

SPANISH police are puzzled by the death of tourist George Stocking, 32, whose body was found in a seaside cave in Minorca. Mr. Stocking, of Hastings, Sussex, apparently fell from a nearby hotel but how he came to be in the cave is a mystery. Daily Star – 6-12-81

Mars for energy

Mars could soon solve the energy crisis. For scientists have discovered a natural laser beam on the planet's surface. Its power—five times as great as America's entire output—could heat and light cities and factories and provide energy for transport say NASA boffins.

DAILY STAR WED, JULY 15, 1981

THE FAR SIDE / GARY LARSON

Thank God, Sylvia. We're alive!

WITCHES' DEATH RIDDLE

POLICE were puzzling last night over the massacre of a witches' coven. Four people were found shot to death and two others wounded at a mansion in Columbia, South Carolina, furnished with a black magic altar and a library of occult books.

The victims had been shot in the back of their heads after being forced to stand facing a wall. "It was like something out of a horror movie," one detective said. "Really eerie."

18